The Lives of Guns

Harel Shapira is Assistant Professor in the Department of Sociology at the University of Texas at Austin. Shapira is an ethnographer who uses long-term participant observation in order to study political life in contemporary America, with an emphasis on right-wing politics. He is the author of *Waiting for José: The Minutemen's Pursuit of America* (Princeton University Press, 2013), which explores the civilians who patrol the United States–Mexico border. He is currently writing a book on gun owners, which explores how the notion of self-defense is deeply connected to group identity. Through fieldwork at gun schools, Shapira considers how people train their minds and bodies to use guns, and what such an education means for the future of American democracy. His previous research has been funded by the National Science Foundation as well as the Harry Frank Guggenheim Foundation. Harel Shapira earned his PhD and Master of Arts degrees in Sociology from Columbia University, and a Bachelor of Arts degree from the University of Chicago where he majored in Sociology.

David Yamane is Professor of Sociology at Wake Forest University. Professor Yamane's primary scholarly interest has been in sociologically understanding organized religion, particularly Roman Catholicism in the post-war United States. His books in this area include *The Catholic Church in State Politics: Negotiating Prophetic Demands and Political Realities* (Rowman & Littlefield, 2005), *Real Stories of Christian Initiation: Lessons for and from the RCIA* (Liturgical Press, 2006), and *Becoming Catholic: Finding Rome in the American Religious Landscape* (Oxford University Press, 2014). In a recent departure from his previous work, Professor Yamane has undertaken a study of American gun culture. With support from Wake Forest University, he is exploring the phenomenon of armed citizenship as part of what has been called "Gun Culture 2.0"—a new group of individuals (including an increasing number of women) who have entered gun culture through concealed carry, self-defense, and the shooting sports. Professor Yamane earned his BA ('91) in sociology from the University of California at Berkeley and his MS ('94) and PhD ('98) in sociology from the University of Wisconsin at Madison. After teaching at the University of Notre Dame and holding a postdoc at the University of Virginia's Center on Religion and Democracy, he joined the sociology faculty at Wake Forest in 2005. He served as department chair from 2009–2011 and is currently an affiliated faculty member in the Department of Religion and School of Divinity.

Franklin E. Zimring is the William G. Simon Professor of Law and Director of Criminal Justice Studies at Boalt School of Law at the University of California, Berkeley. He was a member of the University of Chicago law faculty as Llewellyn Professor of Law and director of the Center for Studies in Criminal Justice. He joined the Boalt faculty in 1985 as director of the Earl Warren Legal Institute.

Professor Zimring was appointed the first Wolfen Distinguished Scholar in 2006 and served in that capacity until 2013. He has been a visiting professor at the University of Pennsylvania and Yale University, and a fellow of the Center for Advanced Studies in Behavioral Sciences. He is a fellow of the American Society of Criminology and a member of the American Academy of Arts and Sciences. From 2005 until 2011, he was the principal investigator for the Center on Culture, Immigration, and Youth Violence Prevention, supported by the Centers for Disease Control. Zimring is the author or co-author of many books on topics including deterrence, the changing legal world of adolescence, capital punishment, the scale of imprisonment, and drug control. His recent books include *The Contradictions of American Capital Punishment* (Oxford University Press, 2003), *The Great American Crime Decline* (Oxford University Press, 2007), and *The City That Became Safe: New York's Lessons for Urban Crime and Its Control* (Oxford University Press, 2012).

The Lives of Guns

EDITED BY JONATHAN OBERT

ANDREW POE

and

AUSTIN SARAT

OXFORD
UNIVERSITY PRESS

Oxford University Press is a department of the University of Oxford. It furthers the University's objective of excellence in research, scholarship, and education by publishing worldwide. Oxford is a registered trade mark of Oxford University Press in the UK and certain other countries.

Published in the United States of America by Oxford University Press
198 Madison Avenue, New York, NY 10016, United States of America.

Library of Congress Cataloging-in-Publication Data
Names: Obert, Jonathan, editor. | Poe, Andrew, editor. | Sarat, Austin, editor.
Title: The lives of guns / [edited by] Jonathan Obert, Andrew Poe, Austin Sarat.
Description: New York, NY: Oxford University Press, [2019] |
Includes bibliographical references and index.
Identifiers: LCCN 2018003060 | ISBN 978-0-19-084292-5 (hardcover) |
ISBN 978-0-19-084294-9 (epub)
Subjects: LCSH: Firearms ownership—United States. | Firearms—Social aspects—United States. | Gun control—United States.
Classification: LCC HV7436.L58 2019 | DDC 323.4/32—dc23
LC record available at https://lccn.loc.gov/2018003060

9 8 7 6 5 4 3 2 1

Printed by Sheridan Books, Inc., United States of America

To Ben, with hope that he will live in a saner and safer world.
(A.S.)

Contents

PART III   THE PRIVATE LIFE OF GUNS

Acknowledgments

This book is the product of a wonderful year of collaborative inquiry under the auspices of Amherst College's 2016–2017 Copeland Colloquium. We are grateful to Copeland Fellows Jennifer Yida Pan, Nathan Shelton, Alex Young, and Chad Kautzer, as well as to our Amherst colleagues Leah Schmalzbauer and Nusrat Chowdhury, for their intellectual companionship during this year.

Contributors

Elisabeth Anker is Associate Professor of American Studies and Political Science at George Washington University. Her research and teaching interests are at the intersection of political theory, critical theory, cultural analysis, and media studies. Professor Anker received her PhD in Political Theory from the University of California, Berkeley, where she also received a Designated Emphasis in Film Studies. She has held research fellowships at Brown University's Pembroke Center for Teaching and Research on Women and UC Berkeley's Charles Travers Fellowship in Ethics and Politics. Her research has also been supported by multiple faculty grants from George Washington University. Professor Anker's book *Orgies of Feeling: Melodrama and the Politics of Freedom* (Duke University Press, 2014), which examines the role of melodrama in US politics, was a finalist for the 2015 Lora Romero Prize for Best First Book in American studies.

Joanna Bourke is Professor of History in the Department of History, Classics, and Archaeology at Birkbeck College, where she has taught since 1992. She is a Fellow of the British Academy. Over the years, her books have ranged from the social and economic history of Ireland in the late nineteenth and early twentieth centuries, to social histories of the British working classes between 1860 and the 1960s, to cultural histories of military conflict between the Anglo-Boer war and the present. She has worked on the history of the emotions, particularly fear and hatred, and the history of sexual violence. In the past few years, her research has focused on questions of humanity, militarization, and pain. She wrote a book entitled *What It Means to Be Human*. In 2014, she published two books: *Wounding the World. How Military Violence and War Games Invade Our World* and *The Story of Pain: From Prayer to Painkillers*.

Heather Ashley Hayes is Assistant Professor of Rhetoric at Whitman College. Professor Hayes is a rhetoric and communication studies scholar, working across the intersections of rhetorical materialism, race, violence, the global war on terror, and argument studies. Since 2013, Professor Hayes has delivered a number of talks and presentations including work on the revolutionary events in Egypt's Tahrir Square that ousted Hosni Mubarak in January of 2011 and work on the rise of unmanned aerial vehicles (also known as drones) as a new technology of the global war on terror. Her first book, *Violent Subjects and Rhetorical Cartography in the Age of the Terror Wars,* was published in 2016 by Palgrave Macmillan Press.

Timothy W. Luke is University Distinguished Professor of Political Science in the College of Liberal Arts and Human Sciences as well as Program Chair of the Government and International Affairs Program, School of Public and International Affairs at Virginia Tech University. Professor Luke's areas of research include environmental politics and cultural studies as well as comparative politics, international political economy, and modern critical social and political theory. He is the author of eight books and over 150 articles and book chapters on a variety of topics including, most recently, *Gun Violence and Public Life,* eds. Ben Agger and Timothy W. Luke (Paradigm, 2014). He serves on the editorial board of *Capitalism Nature Socialism, Critical Social Policy, Culture and Politics: An International Journal of Theory, Current Perspectives in Social Theory, e-Learning and Digital Media, Fast Capitalism, International Political Sociology, Journal of Information Technology and Policy, Open Geography Journal, Organization & Environment, New Political Science, Peace Studies Journal, Public Knowledge Journal, Spectra, Telos,* and *the minnesota review.* He is an associate editor of *New Political Science,* and he also is a founding editor of *Fast Capitalism* located at the Center for Theory with the University of Texas.

Jonathan Obert is Assistant Professor of Political Science at Amherst College. He is the author of *The Six-Shooter State: Public and Private Violence in American Politics* (Cambridge University Press, 2018).

Andrew Poe is Assistant Professor of Political Theory at Amherst College. Professor Poe received his PhD in Political Science of the University of California (San Diego) in 2010 and is currently completing a book titled *The Release of Political Enthusiasm.*

Austin Sarat is Associate Dean of the Faculty and William Nelson Cromwell Professor of Jurisprudence and Political Science at Amherst College. Professor Sarat is author or editor of more than ninety books, including *Gruesome Spectacles* (2014), *Re-imagining* To Kill a Mockingbird (2013), *Mercy on Trial* (2005), *When the State Kills* (2001), and *Guns in Law* (forthcoming, 2019).

The Lives of Guns

The Lives of Guns

An Introduction

JONATHAN OBERT, ANDREW POE, AND AUSTIN SARAT

Guns affect our lives as never before.[1] In the contemporary United States, for example, gun violence has become commonplace, with 13,282 homicides by firearms and 372 mass shootings documented in 2015.[2] Almost all current scholarship on guns and gun violence focuses on the gun as a site of legal regulation,[3] or as a tool used in mass killings,[4] or as a thing afforded a right of ownership.[5] Yet in all this attention, scholars treat the gun as if it were simply a passive object, problematically ignoring a vital agency in the gun itself. They fail to appreciate how guns themselves might be active, how they might have their own "lives."

Evidence of this neglect is most apparent in the literature on violence in the social sciences. Much of this scholarship on violence focuses on its etiology or effects, rather than the various modes of its production.[6] It deploys a variety of legal, anthropological, philosophical, economic, sociological, and psychological

---

[1] Firmin DeBrabander, *Do Guns Make Us Free? Democracy and the Armed Society* (New Haven, CT: Yale University Press, 2015).

[2] "Guns in the US: The Statistics behind the Violence," BBC News, January 5, 2016, http://www.bbc.com/news/world-us-canada-34996604.

[3] Michael Waldman, *The Second Amendment: A Biography* (New York: Simon and Schuster, 2014); Adam Winkler, *Gunfight: The Battle Over the Right to Bear Arms in America* (New York: W. W. Norton, 2011).

[4] Bernard E. Harcourt, ed., *Guns, Crime, and Punishment in America* (New York: New York University Press, 2003).

[5] Philip J. Cook and Jens Ludwig, eds., *Gun Violence: The Real Costs* (New York: Oxford University Press, 2000).

[6] Randall Collins, *Violence: A Micro-Sociological Theory* (Princeton, NJ: Princeton University Press, 2009); James Gilligan, *Violence: Reflections on a National Epidemic* (New York: Vintage Books, 1996); Geoffrey Canada, *Fist Stick Knife Gun: A Personal History of Violence* (Boston: Beacon Press, 1995).

frames to explain how and why violence matters. The focus on the causes of violence connects to attempts at prevention or management, and usually treats physical or cultural destruction as motivated, rational, or at least sensible.

What exactly produces this destruction—the material technologies (the drones, knives, bombs, and, especially, guns) that constrain and enable violence—seems lost in the excessive attention to causes and consequences of violence. When used to inflict harm, knives are no longer abstract instruments, used merely for "cutting." Instead, they take on a particular symbolic value, standing in for honor, or intimacy, or blood.[7]

Moreover, weapons not only impose technical constraints on the distribution of violence, they also draw questions of agency and strategy into question. The history of, for instance, the suicide bomb, suggests that humans not only "use" weapons, but sometimes they can become weapons.[8] The recent militarization of drones points to the further alienation of subjects from the effects of their actions, the result of the global spatial distances such technologies impose between the "shooter" and the "target."[9] Indeed, the very material conditions of violence may well affect both why it happens and what the results might be.

This book investigates the material production of violence by "guns" or ballistic weapons, a category that, for our purposes, includes not only firearms but also targeted drones, missiles, and the like. Such weapons involve propulsion (killing at a distance), as well as the potential for targeting (selecting specific victims). "Guns don't kill people . . . people kill people" is the old gun-rights adage, a defense of the view that we must separate the mode of the production of violence from the motives behind pulling a trigger or pushing of a button.[10] Guns are, in this view, neutral. They are tools and not much else. And, on a superficial level, this seems to be true. Guns do not, at least yet, shoot people without some kind of obvious human intervention (though advances in drone technology and artificial intelligence seem to be rendering even the human finger passé).[11] But the view of guns as

---

[7] Mika LaVaque-Manty, "Dueling for Equality: Masculine Honor and the Modern Politics of Dignity," *Political Theory* 34, no. 6 (December 1, 2006): 715–740; Thomas W. Gallant, "Honor, Masculinity, and Ritual Knife Fighting in Nineteenth-Century Greece," *American Historical Review* 105, no. 2 (2000): 359–382; Steven C. Hughes, *Politics of the Sword: Dueling, Honor, and Masculinity in Modern Italy* (Columbus: Ohio State University Press, 2007).

[8] Banu Bargu, *Starve and Immolate: The Politics of Human Weapons* (New York: Columbia University Press, 2016), 15, 297.

[9] Nasser Hussain, "The Sound of Terror: Phenomenology of a Drone Strike," *Boston Review* 16 (October 16, 2013); Michael S. Sherry, *The Rise of American Air Power: The Creation of Armageddon* (New Haven, CT: Yale University Press, 1987).

[10] Evan Selinger, "The Philosophy of the Technology of the Gun," *The Atlantic*, July 23, 2012, http://www.theatlantic.com/technology/archive/2012/07/the-philosophy-of-the-technology-of-the-gun/260220/.

[11] Hogwit, *Flying Gun*, YouTube, 2015, https://www.youtube.com/watch?v=xqHrTtvFFIs&feature=youtu.be.

tools also assumes that the distribution of guns, their presence and physical form, has no independent effect on the opportunities and choices of the human agents who deploy their force. While we know this is not correct—increasing availability of guns in the home is a reliable predictor of greater than expected rates of suicide, for instance[12]—those who purport the view that guns are merely tools remain preoccupied with the human choice to act, not the material relationship between the gun and that action. Our book highlights how crucial the material relationship between the gun and the subject who possesses it may really be.

Even those who agree that the presence of guns has an independent and irreducible effect on the making of violence often still view them primarily in instrumental ways. For instance, many scholars would argue that it is not the gun that ultimately matters but the coercive or deterrent power inherent in firearms technology that determines how the "availability" of technology shapes action—violence as physical destruction is only important, that is, strictly through its effects on strategic choices or social processes.[13] While many anthropologists and sociologists pay close attention to how, for instance, "gun culture" shapes the civic ideologies of participants,[14] or identify the key role of guns as signifiers in social rituals and discourses,[15] guns in these accounts are still often mostly just a means to get at larger ideological or symbolic worlds.[16]

But what of the guns themselves? What if guns are not merely the carriers of action, but also actors themselves? How might this affect our theories of the causes and consequences of violence? To take one example, the great Russian playwright Anton Chekhov provides a set of tools to think about these questions in his own comments on the place a gun should have in a narrative—when any gun appears in the first act of a theatrical play, he contends, someone will fire

---

[12] Arthur L. Kellermann et al., "Suicide in the Home in Relation to Gun Ownership," *New England Journal of Medicine* 327, no. 7 (August 13, 1992): 467–472.

[13] David Hemenway and Matthew Miller, "Firearm Availability and Homicide Rates across 26 High-Income Countries," *Journal of Trauma and Acute Care Surgery* 49, no. 6 (2000): 985–988; Arindrajit Dube, Oeindrila Dube, and Omar García-Ponce, "Cross-Border Spillover: U.S. Gun Laws and Violence in Mexico," *American Political Science Review* 107, no. 3 (August 2013): 397–417; David M. Kennedy, Anne M. Piehl, and Anthony A. Braga, "Youth Violence in Boston: Gun Markets, Serious Youth Offenders, and a Use-Reduction Strategy," *Law and Contemporary Problems* 59, no. 1 (1996): 147–196.

[14] Abigail A. Kohn, *Shooters: Myths and Realities of America's Gun Cultures* (New York: Oxford University Press, 2004); Joan Burbick, *Gun Show Nation: Gun Culture and American Democracy* (New York: New Press, 2006).

[15] Laura Browder, *Her Best Shot: Women and Guns in America* (Chapel Hill: University of North Carolina Press, 2009); Jennifer Carlson, *Citizen-Protectors: The Everyday Politics of Guns in an Age of Decline* (New York: Oxford University Press, 2015); Bernard E. Harcourt, *Language of the Gun: Youth, Crime, and Public Policy* (Chicago: University of Chicago Press, 2006).

[16] Richard Slotkin, *Gunfighter Nation: The Myth of the Frontier in Twentieth-Century America* (Norman: University of Oklahoma Press, 1992).

it by the third. In explaining or understanding violence, we are also explicitly building narratives, which assume that we have correctly chosen the elements that make up our causal story. And this causal story must pay attention to the entity without which there can be no violence. How we describe violence, in other words, necessarily attributes a role to the objects in our inquiry as well as the human agents.[17]

Guns also claim an autonomous space within those narratives, becoming carriers of their own action. When guns appear, *must* they go off? Or, to rephrase the question, might the appearance of a gun in a social situation or interaction reshape the human actors who share the stage with the object, inciting them to pull the trigger? Like all objects, guns shape possible futures, changing the set of outcomes in a social interaction or game, and, in so doing, they also seem to change the players.[18]

That guns transform those who choose to use them is a central claim of this book. Scholars of material culture emphasize the ways in which things not only reflect social identity and organization, but also construct constraints through which social life is itself ordered. Guns at first seem to be simply part of an interaction that is fundamentally about shooters, targets, and observers.[19] This is the source of the notion that guns themselves are not capable of moral agency but instead are simply "tools," that they alone "don't kill people" and, therefore, should not be subject to legal regulation. But, as recent scholarship in material culture points out, part of the power of guns is that, like all products of labor, they can be treated as purely *external* points of reference as well; that is, technologies like guns (and telephones and computers) are similar to other, more abstract products of human labor, like language and law: they provide a medium outside of ourselves through which we both change the world and understand how those changes occur.[20] This process of "objectification" is crucial in understanding how guns can become so symbolically important, while at the same time appearing to simply mediate decisions ultimately made solely by humans.

Take, for instance, the famous Rifleman's Creed, a key element of the training process for new Marine Corps recruits (and made famous in *Full Metal Jacket*). The current version reads:

[17] Allen Feldman, *Formations of Violence: The Narrative of the Body and Political Terror in Northern Ireland* (Chicago: University of Chicago Press, 1991).

[18] Bruno Latour, "On Technical Mediation—Philosophy, Sociology, Genealogy," *Common Knowledge* 3, no. 2 (1994): 29–64.

[19] Alfred Gell, *Art and Agency: An Anthropological Theory* (Oxford, UK: Oxford University Press, 1998), 17–21.

[20] Daniel Miller, *Stuff* (Cambridge: Polity Press, 2010).

This is my rifle.

There are many like it, but this one is mine.

My rifle is my best friend. It is my life. I must master it as I must master my life.

My rifle, without me, is useless. Without my rifle, I am useless. I must fire my rifle true. I must shoot straighter than my enemy who is trying to kill me. I must shoot him before he shoots me. I will . . .

My rifle and myself know that what counts in this war is not the rounds we fire, the noise of our burst, not the smoke we make. We know that it is the hits that count. We will hit . . .

My rifle is human, even as I, because it is my life. Thus, I will learn it as a brother. I will learn its weaknesses, its strengths, its parts, its accessories, its sights and its barrel. I will ever guard it against the ravages of weather and damage as I will ever guard my legs, my arms, my eyes and my heart against damage. I will keep my rifle clean and ready. We will become part of each other. We will . . .

Before God, I swear this creed. My rifle and myself are the defenders of my country. We are the masters of our enemy. We are the saviors of my life.

So be it, until victory is America's and there is no enemy, but peace![21]

The creed offers both an account of objectification, asking recruits to think in new ways about the distances separating the gun as an object and the gun as a "human," while also trying to enhance the power and effectiveness of the object as a weapon in service of a larger, strategic aim. By treating the gun as an extension of the self—by taking seriously the notion that one should care for a gun like one cares for "legs" and "arms"—the gun and the person fuse, becoming "masters of our enemy." As part of the soldier's agency and an enhancement of military effectiveness, guns connect the private sphere of the individual's body to the political sphere of collective friends and enemies.

While other material objects—clothing, cookware, and cars, for example—all have potentially violent biographies, unlike weapons, such things do not usually circulate violence. In this way, guns may be unique, directing violence across distances through intentional targeting by a shooter. In this way, personal gun ownership challenges the fundamental presuppositions of the Weberian schematic of the state as the sole, legitimate protector of a populace. Indeed, many gun owners take seriously the risks and rewards of this power, adopting elaborate procedures to manage the cultivation of skills in gunplay and creating special spaces (ranges) in which to hone those skills. The end goal of this normative system is to prepare for the *gun fight*: the highly contingent, unpredictable, and often purely imaginary moment in which a gun owner will put the gun to use. Here, the myth of the utility of the gun disguises the agentic transformation of

---

[21] http://bootcamp4me.com/the-riflemans-creed/

the gun, and of its potential shooter. It is in this moment that the power to decide life and death—a key definition of sovereignty—becomes the provenance of an individual. Indeed, the allure of weapons as craft goods, as objects of ballistic inquiry, and even as cinematic mythologizing,[22] all contribute to a generalized narrative among gun-rights advocates that guns are ultimately useful because they may be needed in an armed interaction. Yet the promise of this power complicates both the idea of the gun and the identity of the gun owner.

Even if one has the "right" to protect oneself through carrying a gun, how can one know when a moment requiring self-protection will arise? The answer most gun-rights proponents give is that there is no way to know. Hence, as self-protection has become more important as a reason for buying guns in the United States, rather than hunting or recreation, owners have sought legal and technical means to carry guns everywhere. The *concealed-carry* movement— which advocates for the right to carry hidden weapons in public places on one's person—links the potential violence of the gun to its materiality as an object. As a result, unlike many other "things," guns rarely recede into the background. The power and responsibility of carrying an instrument of violence in one's pocket entails serious consequences for how one comports oneself; those who carry a concealed weapon are continually aware of the presence of the gun. They want the weapon to remain hidden from view, but also be accessible at all times. Gun culture is thus more than simply a semiotic system in which guns come to possess symbolic meanings; instead, it is a material, practical element of day-to-day life to which gun owners and users must continually adapt themselves.

By taking the gun seriously, as both a material and symbolic object, we are therefore pushing beyond approaches focused purely on the legal, discursive, or functional status of the weapon. At the same time, because guns and their associated material worlds are, ultimately, embedded in the production of violence, they frequently become objects of physical struggle, proudly displayed badges of pride, and obstacles and facilitators of day-to-day comfort. Guns can act with agency because, in their materiality, they impose themselves undeniably on the habits, emotions, and decisions of the people with whom they come in contact.

The contributions to this volume sketch out several kinds of "lives," arguing that guns live through the ways they inscribe and rewrite sovereignty (what we call political), through the modes by which they both destabilize and reproduce domination and division (what we call social), and by way of the consumptive and bodily practices they induce (what we call personal). Each of these "lives" highlight the simultaneous material and symbolic nature of ballistic weapons and trace their narrative lives. We will address each in turn.

---

[22] Consider such Hollywood productions as Anthony Mann's *Winchester '73* or Robert Altman's *Gun*, both of which narrate the biographies of particular weapons.

The Political Lives of Guns

As producers of violence, guns "live" in a condition intimately connected to the state; the capacity for relatively unskilled users to do immense damage, relatively quickly, creates new questions for who can and is able to kill. Since the state seeks to exercise a legitimate monopoly of force, the lethality of the gun makes it an intrinsically political object. Where guns differ from other objects (regulated or otherwise) is in how acute and active their political lives have become, particularly in the contemporary American context.

In her chapter on the politics of personal gun ownership in the United States, Elisabeth Anker draws attention to how guns become crucial to what she calls "mobile sovereignty," which is particularly appealing in moments of economic and political vulnerability. That is, guns are more than a totem of masculinity or a symbolic nexus of racial power or supremacy; they, quite literally, produce the feeling that carriers can act in the absence of state protection. They allow for a decentralization of political power. Unlike traditional nation-state forms of sovereignty, the perceived sovereignty of the gun owner remains disconnected from a bounded territory. Instead, the power to kill becomes linked to the personal space and field of vision (and action) of those who carry them.

Anker's argument draws on a wealth of material related to how gun-rights advocates conceptualize and broadcast their commitments to personal protection. But by introducing the notion of the mobile sovereign, she also provides an important conceptual vocabulary to link the gun as a necessarily specific object with the collective experience of vulnerability. Only by understanding the ways in which guns act as material and mobile containers for violence, a potential source of stateless protection, can we understand the politics behind controversial issues like "stand-your-ground" laws. Such laws allow people to respond to threats they perceive as deadly, without retreating (as required by other common law systems). In addition, they allow the gun owner to feel proactive rather than reactive, to embody a hope of civic agency that can substitute for a state failing in its core duty to protect.

This line of inquiry, however, leads to another question: why and when do guns become political markers of sovereignty to begin with?

In his chapter, Andrew Poe explains how guns especially might be a remaining site of enchantment that manifests this mode of political sovereignty. Such enchantment is especially apparent in the mode of production of guns. A recent transformation in gun production seen in 3D printing may have opened a new framework. The technology of 3D printing returns the manufacturing of firearms to owners, augmenting the agency of the gun. This changing relationship between gun owners and guns, into gun crafters and guns, produces a new threat to the monopoly of sovereign force that once defined the modern state.

Counter to a Weberian logic of disenchantment, Poe examines the manufacturing of firearms through advances in printing technologies, and the consequences of these new modes of gunsmithing for self-sovereignty. He claims that the radical printing (both of gunsmithing instructions, as well as of firearms themselves) diversifies the means of production of firearms. The self-production of plastic firearms, capable of ballistic force, opens the possibility that the actual matter of made things—from metal to plastic, and from tool (like a plow) to luxury item (and the idea of security), and finally to disposable/home-made—fundamentally transforms what constitutes the gun. It also empowers sovereign actors who might deploy this potentially violent force, liberating actors from the confines of state control.

In his chapter, Timothy Luke extends this argument further, arguing that the capacity for mass violence inherent in particular kinds of guns—"assault rifles"—is inextricable from the appeal of these objects in civilian life. Luke uses a "material genealogy" of AR-15 and M-16 rifles to show how, in moving from military use to civilian consumption, assault rifles become subjects in new kinds of cultural positions. For instance, the AR-15 is a hobbyist's platform, allowing for craft, artistic attention, and modification. Assault rifles provide opportunities for their owners to enjoy their technical and physical properties, to collect and learn about them as objects.

Even when owners use such guns in shooting activities (target shooting, hunting, and the like), these activities are seen as healthy, socially productive, and relaxing pursuits. These weapons, though implicated in very real and tragic events like the 2012 massacre at Sandy Hook Elementary in Connecticut, are aesthetic as well as political objects. Thus, when these guns move from military battlefields to household garages and Hollywood movies, their material "continuity"—the fact that they maintain their physical form across different contexts—allows users to draw on their origin as tools of war to construct fantasies that violent destruction can also be personal and fun.

In examining guns and their materiality, Luke also points out that guns gain a kind of "subject" status as part of an intricate social formation, in which the weapon, bullets, targets, and the shooter form a kind of social system, with agency distributed across each of the components. While the shooter remains the primary mover in this social system (the root of the notion that guns don't themselves kill people), he concludes that guns mediate and transform human agency.

Bringing Luke, Anker, and Poe's chapters together helps us reframe the political stakes of guns in the contemporary American context. Luke shows us that, even as they move from the battlefield to the target range, their tangibility as objects roots the appeal of guns. Users perceive such weapons as violent instruments possessing a ludic quality, retaining the mark of both their political and recreational uses. Anker in turn links this quality—which can give the user the feeling that the gun is itself an agent—to the logic of gun *rights*. The political nature of guns is a function of their capacity to produce feelings of power, felt as joy, fun, and freedom (as well as terror). Those feelings intrinsically connect to visions of personal agency and the relationship individuals have to the state. Poe highlights the ways in which shifting control of the very means of production of guns helps transform those modalities of agency. The inequalities produced by state hierarchies depend on control of both the monopolies of force, but also on the material conditions of the production of force itself.

The "political" life of the gun, then, requires us to think seriously about the materiality of the weapon and the violence it produces in the affective experiences of political subjects. But the feeling of sovereignty produced by guns is necessarily incomplete. A society of armed actors, each claiming the right to self-defense, produces more rather than less fear. Here, the presence of the gun itself becomes able to achieve those feelings of protection. Moreover, such a social system, when backed up by a legal regime protecting the right to "stand your ground," reproduces existing inequalities among genders, races, and classes. The very choice to use deadly force is, in fact, always at least in part a response to socially constructed threats, which often accompany these cleavages. It is to this issue that we now turn.

The Social Lives of Guns

Who "shoots" and who is "shot" is rarely random; but while guns have been critical in toppling and revising political hierarchies and promoting visions of civic agency, the distribution of ballistic coercion just as often reflects and reproduces existing forms of social organization. The relations among those who own, make, and use guns, as well as those targeted by guns, construct a social life that embeds weapons to complex projects of power, moving them beyond discussions of political rights and sovereignty and into the realm of domination and resistance.

Heather Hayes explores this point by analyzing the links between military drone technology and civilian policing. For Hayes, drones (the military variant of which usually include some form of self-flying ballistic technology) not only possess a form of autonomy and remoteness lacking in previous weapons systems, they also challenge how we think about violence itself. We should not limit the coercive violence of drones to the impact of a ballistic explosive, but extend it also to how they "speak." This constant, ominous noise, like the click of a gun trigger, indicates the potential for imminent pain, but also suggests, according to Hayes, that weapons are more complex social actors than we give them credit for. They can "see"—in the sense that they include optical and tracking technologies—they can "move," and they can "speak," all without human intervention.

To highlight how a weapon's "speech" contributes to its coercion undermines one of the key distinctions in political thought: the idea that violence starts where speech ends, and that somehow the two modalities of political life offer us clearly distinctive ways of resolving conflicts and producing consensus.[23] But the fact that algorithmically adept drones can seemingly also make decisions draws attention to instability in the boundaries separating human decisions about killing from the material through which that killing is carried out.

Hayes also shows, however, that the circulation of such weapons from the battlefield to neighborhoods in American cities significantly undermines the distinction between the domestic and international spheres of state power. In particular, she argues that pilots deploy these semi-autonomous drones dispro-portionately against racial minorities. Drones allow the state to practice a diffuse form of control, one in which the general, seemingly ubiquitous threat of "death from the skies" replaces more personalized forms of coercive interaction tra-ditionally used by police or military forces. Precisely because this kind of state terror does not depend on any such interaction, but instead simply the presence of the weapon itself (controlled remotely), drones upend practical differences in state coercion against both citizens and foreigners.

Ballistic technologies create spatially extensive forms of violence, allowing killing at a distance. This distance, in turn, is essential in maintaining the social distinctions between vulnerable targets (like minority populations) and shooters (like state authorities), since it can help dehumanize the targets of violence. But killing is, as Joanna Bourke reminds us in her chapter, ultimately a visceral and bodily process, and even the remoteness of ballistic technology only incompletely avoids the complex and messy implications of using physical harm to enact political power.

Bourke traces international legal debates in the late nineteenth century to show how British authorities defended a new killing technology—the Dum-Dum bullet—in the midst of widespread opposition from other "civilized" powers. Dum-Dums—semi-jacketed ammunition developed by British Lieutenant Colonel Neville Sneyd Bertie-Clay in aid of the colonial struggle in India—became both a symbol of British imperial power and an object of conten-tion on the international stage, where delegates at the Hague Peace Conference in 1899 labeled it as inhumane.

---

[23] Hannah Arendt, *On Violence* (San Diego, CA: Harcourt, Brace, and World, 1970).

Ballistics scientists, legal scholars, and military thinkers saw Dum-Dums as uniquely capable of imposing undue amounts of physical pain in addition to killing the target. Opponents of the British Empire seized on this evidence to argue that such technology was unfit for use against other European powers. British "experts" responded not only by arguing that *all* forms of killing were, in a way, inhumane, but also by claiming that the bullet's "stopping" power was of great use against "savage" colonial opponents. The net effect of these debates was to link the destructive materiality of the Dum-Dum to a discourse about civility. Ironically, over time the Dum-Dum's reputation as an instrument of terror took on a life of its own, and actually increased the appeal of the weapon to future military and police strategists. They used its taboo status as a signal of their own willingness to confront a "barbarous" opponent in an insurgency or civil war.

While Bourke focuses attention on the level of discourse about ballistics, Franklin Zimring draws our attention to the level of personal interaction. Specifically, he demonstrates how police are more likely to use deadly force against unarmed African American men, whose bodily movements and physical proximity they view as particularly threatening. Heated interactions involving struggles to control guns, somewhat ironic given the putative role of the firearm as a means of *protecting* the officer, make police more rather than less likely to use them against seeming threats.

Zimring suggests that the ways agents of the state use violence are intimate, emotional, and ultimately social. While scholars often tie the killing of African Americans to large-scale structural and demographic factors, such killings are also a result of how police think and act *with their guns* in moments of danger. In this, Zimring follows in the spirit of recent sociological work on the importance of contingent, interactive events as building blocks in social life.[24]

But Zimring does not stop there; because prosecuting police officers for such deaths reintroduces *structural* problems of unequal power and access to courts, he argues that new rules of engagement—practical, embodied techniques of acting enforced by rules and regulations—offer a better path forward than judicial redress. He thus proposes a series of such rules which require that police officers learn to use their own guns correctly. Habits of use matter in both explaining and preventing violence.

For police officers, like officials in the British Empire or the American military, ballistic weapons thus rarely play a neutral or purely instrumental role. Instead, police use guns to help draw distinctions among communities or groups. Moreover, Zimring links these social distinctions, core to the operation of political power, to their materiality. In some cases, the mere presence

---

[24] Robin Wagner-Pacific, *What Is an Event?* (Chicago: University of Chicago Press, 2017).

of a gun serves to change an interaction, as Zimring points out, while in others, the sound, power, and even the aesthetics of guns, help give them reputations as instruments of terror.

Guns connect macro-social structures of power and domination, like race, colonialism, or the state, to particular situations and transactions. At the same time, guns are also objects which people acquire, carry, and learn to use. The next section explores these more personal and quotidian aspects of the lives of guns.

The Private Lives of Guns

The private lives of guns involve the ways in which subjects embed guns in circuits of production, marketing, and sales, as well as other material and bodily practices involved in making weapons continuously available and useful. This path, too, necessarily connects the material experience of violence with the politics of personal protection and the social organization of domination and resistance. However, ballistic weapons, which enter the worlds of training and consumption, also forge a different set of relations to users than those conceptualized primarily as political "actors."

David Yamane's chapter, an ethnographic exploration of a gun show specializing in concealed-carry paraphernalia, demonstrates these relations in several ways. First, there are the complexities involved in producing weapons that owners could ever even conceal. These guns must be small and relatively light, but the smaller and lighter the weapon, the less lethal it is. This, of course, defeats the whole purpose of concealed carry. Gunmakers produce weapons for the concealed-carry market that push the technical envelope. And yet the solutions produced often open up new problems in terms of use and access. Gunmakers find them in a complex arms race to provide maximum "stopping power" with minimal size.

These technical problems are, as Yamane shows, also cultural; committing to the "concealed-carry lifestyle" involves a huge array of devices, gadgets, political pamphlets, bumper stickers, fashion accessories, and other accoutrements, which the exposition concentrates into a single setting of display and commercial exchange. Guns are in reality only a small part of what Yamane refers to as "gun culture 2.0," a term practitioners use to describe the shift away from firearms as sporting devices to guns as means of self-protection.

While guns at concealed-carry shows are commodities, in the sense that they are exchangeable and interchangeable in terms of value, the violence they produce—and their potential to "save lives"—also makes them peculiar and fascinating objects on their own. Thus, much of the material culture that surrounds concealed-carry weapons involves personalization and customization of both the weapon itself and the holsters, carriers, and ammunition needed to make such a lifestyle possible.

Finally, Yamane shows how the expo links different kinds of consumers to a notion of "armed citizenship" while also providing for individual expression and consumer choice. Politics plays a key role in the discursive environment of the concealed-carry expo; the armed citizen naturally invokes the cluster of concepts of sovereignty and personal responsibility. As Yamane observes, in order for armed citizens to be "self-reliant," they must also participate in a shared material culture, making such individual responsibility possible.

Thus, armed citizens are not just political subjects; they are also shoppers. As such, a key imperative of the expo is to meet the "demands" of individual consumers while simultaneously forging an abstract community of armed citizens from a variety of backgrounds. For instance, Yamane demonstrates how manufacturers explicitly address the "carry needs" of women by designing particular accessories like purses and special holsters intended to facilitate a "feminine" version of concealed carry. In addition, the show features a huge array of customizable holsters and guns, each of which provides the possibility that consumption can preserve individuality while sustaining a shared political vision. In this sense, expos are indeed expository, transforming commercial experience into a political event and, in turn, using the political logic of self-sufficiency and personal agency to sell guns and associated goods.

Concealed carry is thus, in part, a matter of consumption. But, as Harel Shapira reveals in his own ethnographic work at a gun range in Texas, learning to carry and use guns for self-protection is also a matter of bodily practice. Building on Marcel Mauss's conception of the "technique of the body," Shapira focuses on the emotional and physical experience of carrying and shooting guns, and the ways in which participants in training programs discipline their movements and posture to accommodate the weapon.

It turns out that guns are intimidating objects, which rarely allow their users to forget or ignore them. This fear is, in part, socially produced. Shapira shows how gun training helps to make users acutely aware of the gun's violent potential, while also providing them with techniques to make the weapon useful and controllable. But guns make loud and terrifying noises, and the act of shooting is physically demanding and destabilizing. Shapira describes how the first interaction with guns in a training scenario lends itself to fear and exhilaration, both of which are key emotional components for the training process itself.

More specifically, training in armed self-protection means experiencing scenarios or imaginary interactions of danger, in which users develop skills necessary to respond to unforeseen contingencies. Shapira describes how trainers purposefully create complications in shooting and use—such as a jammed gun or one that misfires—in order to accustom users to the imaginary "gun fight" in which they must use their concealed firearm in an unpredictable and uncontrolled context. These imaginary interactions code victims and perpetrators along racial and gender lines and help propagate the notion that only through constant vigilance and preparedness can one properly address the dangers of everyday life. The hope is that training and carrying will reduce the fear many gun owners have about finding themselves in a predatory interaction.

Ironically, carrying concealed guns in public places also imposes psychic and physical costs on those who do so, and many find themselves in situations for which training has not equipped them. How, Shapira asks, does one go to the bathroom while holstering a concealed weapon, without unintentionally revealing it to precisely those "bad guys" who might take advantage of such a moment of vulnerability? In Shapira's telling, there is no clear solution to this problem; carrying guns is a very complex bodily process requiring constant adaptation and attention. By design, concealed guns recede into the background, but they become a focus for almost every physical movement and choice that adherents make.

Concealed weapons, then, "act" in multiple ways. As functionally dangerous objects, they entice their users to adopt particular bodily habits, buy helpful holsters and accessories, and align with certain political schemas. But secret self-defense guns also reflect the desire of owners to extend a sense of agency into a threatening world without drawing attention to these alterations in bodily and material style. When guns appear in a social setting, they change it; their very existence can transform the emotional content of an interaction between police and suspects, or trigger terror through their appearance or sound. The very logic of concealed carry presupposes the notion that guns have a certain social power *on their own*.

Concealed weapons also reveal the intersection of the political, social, and private lives of the gun in stark detail, for there is a direct connection between the concealed gun purchased at an expo and hidden while using the bathroom and the distinction between "good guys" (often white) and "bad guys" (usually not). Other weapons, too, connect these domains—Dum-Dum bullets are both objects of a civilizational discourse as well as a commodity produced and distributed. Drone technology produces terror for targets and delight for amateur hobbyists. In these situations, the political and private lives of guns reinforce and affirm one another. At other times, of course, they might come into conflict, as when the arms possessed by police actually *cause* a (perceived) practical threat and a potential escalation with African American men.

A source of the uniqueness of guns reveals itself in how these private, social, and political domains never quite collapse into one another. The portable violence of the gun, while an object requiring bodily and commercial accommodations, also necessarily brings up questions of protection and threat for owners, potential targets, and bystanders. Even when sitting on a table, out of the reach of any potential users, a gun is often impossible to ignore. Is it loaded? Has anyone fired it? Is it a threat or a comfort? These questions are unavoidable, as the sight of the ballistic weapon possesses its own allure. And they highlight a lurking agency in these various lives of guns.

Conclusion

The lives of guns addressed by contributors to this book are only some of the many ways in which guns "live"—we can only cursorily address many of the legal and cultural modes through which we might understand guns and their position in human life. Moreover, most of the owners, makers, and users of guns in our account are white and male, while we know from scholars like Bernard Harcourt that women, young people, and people of color have very different discursive engagements with the gun as an object.[25]

Nevertheless, in addressing how guns live, the contributors to this book draw our attention to several important things. First, while some owners and users may perceive guns in contemporary America as "tools" capable of achieving particular ends, the protection they offer is necessarily incomplete. This is largely because the sales, manufacture, distribution, purchase, and production of guns, as well as the socialization of their owners, are responses to a perceived weakness of the state, and thus a need for constant vigilance and a concomitant interpersonal fear. While it is undoubtedly true that concealed-carry weapons have saved some lives, and that proper training in gun storage and use can reduce accidents, at the root of contemporary gun culture is a belief in mutual threat, deterrence, and the occlusion of the state as a locus for protection. The problems many policy and health experts have with private gun ownership, rooted in a logic of self-protection rather than sport or recreation, seemingly fail to reckon with a Hobbesian schema that is simultaneously ideological and materially embedded in the practices of activists.

This schema is not merely a matter of locating the individual's agency in contemporary society. States and communities make and use weapons to contend with and enforce political power in a world where violence serves as a key medium of exchange. Because ballistic weapons involve *targeting*, victims are rarely random or unintentional; this very fact links the materiality of the weapon to discourses, bodily reactions, and ideological presuppositions that privilege

[25] Harcourt, *Language of the Gun.*

certain identities. Scholars of nuclear weapons have explored the ways in which mass violence encodes and reflects these assumptions about civilization, barbarism, and racial or ethnic superiority; our contributors demonstrate that the same logic of deterrence and first use apply at the more intimate scale of the gun.[26]

A second point suggested by the work collected in this book is that guns connect as well as divide people. As objects of exchange, firearms (like all other commodities) link potentially distant producers, manufacturers, and purchasers into a shared and interdependent set of social relationships, a phenomenon Mauss analyzed many years ago in his important work on the gift.[27] But because of their danger and allure, guns also draw adherents directly together in spatially and temporally bound contexts like expos, gun ranges, and online chat rooms, where participants can forge a shared commitment to armed citizenship or can indulge in hobbyist debate and discussion. Those who seek to meet the practical demands of getting access to and learning to control deadly force, somewhat ironically, can do so through social engagement; indeed, many such actors actively bond over their shared fear of diffuse and unpredictable threats of contemporary life.

Third, while guns move through many registers and link various social domains in contemporary America, they are, like objects of art, ultimately unstable objects. By unstable, we are referring to the fact that even seemingly inert or inactive guns, like those hanging on a museum wall, provoke feelings of terror and fascination. The defining feature of the ballistic weapon is its potential for both explosive *and* targeted violence; as a result, guns almost always both appear "objective," in the sense that they are material objects capable of killing at a distance, and "subjective," in the sense that their production and use ultimately reflect human choices and decisions. Such instability in what guns are and how we should respond to them helps us understand differences in how they might be classified socially and legally. Because knives, for example, preserve the intimacy of killing—connecting them much more to the subjective side of material culture—they produce a different politics than the ballistic weapon, which enables distant foes (socially and otherwise) to engage with one another.[28] As a

---

[26] Hugh Gusterson, "Nuclear Weapons and the Other in the Western Imagination," *Cultural Anthropology* 14, no. 1 (1999): 111–143; Andrew J. Rotter, *Hiroshima: The World's Bomb* (New York: Oxford University Press, 2009).

[27] Marcel Mauss, *The Gift*, W. D. Halls, trans. (New York: Routledge Press, 1990).

[28] In nineteenth-century Argentina, for instance, the use of a knife by the gaucho became a way of linking personal to national honor, precisely *because* of the intimacy of knife fighting as a technique of dueling. See Sandra Gayol, " '*Honor Moderno*': The Significance of Honor in Fin-de-Siècle Argentina," *Hispanic American Historical Review* 84, no. 3 (2004): 475–498.

result, in the United States at least, guns relate directly, and in a unique way, to stories about citizenship, revolutionary sentiment, and individualism.

Finally, while many of our contributors agree that guns may have some "agency," most do not call them "agents." The notion that "people kill people" is, in other words, obviously right; people are inevitably agents in gun violence. But, as Latour points out, the corollary that "guns don't kill people" cannot be quite correct; this slogan only matters if guns are also something more, something worth defending or attacking precisely because their material effects themselves are transformative.[29] The gun's capacity to affirm or challenge an existing social order or social interaction merely by its appearance instead suggests that it is embedded in what Kenneth Burke might call an "agency-act" ratio; a narrative or causal structure in which the instrument of agency (the appearance of the gun) irreducibly shapes the action (of killing, or shooting) that engenders it.[30] While this may seem a straightforward claim, if taken seriously it would force us to rethink many of the ways we think about the causes of violence as strictly a product of human decision, external to the particular material conditions facilitating those choices to begin with.

Focusing analytic attention on the relationship between the agency of the gun and the acts of violence, intimidation, joy, and allure they create offers us a new way to think about the problem of firearms in both the United States and abroad. Scholars miss too much in the study of guns as merely objects of legal regulation, or as causes of public health crises, or as bases for political movements that focus solely on solutions like "gun control" or "accident prevention." Moreover, these approaches rarely register with gun-rights supporters, who consider guns to be the material embodiments of civic agency. For such advocates, the world is a forbidding and dangerous place, and the state is, at best, an incomplete protector. Such fundamentally different understandings of the gun, on the part of rights activists (more inclined to appreciate and understand guns in personal and material ways), and on the part of many policy and legal analysts (for whom guns are abstract and threatening tools), play a significant role in the stalemate in gun-politics discussions in the United States. By identifying the multiple lives of the gun, this problem becomes even more complex; for it remains a simple fact that the political, social, and personal lives of guns help make some visions of society possible while threatening to destroy others.

---

[29] Latour, "On Technical Mediation."

[30] Kenneth Burke, *A Grammar of Motives* (Berkeley: University of California Press, 1969).

Part I

THE POLITICAL LIFE OF GUNS

1

Mobile Sovereigns

Agency Panic and the Feeling of Gun Ownership

ELISABETH ANKER

There are more guns in the United States than there are citizens.[1] Most gun owners state that they own guns for "protection," unlike in earlier generations when gun ownership was significantly lower and the primary reason for ownership was "recreation."[2] Now, more people than ever own guns, and they do so for safety and security. Having a gun, as many studies have shown, does not make a person safer; in fact, people are much more likely to die by gunshot, whether accidentally or intentionally, if they own a gun.[3] By some measurements, one's

[1] Gun ownership has been on the rise since the 1970s when rates of ownership dramatically increased at the same time that restrictions for carrying guns in public were weakened across the country. Now, more Americans own guns and are licensed to carry guns than at any other time in US history. See *Report from the Crime Prevention Research Center*, July 9, 2014, http://crimeresearch.org/wp-content/uploads/2014/07/Concealed-Carry-Permit-Holders-Across-the-United-States.pdf.

[2] Greg St. Martin, "Study: 70M More Firearms Added to US Gun Stock over Last 20 Years." *News@Northeastern*, September 26, 2016. https://news.northeastern.edu/2016/09/study-70m-more-firearms-added-to-us-gun-stock-over-past-20-years/. As reported by the study investigators, "these findings are in stark contrast to the mid-1990s, when the last comprehensive survey to assess reasons for gun ownership, the 1994 National Firearm Survey, found that 46 percent of gun owners cited protection as the principal reason for gun ownership (the majority cited recreation, such as hunting or target shooting)."

[3] A. L. Kellerman et al. "Gun Ownership as a Risk Factor for Homicide in the Home" *New England Journal of Medicine* 329 (October 7, 1993): 1084–1091; Garen J. Wintemute, "Guns, Fear, the Constitution, and the Public's Health, " *New England Journal of Medicine* 358, no. 14 (April 3, 2008): 1421–1424; Linda L. Dahlberg, Robin M. Ikeda, and Marcie-jo Kresnow, "Guns in the Home and Risk of a Violent Death in the Home: Findings from a National Study," *American Journal of Epidemiology* 160, no. 10 (November 15, 2004): 929–936; Madeline Drexler, "Guns & Suicide: The Hidden Toll," *Harvard Public Health*, Spring 2013, https://www.hsph.harvard.edu/magazine/magazine_article/guns-suicide/; Abhay Aneja, John J. Donohue III, and Alexandria Zhang, "The Impact of Right to Carry Laws and the NRC Report." *National Bureau for Economic Research*, September 4, 2014, http://crimeresearch.org/wp-content/uploads/2014/11/SSRN-id2443681.pdf;

chance of dying by homicide doubles the minute a gun is brought into a home.[4] Yet most people report that buying a gun makes them feel more secure, and that carrying a gun grants them protection and authority.[5] What can explain the *feeling* of security that gun ownership confers, and the more general rise in gun ownership across the United States?

Gun ownership, I will argue, has become a way for people, especially white men who make up the vast majority of owners, to feel as if they are personally sovereign over many of the precarious yet confusing economic and political experiences that shape their daily lives. The last few decades have been called an era of uncertainty in the United States, when long-standing political, economic, and social structures, initially created to support a flourishing citizenry, have been eviscerated, leaving people feeling isolated and vulnerable. As Wendy Brown has detailed, we live in an era of "waning sovereignty" in which visible manifestations of state and economic power are weakening, which leaves people feeling confused and unprotected, and looking for new promises of security.[6] Many people, particularly white men, now feel unable to live up to the promise of individual sovereignty and economic success they have been promised as privileged members of the American electorate, a feeling that they are not about to achieve what is rightfully theirs. Gun ownership, I suggest, often carries the implicit promise of counteracting increasing economic and social insecurity. Owning, and especially carrying, a gun buffers against declining sovereignty. If sovereignty, classically defined, is the final authority to make decisions within a given sphere, then gun owners feel as if guns can restore their personal capacity for self-determination and success against a backdrop of waning economic and social sovereignty.[7] Carrying a gun re-instantiates a type of individual sovereignty when other forms of sovereign power might seem out of reach.

Scott R. Kegler and James A. Mercy, "Firearm Homicides and Suicides in Major Metropolitan Areas—United States, 2006–2007 and 2009–2010," *Center For Disease Control and Prevention MMWR*, August 2, 2013, https://www.cdc.gov/mmwr/pdf/wk/mm6230.pdf; Jennifer Carlson, *Citizen-Protectors: The Everyday Politics of Guns in an Age of Decline* (New York: Oxford University Press, 2015), 5.

[4] Rates of suicide are almost ten times higher with a gun in the home. See Andrew T. Anglemyer, Tara H. Horvath, and George Rutherford, "The Accessibility of Firearms and Risk For Suicide and Homicide Victimization among Household Members: A Systematic Review and Meta-Analysis" *Annals of Internal Medicine* 160, no. 2 (January 21, 2014), 101–110; and Dahlberg, Ikeda, and Kresnow, "Guns in the Home."

[5] Alan Leshner et al., *Priorities of Research to Reduce the Threat of Firearm-Related Violence*, Washington, DC: National Academies Press, 2013, http://www.ncdsv.org/images/IOM-NRC_Priorities-for-Research-to-reduce-the-threat-of-firearm-related-violence_2013.pdf.

[6] Wendy Brown, *Walled States, Waning Sovereignty* (Brooklyn, NY: Zone, 2010).

[7] Jean Bodin, *On Sovereignty* (Cambridge: Cambridge University Press, 1992); Thomas Hobbes, *Leviathan* (New York: Penguin, 1982).

When scholars discuss the appeal of gun ownership and the feeling of security it confers, they often turn to masculinity as an explanatory force. Michael Kimmel's important work sees guns as a key factor in the performance of contemporary masculinity, where showing fear is tantamount to feeling emasculated; owning a gun counters that fear with a supposition of strength.[8] James Gibson argues that the popularity of gun ownership in the United States reflects the post-Vietnam militarization of masculinity, implicitly suggesting that weakened state power encourages gun ownership as a compensatory mechanism.[9] Scott Meltzer examines how gun manufacturers and the National Rifle Association pair gun ownership and masculinity, as if the former proves the gendered toughness of the latter and grants individual freedom understood as a performance of masculine fearlessness.[10] Jennifer Carlson argues that a nexus of historical and social factors, including downward mobility, women as breadwinners, and a deep investment in outmoded visions of America, contribute to a sense of weakened masculinity that is countered by carrying a gun.[11] Each of these analyses of gun ownership and masculinity are important for interpreting the reasons behind increases in gun use. Yet the *feeling of regained sovereignty* that gun ownership offers is not subsumed by masculinity, for sovereignty is a somewhat different alignment of power than a performance of masculinity alone. It connects increased gun ownership with the geopolitical and economic instabilities that help to fuel a sense of *lost* power, and can explain why our era has seen such a steep increase in ownership relative to the 1970s.

A desire for sovereignty, I suggest, undergirds the increasing allure of guns and the feelings of security they confer. For what is a gun but an instrument of sovereignty for determining life and death? It is a mechanism for sovereign control over the self through sovereign power over the life of another. Guns allow owners who carry them to determine at any given moment who shall live and who shall die. It grants the fantasy of individual sovereignty, if not the very power of sovereignty, over and against others with whom they would otherwise be in a putatively equalized relationship, or from whom they would otherwise feel vulnerable and/or threatened. As political theorists from Thomas Hobbes to Giorgio Agamben have argued, to have the power to determine who can be killed is to be sovereign over what can be killed and what is allowed to live.[12]

---

[8] Michael Kimmel, *Angry White Men: American Masculinity at the End of an Era* (New York: Nation Books, 2013).

[9] James William Gibson, *Warrior Dreams* (New York: Hill and Wang, 1994).

[10] Scott Melzer, *Gun Crusaders: The NRA's Culture War* (New York: New York University Press, 2012).

[11] Carlson, *Citizen-Protectors*.

[12] See Hobbes, *Leviathan*; and Carl Schmitt, *Political Theology: Four Chapters on the Concept of Sovereignty* (Chicago: University of Chicago Press, 2006); Michel Foucault *History of Sexuality, Vol 1.*, Robert Hurley, trans. (New York: Vintage, 1990).

Carrying a gun echoes this power and suggests that the relationship between self and other is hierarchical and one of domination and control, rather than equality or vulnerability.

Yet the very concept of sovereignty does not remain stable in idea or in practice when carrying a gun. It produces a different type of sovereign power, one that is mobile and without predetermined boundaries except the range of a bullet and the movement of the body. Gun ownership in an era of concealed-carry and Stand Your Ground laws challenges the idea that our current era is only one of waning sovereignty. Instead, gun ownership confers a *fragmented and mobile sovereignty* that constantly changes the boundaries of final authority. Carrying a gun produces a portable and privatized sovereignty without a fixed territory or known borders, setting up an ever-shifting and unpredictable range of individual control that is unknown to others who may enter it. The increase in violence this enables, however, deepens the instability and insecurity that carrying a gun intends to challenge, contributing to the vulnerability and powerlessness it aims to counteract.

In this chapter, I examine four of the factors contributing to a feeling of lost sovereignty, and then show how the mobile sovereignty of gun ownership aims to rehabilitate individual sovereignty even as it changes the conceptual apparatus of sovereign power and territory.

Agency Panic and Lost Sovereignty

In an era of decreasing crime, the increase in gun ownership and gun carrying over the last twenty years, especially for "protection," might seem contradictory or misplaced. But when we turn to a different optic, and view our moment as an era of decreasing state and individual sovereignty, the rise in gun ownership makes more sense. We are living in what some scholars call a "post-sovereign" era in which the ability of states to control their territory has significantly weakened, as has the concomitant fantasy of individual control over one's destiny.[13] States are losing power to global capital flows, technological developments,

[13] On this point see Elisabeth Anker, "Sovereign Longings: Violence and Desire in the Trump Era," *theory@buffalo 20: Doing Theory*. Spring 2018. http://gsa.buffalo.edu/theory/wp-content/uploads/sites/56/2018/04/t@b_20_Elisabeth-Anker-1.pdf; Elisabeth Anker and William Youmans, "Sovereign Aspirations: National Security and Police Power in a Global Era," *Theory & Event* 20, no. 1 (January 2017): 3–18; Richard Bellamy, "Sovereignty, Post-Sovereignty, and Pre-Sovereignty: Three Models of the State, Democracy, and Rights within the EU," in *Sovereignty in Transition*, ed. Neil Walker (Oxford, UK: Hart Publishing, 2003), 167–190; Michael J. Shapiro, "Moral Geographies and the Ethics of Post-Sovereignty," *Public Culture* 6, no. 3 (1994), 479–502.

international NGOs, nonstate violence, and climate change disasters that make the world feel increasingly chaotic. Individuals feel precarious as they struggle to support themselves while economic inequality has grown exponentially, and communities are torn apart by unemployment as the state has withdrawn support for the vulnerable.[14] In this context, "protection" seems not an incongruous or false claim justifying gun use but an accurate desire on the part of owners to stave off nebulous but deeply felt senses of lost economic, political, and social power, a waning of sovereignty in their world and in themselves. This is not to say that sovereignty has ever been fully achieved, for either individuals or states, and some scholars even argue that sovereignty is always an aspiration if not a fantasy.[15] It is to say, however, that sovereignty serves as a horizon for a form of power that waxes and wanes in accordance with political and social conditions, and amidst current shifts in power seems to be receding past a point of recuperation.

Gun ownership transforms larger geopolitical quandaries that seem to herald a waning sovereignty into a problem of individual power. As I have argued elsewhere, there is a long-standing US tradition of conflating individual and state sovereignty, as if dramatic acts of state violence seem to confer individual sovereignty.[16] Conversely, when state power seems blocked or enervated, as when up against transnational finance or nonstate terrorism, this can be experienced as a loss of individual power for those who identify with state action as an extension and proof of their own personal potency. Gun carrying reflects a desire to regain individual sovereignty in this context by placing the felt experience of geopolitical instabilities onto a scene of individual power over villainous forces.

Gun ownership, I would suggest, aims to salve what Timothy Melley calls "agency panic," a generalized sense, developing out of the later twentieth century up to the present, in which individuals feel increasingly powerless within a complex global society, while the forces of control are difficult to discern.[17] The powers that seemingly sap individuals' agency are nebulous yet omnipotent, controlling but without accountability. In Melley's analysis, agency panic sets in when individuals feel that they have lost power to complex forces they neither know or understand. It is particularly strong in the white American men

---

[14] Sheldon S. Wolin, *Democracy Incorporated: Managed Democracy and the Specter of Inverted Totalitarianism* (Princeton, NJ: Princeton University Press, 2007).

[15] Joan Cocks, for one, argues that sovereignty is always a fantasy and delusion; *Sovereignty, And Other Political Delusions* (London: Bloomsbury, 2014).

[16] Elisabeth Anker, "Heroic Identifications: Or, 'You Can Love Me Too—I Am So Like the State,'" *Theory and Event* 15, no. 1 (2012); Elisabeth Anker, *Orgies of Feeling: Melodrama and the Politics of Freedom* (Durham, NC: Duke University Press, 2014).

[17] Timothy Melley, *Empire of Conspiracy: The Culture of Paranoia in Postwar America* (Ithaca, NY: Cornell, 2000).

who presume self-mastery as an individual and national entitlement, and who implicitly expect to dominate over others, especially the women and minorities who are figured more as dependents than as catalysts of power. An example of agency panic (and the way guns seem to offer a reprieve from it) is described by a journalist recently embedded with gun owners training to be part of a militia: "During two days of conversations, grievances poured forth from the group as effortlessly as bullets from a gun barrel. On armed excursions through sun-dappled forests, they spoke of a vague but looming tyranny—an amalgam of sinister forces to be held at bay only with a firearm and the willingness to use it."[18] Guns seem to salve the agency panic bred by the confusions of globalized power, of a "vague but looming tyranny," by promising to regain control over "sinister forces," and it offers this control as an experience of individual sovereignty. As the premises of sovereign individualism weaken in response to shifting social, geopolitical, and economic powers, compensatory forms of individual strength develop that are tied to gun ownership.

In the specific form of agency panic I track in relation to gun ownership, a felt sense of lost agency comes from multiple factors across the social landscape. First, a sense of lost state sovereignty, that the American state as a global super-power has lost power vis-a-vis other global forms of power like transnational capital and nongovernmental institutions, and it is unable to solve the problems that beset ordinary Americans.[19] The second factor contributing to the agency panic of lost sovereignty is an inchoate but real sense of lost political influence. This is a loss of *popular* sovereignty in the form of liberal democracy. This loss comes from a sense that one no longer has a capacity to shape or participate in governing decisions, as the country's vast decision-making power is both globally dispersed and also more internally centralized and remote from every-day localities. It is a recognition that political decisions are made without one's input, without care for the needs of ordinary people, and that representatives do not represent one's interests in any way. Citizens know that they have little say in governing, that their representational connection to political elites is weak at best, and that their communities are ignored. This loss is powerful, even as popular sovereignty was never, in and of itself, realized in America.[20] Popular sovereignty, as equal and universal power to shape governing decisions across

[18] David Zuccino, "A Militia Gets Ready for a 'Gun-Grabbing' Clinton Presidency," *New York Times*, November 4, 2016, A 12, http://www.nytimes.com/2016/11/05/us/a-militia-gets-battle-ready-for-a-gun-grabbing-clinton-presidency.html.

[19] Zygmunt Bauman, *Liquid Times: Living in an Age of Uncertainty* (Cambridge, UK: Polity Press, 2006); Saskia Sassen, *Losing Control: Sovereignty in an Age of Globalization* (New York: Columbia University Press, 1996).

[20] Wendy Brown, *Politics Out of History* (Princeton, NJ: Princeton University Press, 2001).

a population, has always been an aspirational ideal rather than an actuality. But after decades of neoliberal devaluation of participatory politics, combined with two supreme court decisions, Citizens United in 2010 and the gutting of the Voting Rights Act in 2013, which together empowered corporations to have heretofore unimagined power in campaigns while re-legalizing discrimination against marginalized voters, that loss is even more acute. It is a loss not merely of people's ability to participate in the daily decisions shaping their polity but more specifically the loss of even investing in or desiring a polity that could be truly democratic.

The loss of popular sovereignty is separate from the loss of state sovereignty, even though they can be erroneously conflated.[21] State power—in terms of international relations and domestic order—is quite different than the gradual weakening of the people to shape their polity in a meaningful way.[22] But the conflation of state with popular sovereignty is itself a symptom of the de-democratization of the American polity. Many people feel that their political power has become increasingly minute while corporate and political elites dictate the terms and policies of collective life with little accountability to the populations for whom those policies are supposedly enacted.[23] Even as state power is weakened vis-a-vis transnational capital flows, political power is increasingly centralized in the shadowy registers of national security and the executive branch, rather than in legislative bodies who more directly represent the people and make law from that authority. It is no wonder that even the most touted act of democratic politics—voting for president—garners less than 50% participation from the people, who sense the many ways that the voting system, if not all legislative decision-making, is rigged against them.

A third factor in the feeling of lost sovereignty that powers agency panic is a lost sense of economic sovereignty; this is part of the popular story of globalization and free trade's effects on industrial workers, and it is a factor frequently tied to increased gun ownership.[24] As jobs are outsourced by the millions to

---

[21] Sheldon Wolin, "The People's Two Bodies," in *Fugitive Democracy and Other Essays* (Princeton, NJ: Princeton University Press, 2016).

[22] See, for instance, UN Secretary General Kofi Annan argument in "Two Concepts of Sovereignty"—that one sovereignty is individual and one is state focused—whether run by elites or the people. Kofi Annan, "Two Concepts of Sovereignty," *The Economist*, September 16, 1999, http://www.economist.com/node/324795.

[23] See William E. Connolly, *Identity/Difference: Democratic Negotiations of Political Paradox* (Minneapolis: University of Minnesota Press, 2002), 20–24; Sheldon Wolin, *The Presence of the Past: Essays on the State and the Constitution* (Baltimore, MD: Johns Hopkins University Press, 1989); Jonathan Crary *24/7: Late Capitalism and the Ends of Sleep* (London: Verso, 2013); and Lauren Berlant, *Cruel Optimism* (Durham, NC: Duke University Press, 2011).

[24] Carlson, *Citizen-Protectors*, 10–11.

countries with lower wages and fewer environmental regulations, people lose secure employment, wages stagnate, and benefits decline; at the same time corporate profits skyrocket to top management. Neoliberal forms of governance, which deregulate business practices and weaken state support for the unemployed, promote rampant economic inequality throughout the country, as the less fortunate are unable to support themselves whereas top earners receive virtually all the profits. Workers know this and feel a sense of impotence against impersonal economic powers siphoning their money while they struggle to get by. This feeling of lost sovereignty develops in ways particular to this neoliberal moment. As Zygmunt Bauman has noted, the combination of decreased state support and increasing economic precarity devolve social risk onto individuals, so that economic struggles seem to be personal failures, only solved by individual responsibility.[25] As Foucault defines it, neoliberal rationality contends that if a person does not succeed economically it is their fault, not the fault of transnational finance or rapacious corporate policies that benefit the wealthy or decrease state support for the vulnerable. If people do not have enough money, it is because they have not worked hard enough, indeed they haven't pulled themselves up by their own bootstraps and succeeded in the marketplace of risky entrepreneurialism.[26] This rationality elides complex structures of economic financialization to place blame solely on individual choices.

Gun ownership, as a form of individualized social responsibility, offers one way of responding to feelings of lost sovereignty and the devolution of social responsibility onto individuals. It promises that individuals actually can, on their very own, rehabilitate the lost promise of sovereign power. A 2013 National Rifle Association billboard advertisement (Figure 1.1) reveals some of these losses and promises. It draws upon cultural tropes central to US political imaginaries that idealize a vast unsettled frontier upon which to demonstrate heroic American power. The lone male individual is placed front and center, dominating the image, ever vigilant. He tames the unruly wilds around him, and reigns sovereign over the landscape through his gun, which is his power to kill. In many ways, this ad is a direct reference to the promises of masculine self-reliance that power American norms of rugged individualism. It recuperates a long-standing fantasy of individual power, but links rugged masculinity to a new iteration of individual sovereign power that in this context posits the ability for a gun to wipe away the complex power structures of geopolitics and economic globalization. This image empties the landscape of any power that might threaten or constrain the lone individual. In the billboard, the man literally looms over

---

[25] Bauman, *Liquid Times*, 2007.

[26] Michel Foucault, *The Birth of Biopolitics: Lectures at the Collège de France, 1978–79* (London: Picador, 2010).

Figure 1.1. NRA billboard showing a rugged individual taming a transit center.

and dominates the territory. As one gun owner summarily states in a comment analogous to the billboard, "I refuse to be a victim. I refuse to put myself in a position where . . . someone can exercise that kind of control over me."[27] The similar promise of this ad is not only about a gun's ability to recuperate a rugged potency but about the empty horizon that erases the complexities of the world surrounding the billboard that would otherwise cause one to feel like a "victim." The gun here has the power of controlling turf, making it devoid of challenge and of any competitors, and subduing any potential counter-power.

The fourth factor is more particular to the white men who are the vast majority of gun owners. It includes the relative rise in visibility and public representation of women and minorities in America who, over the last decades, have gained more access to political decision-making and economic stability than they had previously. It is obvious but important to note that women and people of color do not have the same political power or economic capital relative to white men, and never have. And yet, for the latter, the recent and relative rise of women and minorities might seem like a devolution of their power, especially as white men have traditionally dominated social, economic, and political landscapes. Oftentimes the first three factors contributing to feelings of lost sovereignty are displaced onto this fourth factor, so that the white men who feel powerless

---

[27] Stroud, "Good Guys With Guns," *Gender and Society* 26, no. 2 (February 2012), 228. See also Angela Stroud, *Good Guys with Guns* (Chapel Hill: University of North Carolina Press, 2016).

against real and imagined obstacles may blame minorities and women, newly visible, for their own sense of impotence. Men who see trends toward social equality of marginalized groups as displacing their lost sovereignty, view these trends as a form of personal oppression that weakens their own social power.

It could be argued that the feeling of lost sovereignty is a constitutive experience for many white American men, who are influenced by norms of rugged individualism but are almost always enmeshed in social worlds of interdependence and vulnerability.[28] Yet rather than adjudicate whether this vision of individual sovereignty has ever been possible, or postulate that it is always a delusion, as Joan Cocks provocatively argues, what is most important for this paper is to determine why there is *now* such a pervasive feeling that individual sovereignty has been diminished. Angela Stroud's interviews with gun carriers show that a reason many white males carry guns is because they want to feel powerful when confronted by the racialized bodies they deem fearful, or when they are inside minority neighborhoods. Stroud's interviews reveal that many of the more confusing losses of power that are structural in cause are displaced onto minority bodies, who are culturally and historically interpreted as dangerous and threatening.[29] Cultural interpretations of black and brown people as suspicious are not new to American politics.[30] Projecting threats onto racialized others is a pattern that courses throughout US history, but it has a specific connection to individual sovereignty in the case of contemporary gun ownership. Recent diminishments of sovereign power, both real and imagined, are displaced onto minorities (presumably hoarding power) rather than on political and economic systems of inequality. In this displacement, the cause of diminished sovereignty seems to be other people, rather than from financial or political structures. This compensatory mechanism of displacement manages the agency panic produced out of realigning forces at the nexus of gender, race, and nation by suggesting that the biggest threats to one's individual security are those who traditionally have not had that power and don't deserve it, and who can be tamed and dominated through the barrel of a gun.

These four factors contribute to a particular form of agency panic relevant to gun ownership in the present, in which political and economic systems that are expected to uphold individual sovereignty are now seen to be either ineffective

[28] See Cocks, On *Sovereignty and Other Political Delusions*.

[29] Stroud, *Good Guys with Guns*.

[30] Michael Rogin, *Ronald Reagan: The Movie, And Other Episodes of Political Demonology* (Berkeley: University of California, 1988); Cheryl Harris "Whiteness as Property," *Harvard Law Review* 106, no. 8 (June 1993), 1707–1791; W. E. B. DuBois, *Black Reconstruction* (New York: Oxford University Press, 2007); H. M. Blalock, *Toward a Theory of Minority-Group Relations* (New York: John Wiley and Sons, 1967); Allen E. Liska, ed., *Social Threat and Social Control* (Albany, NY: SUNY Press, 1992.

or impotent, while other "undeserving" or dangerous people are seen to gain in power at the expense of those who have traditionally held it. White men who experience this particular form of agency panic are left at a loss for how to feel powerful and how to defend themselves against the real or imagined forces that challenge their assumed rightful agency. Guns may seem a way to remedy these losses of state, political, economic, and individual sovereignty and the fear they incite. As seen in the advertisement for concealed-carry holsters in Figure 1.2, the threat of a surprise attack by a racialized criminal (darkened skin, hoodie) makes it seem as if proper carrying will eliminate the felt vulnerability of contemporary precarity by reinstating individual sovereignty. In the ad, blame for diminished sovereignty is displaced onto the faceless and hooded criminal, but sovereignty is immediately regained by the gun's ability to put the source of vulnerability back in his place: powerless and against a wall. Guns reinstitute the capacity for unchallenged sovereignty back to the men who experience structural changes as personal losses, men who might otherwise feel as if they have failed to live up to the norm of the self-mastering sovereign because undeserving

Figure 1.2. Advertisement for concealed-carry holsters with a racialized criminal, thwarted by a gun.

minorities have taken their rightful power. This displacement helps to understand why, even though US crime is at a historic low, gun ownership and the fear of crime (especially racialized crime) is quite high.

There are, of course, other responses to the feeling of insecurity brought on by these four factors contributing to a feeling of lost sovereignty. Some people aim to strengthen state sovereignty directly, which is how Trump's promises to build an impermeable border wall, deregulate police violence, and deport immigrants have become so influential. For people who find Trump's promises compelling, they often believe that fortifying the boundaries of the nation through strong state power will bring back the security and power they crave. Other responses to the feeling of global complexity and waning sovereignty turn toward bolstering popular sovereignty, aiming to revive practices of civic participation and strengthen political institutions that center on the people as the legitimate bearer of political power.[31] These responses would loosely include Occupy Wall Street and some of the claims made by the presidential candidacy of Bernie Sanders. A third option, which can traverse these other responses, is to strengthen individual sovereignty. For people who idealize the image of the self-sufficient and rugged individual sovereign to no other, one compelling option for revivifying sovereignty becomes gun ownership.

Reviving individual sovereignty through gun ownership is aided by a series of shifts in the legal landscape that make guns easier to procure, carry, and use, especially Stand Your Ground (SYG) laws. SYG laws protect people who feel their lives are at stake in public or in private, and who shoot their assailant in self-defense. These laws only began in 2005, and they grant some autonomy to individuals, not the state, to determine the legitimate use of violence to shoot another person, and to allow individuals to use their own criteria to assess if their life is under threat. Citizens, within Stand Your Ground laws, make their own judgment of danger. Private individuals can enforce their own version of public safety with fewer legal checks if "self-defense" can be seen as a legitimate justification for killing.[32] SYG laws move gun ownership from defense of the home to the defense of individuals in the public realm, and in this sense they are part of a network of juridical changes, especially concealed-carry laws, that allow guns in most common spaces and grant them wide berth for use.

[31] Some people argue that a desire to reinstate state sovereignty is itself part of the problem: that state power alone cannot address fundamental global problems that produce insecurity, such as global economic inequality and climate change. They often want to decenter the state as the primary site of political power to focus instead on a transnational political order where political power is held both locally and supranationally to help solve intractable global problems. See Cocks, *On Sovereignty and Other Political Delusions*.

[32] Chase Madar, "Have Guns, Will Liberate," *The Baffler*, no. 28 (July 2015).

Figure 1.3. Popular NRA T-Shirt: "NRA: Stand and Fight."

If state sovereignty entails, in Max Weber's classic definition, the monopoly over the legitimate use of violence in a given territory, then SYG laws signal the fragmentation of state sovereignty into individual sovereignty, granting the latter the legitimacy and power to determine within loose parameters whom to kill or let live.[33] One of Angela Stroud's concealed-carry subjects argues that he carries because he likes knowing he has "a superior ability to deal with a situation harshly if I have to."[34] Stand Your Ground laws legally empower individuals to "deal with a situation harshly" by telling them they do not have to retreat first. These laws are also known as "Shoot First" laws, as they explicitly state that individuals who find themselves in threatening situations do not need to retreat, the typical norm for self-defense—instead they can shoot first. It allows individuals to feel justified in making the ultimate sovereign adjudication about whether another human being shall live or die. Indeed, as the popular NRA T-shirt advertises (Figure 1.3), it is the capacity to stand and fight once someone is determined to be a threat, to have final say over life and death by shooting first, that marks a true gun owner. The gun owner determines who is safe and who is threatening at any time through his or her capacity for sovereign action, with the lethal power to act on that determination in the moment.

The NRA has been crucial to the creation and popularization of SYG laws, and the power they supposedly grant individuals, in part through its advocacy channels like its popular "Armed Citizen" column, which culls stories from

[33] Max Weber, "Politics as a Vocation," in *The Vocation Lectures,* eds. David Owen and Tracy B. Strong (Indianapolis, IN: Hackett, 2004).

[34] Stroud, *Good Guys with Guns,* 227.

around the country where guns have supposedly stopped intruders, robbers, and criminals (Figure 1.4). Armed Citizen intentionally depicts a dangerous and violent world, staved off by individual gun use alone, in which only "armed citizens" stand between the forces of freedom and oppression, order and chaos. Within this narrative, armed individual citizens are required to protect themselves and the public, and must be ready at any time and in any public space: a mall, a school, a restaurant. They are the final authority against injustice when the state is too weak to enforce it.

Yet Stand Your Ground laws have most often been used to justify the murder of black men.[35] This happened most notoriously in the Trayvon Martin case. Martin's murderer, George Zimmerman, was acquitted using a SYG defense, even though the teenager, whom Zimmerman found "real suspicious," was only carrying candy, and was running away from Zimmerman when Zimmerman caught up to him, engaged him in a fight, and then shot him. Studies have shown that Stand Your Ground laws in Florida alone have acquitted the killing of black men at a rate of 73%, and acquitted the killing of white men at 59%.[36] There is a long history in the United States of equating blackness and criminality, and SYG laws both draw from that history and reshape it to fit twenty-first century dynamics.[37] If feelings of political powerlessness, loss of economic control, and fear of unknown others are common affective experiences in twenty-first century America, then SYG laws legally enable white gun owners to counteract that feeling, making it easier for them to use a gun in public when they feel threatened by the often-racialized others upon whom they have already displaced their social and economic insecurities.

The four factors listed in this section take shape in a changing legal landscape to enable a rise in gun carrying and gun use, which is often experienced as a performance of individual sovereignty within an unsecure social and geopolitical order. SYG laws, concealed-carry laws, and increasing gun ownership speak to a

---

[35] Adam M. Butz, Michael P. Fix, and Joshua L. Mitchell, "Policy Learning and the Diffusion of Stand-Your-Ground Laws," *Politics & Policy* 43, no. 3 (June 5, 2015), 347–377.

[36] Darla Cameron and William Higgins, "Florida Stand Your Ground Law Cases—Those Who Stood, Those Who Fell: Fatal Cases," *Tampa Bay Times*, last updated October 1, 2014, http://www.tampabay.com/stand-your-ground-law/fatal-cases. The *Tampa Bay Times* writes, "In nearly a third of the cases the *Times* analyzed, defendants initiated the fight, shot an unarmed person or pursued their victim —and still went free." See also Patrick Johnson, "Racial Bias and 'Stand Your Ground' Laws: What the Data Show," *Christian Science Monitor, August 6, 2013,* http://www.csmonitor.com/USA/Justice/2013/0806/Racial-bias-and-stand-your-ground-laws-what-the-data-show.

[37] See, among many others, Saidiya V. Hartman, *Scenes of Subjection: Terror, Slavery, and Self-Making in Nineteenth Century America* (New York: Oxford University Press, 1995) and Elisabeth Anker, "Three Emancipations: Manderlay, Slavery, and Racialized Freedom," *Theory & Event* 8, no. 2 (Spring 2015).

☰ MENU

Armed homeowner confronts suspicious man, van ☑

An armed Port St. Lucie homeowner chased away several would-be burglars Wednesday morning, according to police. The homeowner ...

PA | 6 ABC   FRIDAY, FEBRUARY 10, 2017

Deli Owner Shoots Armed Robbery Suspect ☑

A Philadelphia deli owner shot an armed man who was attempting to rob him, police say. It happened ...

MI | FOX 17   FRIDAY, FEBRUARY 10, 2017

Customer armed with handgun shoots assault suspect in local party store ☑

A man who walked into a party store on the lake shore ended up breaking up an assault ...

TX | ALICE TX   WEDNESDAY, FEBRUARY 8, 2017

Homeowner shoots attempted burglar ☑

A 19-year-old San Antonio man was shot Saturday night as he attempted to enter a residence on the ...

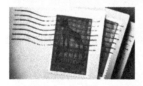

IN | THE INDY CHANNEL   TUESDAY, FEBRUARY 7, 2017

Resident, suspected intruder shot during attempted home invasion on Indianapolis' south side ☑

A resident and a suspected home intruder were both shot during an attempted home invasion on Indianapolis' south ...

OK | NEWS ON 6   MONDAY, FEBRUARY 6, 2017

Mother Shoots At Woman Trying To Break Into Tulsa Home ☑

A Tulsa mother is urging others to teach their kids to never answer the door if a stranger ...

Figure 1.4. A typical list of NRA Armed Citizen articles.

fear that public safety can no longer be ensured by the state, which has become weak and ineffectual at the same time that the population is presumed to be increasingly violent. Again, this is where geopolitics comes in. If the expectation of state sovereignty is a wall of impermeable protection to ensure the safety of individuals, then when that expectation fails, the people must protect themselves and others—through their guns—creating their own wall. Gun owners are the ones who will attack the (racialized) forces diminishing their sovereignty; they will stand and fight.

Mobile Sovereignty

Something more, however, is going on with gun ownership than a transfer of sovereignty over life and death from state to the individual. When combined with the new changes in the legal landscape for concealed carry and Stand Your Ground, this transfer actually changes the very nature of sovereignty. Sovereignty shifts from supreme authority over a fixed territory to a mobile jurisdiction dependent on the location of the body carrying a gun. Carrying a gun turns the boundary of sovereignty into an unstable, movable space. Rather than having sovereignty extend throughout a fixed landscape regardless of where the sovereign resides, guns offer a portable sovereignty that can be carried by individuals throughout a seemingly hostile territory. Carrying a gun produces a sovereignty that spatially changes moment-by-moment and is determined by the carrier's immediate topographical location plus the range of the gun. Guns make sovereignty roving and transportable.

With gun carrying, sovereignty becomes the power to determine who can justifiably be shot for intruding on the owner's mobile sovereign territory, a territory that no one else knows but the carrier of the gun. In mobile sovereignty, the border of sovereign power is invisible to everyone except the carrier. In concealed-carry laws, a gun can be carried in many public spaces, but *must* be hidden; others will likely not know that one is carrying it. It creates an *unknown* and *unseen* boundary to all but the gun carrier. By carrying a hidden gun, combined with the incitement to Stand and Fight rather than retreat that is emblematic of SYG laws, the gun owner becomes the sole decision maker both of who is within the border and who is deemed a threat serious enough to be shot. Whereas the geopolitical shifts listed in the prior section suggest that sovereignty is waning—that complex geopolitical powers erode the sovereignty of individuals, states, and polities—mobile sovereignty resurrects a new form of fragmented and moving sovereignty by setting up an ever shifting personal boundary that can constantly defend the individual no matter what social powers might otherwise ensnare his agency.

It is generally presumed that sovereignty requires fixed, stable boundaries. Sovereignty, it is often claimed in political theory and international relations, must be tied to a distinct territory or else it vanishes into thin air. John Agnew's definition of sovereign power as "lodged in a *central place* and exercised over a *definite territory*" is but one variation.[38] Yet now, mobile sovereignty offers a sovereignty that has no definite territory. Instead it offers a probable range of action. One key to this change is the dramatic increase in concealed-carry laws, which now traverse all fifty states and the District of Columbia, as well as the ease of getting a concealed-carry permit. Donald Trump gained many supporters in his presidential bid when he pushed for a national concealed-carry law that would cover the country, and he is now promising to follow through on it. Concealed-carry grants owners a license to carry a gun in many public spaces that used to be off limits. The body of the gun-carrying sovereign has no fixed point of reference within that public space, and the territory of the sovereign's reach is also in a state of constant flux, even as its relation to the individual remains a set circumference.

Whereas territorial sovereignty is physically fixed and stable, and it demarcates clear geographical boundaries where sovereignty is and is not held, mobile sovereignty changes location in every moment. Sovereignty here is not the exclusive use of force in a given territory, but the supremacy over others through the potential use of force in a mobile range that constantly surrounds the gun holder. In mobile sovereignty it is therefore not the territory that retains integrity, as in foundational discourses of sovereign power;[39] instead, the gun allows the body of the gun owner to hold sovereign power regardless of a particular territory. Sovereignty is carried like a turtle shell; it offers the feeling of invulnerability as one moves through any space at any time.

In mobile sovereignty, the range of the gun at any moment IS the border of sovereignty. Gun-carrying individuals redetermine the border at each moment by where they move. The effective range of a bullet determines the sovereign border, but it is a border without clear markers or external signposts. The range of one's guns and ammunition are thus increasingly important, as in Figure 1.5, because they mark the very turf of one's sovereignty. Greater firepower means more than safety; it extends the possibilities of command. It helps to explain why military assault weapons have become so much more prevalent in the last

---

[38] John Agnew, *Globalization and Sovereignty* (Lanham, MD: Rowman and Littlefield, 2009), 47 (italics mine).

[39] Sara Kendall, "Cartographies of the State: 'Contingent Sovereignty' and Territorial Integrity," in *Netherland Yearbook of International Law 2016*, eds. M. Kuijer and W. Werner (The Hague, Netherlands: T. M. C. Asser Press, 2017).

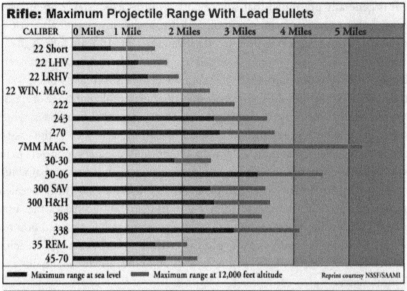

Rifle: Maximum Projectile Range With Lead Bullets

Maximum range at sea level / Maximum range at 12,000 feet altitude   Reprint courtesy NSSF/SAAMI

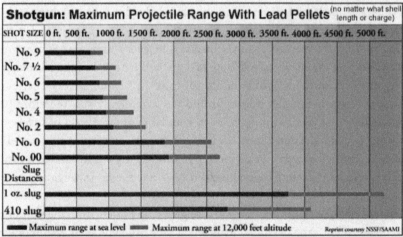

Shotgun: Maximum Projectile Range With Lead Pellets (no matter what shell length or charge)

Maximum range at sea level / Maximum range at 12,000 feet altitude   Reprint courtesy NSSF/SAAMI

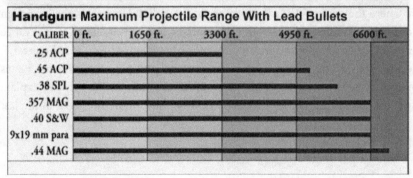

Handgun: Maximum Projectile Range With Lead Bullets

Figure 1.5. The range of mobile sovereignty: a list of projectile ranges from various guns. NSSF/SAAMI.

decade.[40] From one optic they are just machines of death that serve no civilian purpose and should be banned. But from the position of agency panic, military assault weapons dramatically expand the range and scope of sovereignty for its holder.

Even compared to canonical versions of individual sovereignty that demarcate each individual's private sphere, guns posit a different relationship. For John Stuart Mill, individual sovereignty is the freedom to do what one wants within one's personal space, without harming another. Individual sovereignty marks off the private from the public and deems the individual the supreme authority in the former. But with gun carrying and SYG laws, an individual can lawfully kill another in one's range even when that range is in the public sphere. Personal space is the space in which one has the lawful capacity to do violence if one feels under threat, whether in public or in private. The circumference of this sovereign sphere holds agency panic at bay by granting the power of control and domination within its ever-shifting bubble that traverses traditional demarcations of public/private spheres. Further, the sphere of sovereignty is not predetermined or equal to others' spheres, but depends on the range of the gun one carries. The boundary of the sovereign sphere is unknown to others who may be walking through it.[41] Within that sphere, the harm principle, so crucial to liberal theory, is reconfigured: individual sovereignty does not stop if one harms another. Rather, individual sovereignty is now marked by the very capacity for one to harm another. This is a sovereignty that does not stabilize a polity but radically destabilizes it, as it increases the range of tolerable violence against others, and makes the *capacity for harm* the very condition of individual sovereignty.

The rise in gun ownership is not necessarily about vigilante justice, however, because it operates according to a different logic: not justice but risk and probability. In mobile sovereignty, it is up to individual sovereigns to determine the threat of others by risk assessment. The individual gun carrier decides whether someone seems risky or menacing, and whether a situation warrants use of a gun, even as that determination may later be subject to legal scrutiny. As one concealed-carry permit teacher states, in terms of the permanent risk assessment placed on the armed citizens, "There is no safe place." He asks his students to evaluate rooms: "Does it have plants? Are they fake or real? If they're real, does it have potting soil? I'm always thinking."[42] This teacher emphasizes that carrying

[40] Alan Feuer, "AR-15 Rifles are Beloved, Reviled, and a Common Element in Mass Shootings," *New York Times*, June 13, 2016, https://www.nytimes.com/2016/06/14/nyregion/ar-15-rifles-are-beloved-reviled-and-a-common-element-in-mass-shootings.html.

[41] The circumference of this newly formed sovereign sphere holds agency panic at bay by granting the power of control and domination within a shifting bubble that traverses public/private spheres.

[42] Evan Osnos, "Making a Killing: The Business and Politics of Selling Guns," *New Yorker*, June 27, 2016.

demands a heightened level of attention to potentially vulnerable and dangerous situations, going so far as to turn potted plants into possible safe spaces for shooting assailants or sites for hidden weaponry. The constant vigilance of the individual sovereign is necessary for maintaining the personalized boundaries of securitized territory.

Louise Amoore argues that state sovereignty has become a new type of risk assessment, one that in her analysis is granted to border patrol agents and computer algorithms to determine who is deemed most risky when entering US territory.[43] In the case of guns, by contrast, risk assessment is granted to the individual gun owner, who calculates risk by personal measurements, and classifies each individual who enters his sovereign territory against his own personal database of risk factors. This is why risk assessment for individual gun owners is so often tacked to racial and religious categories, as the people deemed an imminent threat are often those who are black or Latinx, or who display obvious markers or performances of Islamic practice. Cultural significations of danger, devoid of real measurement, determine who is most scary. As another of Angela Stroud's interviewees states, when explaining why he left his gun in the car during their interview, "When I have [my gun] with me, I'm paying a lot more attention to people . . . somebody walks in, looks like they're lookin' for trouble. Somebody that doesn't fit. You know, not to play the race card or anything but there aren't too many Black people around here."[44] The sovereignty of gun owners pushes against agency panic by constantly assessing the risk level of individuals who happen to enter one's mobile territory, in order to determine who feels most threatening. The risk assessment of individual agents, no matter how objectively racist or unjust, legitimizes preemptive action if they seem a probable threat, and justifies a more relaxed comportment or decreased sense of agency panic when racialized others are not physically present.

Taking mobile sovereignty to a new level, "sovereign citizens" is a new and growing movement of primarily white men who believe that they alone determine justice irrespective of the law.[45] Sovereign citizens claim that they can choose which laws to obey and which not to, as it is their sovereign right to make those determinations for themselves.[46] They are thickly armed, and believe that government is illegal and does not have power over them. For sovereign citizens,

[43] Louise Amoore, *The Politics of Possibility: Risk and Security beyond Probability* (Durham, NC: Duke University Press, 2013).

[44] Stroud, *Good Guys with Guns*, 232.

[45] J. M. Berger, "Without Prejudice: What Sovereign Citizens Believe," George Washington University Program on Extremism, Occasional Paper, June 2016. https://cchs.gwu.edu/sites/cchs.gwu.edu/files/downloads/Occasional%20Paper_Berger.pdf.

[46] "Sovereign Citizens Movement," *Southern Poverty Law Center,* https://www.splcenter.org/fighting-hate/extremist-files/ideology/sovereign-citizens-movement.

the source of their feelings of lost sovereignty and agency panic is an evil and illegitimate state that aims to sap their power, so sovereign citizens array against state power using guns in an effort to gain their individual sovereignty back. Sovereign citizens see their sovereignty as self-generating and mobile, carried with them wherever they go and ensured only by the guns they carry. Guns determine their interactions with all other people, including and especially those vested with some form of state authority. They view themselves as the only authority of justice, and often commit acts of violence against police officers and even postal workers if they feel threatened. The sovereign citizens movement is less than twenty years old, but it spins out to its endpoint the logic already inherent in much contemporary gun ownership, with its focus on the individual as a mobile sovereign who has final authority demarked by the gun one carries.

Sovereign citizens fantasize away the complexities of global powers, economic insecurities, loss of democratic authority, rising relative power of women and minorities, and waning state sovereignty that shape our globalized era, to instead reimagine themselves as sovereign individuals who can make their own juridical order on the run through the barrel of a gun. They see most other people as threatening enemies and have their origins in anti-Semitic beliefs that government finances are controlled by Jews—a clear example of displacing complex global power structures onto racialized others. By 2014, "sovereign citizens" were considered the top domestic terrorist threat in the United States.[47] Their violent displacements deem government workers and minority groups the source of their long-standing insecurities, and they presume that if they have the power to shoot other people then they have therefore regained their sovereignty.

. . .

Guns, for many people, provide a feeling of sovereignty seemingly at odds both with the real dangers guns confer on those who own and carry them, and with the insecurity that gun ownership paradoxically incites on those who buy them for safety.[48] Gun carriers often experience *more* feelings of vulnerability and fear, as they become more watchful and suspicious when carrying, and in turn begin to find other people's daily actions more threatening.[49] Many carriers

[47] "Understanding Law Enforcement Intelligence Processes," National Consortium for the Study of Terrorism and Reponses to Terrorism, Department of Homeland Security Science and Technology Center of Excellence, July 2014, https://www.start.umd.edu/pubs/START_Understa ndingLawEnforcementIntelligenceProcesses_July2014.pdf.

[48] Abhay Aneja, John J. Donohue III, and Alexandria Zhang, "The Impact of Right to Carry Laws and the NRC Report: The Latest Lessons for the Empirical Evaluation of Law and Policy," National Bureau of Economic Research Working Paper, no. 18294, August 2012 (revised in November 2014), http://www.nber.org/papers/w18294.

[49] See Harel Shapira, "How to Use the Bathroom with a Gun and Other Techniques of the Armed Body," in chapter 8 of this volume.

spend much of their public life making threat assessments. As the concealed-carry teacher quoted earlier informed his students, when carrying "there is no safe place." Concealed-carry laws, plus Stand Your Ground laws, encourage gun owners to be permanently suspicious of the environments they navigate, and to see all objects in their world as sources of safety or danger. They thus deepen the very feelings of insecurity that guns supposedly stanch as they make public life more violent.

While guns may at first seem to salve the agency panic bred by a rapidly shifting and manifestly unjust world, they more often lead to instability and violence, especially against women and minorities who bear the brunt of redirected anxiety. Carrying a gun can restore sovereignty only if other people are seen as the source of lost sovereignty. Of course, guns cannot restore sovereignty if the forces weakening sovereignty stem from systems of global finance, or centralizations of political power in a tiny elite, or decreasing job opportunities and diminished political access. Guns can restore the feeling of sovereignty only if those losses are relocated onto other people who are now assessed as threats to one's otherwise trouble-free capacity for self-determination. It creates a situation in which guns are presumed to instate individual sovereignty but leave the real sources of felt vulnerability unexamined.

Guns, and the mobile sovereignty they confer, do little to address the larger problems that contribute to increasing vulnerability and precarity. A gun cannot address neoliberal financialization, global inequality, diminished political influence, and the slow collapse of long-standing localities. Instead, guns increase the isolations and suspicions of a polity seemingly unwilling to productively counteract its growing political powerlessness—except for displacing its effects onto racialized others while heroizing the individual violence of white men.

2

Radical Printings

Future Gunsmithing and the Politics of Self-Manufacturing Firearms

ANDREW POE

> Therefore, no doubt, the sovereignty of man lieth hid in knowledge; wherein
> many things are reserved, which kings with their treasure cannot buy, nor with
> their force command; their spials and intelligencers can give no news of them,
> their seamen and discoverers cannot sail where they grow: now we govern
> nature in opinions, but we are thrall unto her in necessity: but if we would be
> led by her in invention, we should command her in action.
>
> —Francis Bacon

> What human beings seek to learn from nature is how to use it to dominate
> wholly both it and human beings.
> Nothing else counts . . .
>
> —Max Horkheimer and Theodor Adorno

Reproductions

On June 6th, 2015, a US nonprofit corporation, Defense Distributed, in conjunction with the Second Amendment Foundation, Inc., filed suit against the US federal government, claiming that any infringement on either the "creation" or "acquisition" of firearms for lawful purposes was a violation of the Second Amendment of the United States Constitution.[1] At issue in Defense Distributed's initial complaint was the legality of their distribution of materials that would allow for the use of additive printing technology to produce all, or part of, various firearms. But, as the US Court of Appeals briefing later explained, "Defense Distributed's innovation was to create computer files to allow people to easily

---

[1] Defense Distributed v. US Dept. of State, No. 1:15-cv-372 (US Dist. Ct., Western D. Texas, Austin Div., May 6, 2015).

43

produce their own weapons and weapon parts using relatively affordable and readily available equipment."[2]

In their initial complaint, Defense Distributed argued that the federal government had interfered directly in the distribution of printing manuals for the self-manufacturing of firearms. Here, almost by accident, the intersection of the first and second amendments to the US Constitution reveal a complex aporia, and one that the courts are still struggling with. While the federal government may have incentives to limit the production of firearms to those persons approved for such manufactures' licensure, do advances in 3D-printing technologies rupture the very terms of such a limitation through the right to freely distribute information? Or, put differently, what has the gun become, now that anyone can make it?

The self-manufacturing of firearms was itself nothing new. Handmade and primitive guns characterized early American colonial life.[3] While smiths would produce key components of weapons, most colonists in the eighteenth century could not afford to purchase the entirety of pre-made rifles (whether made in the States or shipped from Europe); instead they made most of the gun themselves. Much time would be spent in the slow crafting of the various components of the weapon. Able to provide necessary components through the smelting, forging, and casting of metals, rural blacksmiths became necessary collaborators in the process of self-manufactured firearms. The consequence of this early history of gun manufacturing in the United States was that most guns were individualized (as was the ammunition for such weapons). The advent of mass-produced firearms in the early nineteenth century (Remington in 1816 and Colt in 1836) meant that firearms became cheaper, and that ammunition became interchangeable. In this way, the "gun" then became a manufactured technology, and one that could be regulated (both by market mechanisms, and later, beginning in 1934, by US federal law).

But even after the advent of manufactured firearms, it was still possible (and sometimes useful) to self-produce weapons.[4] While knowledge of metalwork began to decline, access to tools, and later CAD (Computer Aided Design) or CNC (Computer Numeric Control) technologies, still made it possible to produce a weapon capable of propelling lethal ballistics.[5] Labor-intensive, inaccurate,

---

[2] No. 15-50759 Doc. 00513686006, 1 (5th Cir. September 20, 2016), Defense Distributed; Second Amendment Foundation, Incorporated v US, p. 3.

[3] See Gordon S. Wood, *The Creation of the American Republic, 1776–1787* (New York: W. W. Norton, 1993); also Jan E. Dizard, Robert Muth, and Stephen P. Andrews, eds., *Guns in America* (New York: New York University Press, 1999), esp. chap. 1: Michael A. Bellesiles, "The Origins of Gun Culture in the United States, 1760–1865."

[4] See, for example, Keith Krause, ed., *Small Arms Survey 2015: Weapons and the World* (Cambridge, UK: Cambridge University Press, 2015).

[5] J. K. Modi, C. Nigam, and K. Kumar, "Improvised Firearms versus Regular Firearms," *Forensic Science International* 26, no. 3 (November 1984).

and often dangerous to the user, improvised firearms have still continued to be available to those who might desire to avoid regulated firearm markets.

But what 3D printing really changes about the gun isn't that it can be made outside of now traditional regulated manufacturing systems; it is the scale by which weapons can now be produced beyond such regulated markets. As the US Court of Appeals briefing explains,

> Three-dimensional ("3D") printing technology allows a computer to "print" a physical object (as opposed to a two-dimensional image on paper). Today, 3D printers are sold at stores such as Home Depot and Best Buy, and the instructions for printing everything from jewelry to toys to car parts are shared and exchanged freely online at sites like GrabCAD.com and Thingiverse.com. Computer numeric control ("CNC") milling, an older industrial technology, involves a computer directing the operation of a drill upon an object. 3D printing is "additive;" using raw materials, the printer constructs a new object. CNC milling is "subtractive," carving something (more) useful from an existing object.[6]

Such printing makes possible the production of a vast armory of similar, and similarly accurate (and interchangeable), weapons. Multiplying the number of weapons available to any shooter, and the ease by which a user could access and dispose of such weapons, the ability to mass produce arms outside a regulated arms market is a significant transformation in contemporary gun culture. And it is the very change in the material of the gun—the capacity to produce polymer firearms through additive manufacturing—that changes what the gun is. Again, as the US Court of Appeals briefing summarizes,

> Defense Distributed's files allow virtually anyone with access to a 3D printer to produce, among other things, Defense Distributed's single-shot plastic pistol called the Liberator and a fully functional plastic AR-15 lower receiver. In addition to 3D printing files, Defense Distributed also sells its own desktop CNC mill marketed as the Ghost Gunner, as well as metal 80% lower receivers. With CNC milling files supplied by Defense Distributed, Ghost Gunner operators are able to produce fully functional, unserialized, and untraceable metal AR-15 lower receivers in a largely automated fashion.[7]

[6] No. 15-50759 Doc. 00513686006, 1 (5th Cir. September 20, 2016), Defense Distributed; Second Amendment Foundation, Incorporated v. US, p. 3.

[7] Ibid., 4.

The 3D printing of firearms automates a process of gun manufacturing, increasing access to weapons, and to numbers of weapons, where previously such access would have been limited. From being a tool for colonial farmers, to a weapon in militarized combat, to a luxury item for the contemporary middle class, changes in the technologies of manufacturing transform the form and materiality of the gun. By providing access to the production of a new material of weapon, 3D printing, I argue, offers a radical transformation: the 3D-printed gun becomes that gun which is disposable, interchangeable, easily self-produced, and scalable. Just as the printing press transformed societies into literate populations by increasing access to literature and to diverse forms of literature, the additive manufacturing of guns may transform society, increasing access to guns and to a diverse array of guns that any one individual can maintain. Indeed, the difference between the printing of pamphlets and the printing of firearms may not be so great, as both allow for the further dissemination of power beyond those who already possess it (or may hope to regulate it).

How close the processes of 3D printings really are, and what, if any, societal differences might result from new technologies in the self-manufacturing of firearms, is the focus of this chapter. I examine the self-manufacturing of firearms through advances in printing technologies, and the consequences of these new modes of gunsmithing for logics of sovereignty. Defense Distributed claims its central aim is to "produce, publish, and distribute to the public without charge information and knowledge related to the digital manufacture of arms."[8] Through additive manufacturing / 3D printing, the instructions Defense Distributed set out to publish would allow anyone with access to a 3D printer to produce the very firing mechanisms and containment parts that would turn ordinary plastic into a fully functioning firearm. I argue that Defense Distributed's radical printing (both of gunsmithing instructions, as well as of firearms themselves) diversifies the means of production of firearms. Here, I theorize that the transformation of the means of production challenges the notion that the state has a monopoly on the legitimate use of violent force. Control of firearms through management of the means of production, as well as import and export statistics, receive constant analysis from the US Department of Justice Bureau of Alcohol, Tobacco, Firearms, and Explosives. In 2014, the Bureau recorded the production of 10,844,792 firearms in the United States. The diversification of the means of production, into a sphere where firearms production would be unmonitored, would functionally break that monopoly.

---

[8] Defense Distributed website, https://defdist.org/about/.

In the chapter that follows, I pay significant attention to the underlying structure of how the material production of things affect a user's subjectivity.[9] I begin with an analysis of printing.[10] Contrasting the early history of the printing press with 3D printing, I hope to highlight how similar and divergent political consequences might result from the printing of firearms. In the second part of this chapter, I explore how 3D printing of firearms threatens the logic of disenchantment, and the questions then posed to the state's legitimate monopoly on the use of violent force. In the third part of this chapter, following a Rousseauian logic of enchantment, I aim to highlight how 3D printing of guns may make possible an equality, but only one which risks annihilating the very state it requires to preserve that equality. In this way, I hope to illustrate how the self-production of plastic firearms, which are capable of ballistic force, opens the possibility that the actual matter of made things fundamentally transforms the phenomenology of the thing, as well as the subjectivity of its user.

Part 1: Printings

In 1608, Hieronymus Hornschuch published *Orthotypographia,* the very earliest manual for text printing (literally the manual *on correct type writing*). Reflecting on a scene from Hornschuch's *Orthotypographia,* Anthony Grafton narrates, "In one small room a compositor sets type, a corrector reads copy, a warehouseman sorts paper, a printer and an inker work a handpress, and a workman lifts wet sheets to dry on a ceiling-level rack . . . (I)n a corner, an author speaks excitedly to an unidentified companion. In the foreground, dominating the scene, stands the master-printer—a majestic, Prospero-like figure."[11] The image Grafton describes is one of vibrant and shared productive activity. The early processes of printing was, first and foremost, collective. Grafton's reflection highlights the myriad of ways in which the new technology of the printing press created a specific intellectual culture around the very making of the typeset word. Hornschuch's manual helped to narrate this process, explicating the roles of the various characters involved in the printing of words. Where once there was the

---

[9] On debates in new materialism, see Diana Coole and Samantha Frost, eds., *New Materialisms: Ontology, Agency, and Politics* (Durham, NC: Duke University Press, 2010); also Bonnie Honig, *Public Things: Democracy in Disrepair* (New York: Fordham University Press, 2017).

[10] On the history of printing as a radical activity, see Elizabeth Eisenstein, *The Printing Press as an Agent of Change* (New York: Cambridge University Press, 1979).

[11] See Grafton's, "How Revolutionary Was the Print Revolution," *American Historical Review* 107, no. 1 (February 1, 2002): 84–86, for a review of Eisenstein's *The Printing Press as an Agent of Change*; for more on print house practices, also see D. F. McKenzie, "Printers of the Mind: Some Notes on Bibliographical Theories and Printing-House Practices," *Studies in Bibliography* 22 (1969).

author alone, followed by copyists who sat in careful imitation and production of a work, now printing made authorship itself just one part of an engaged activity. Here the collectivity of the press became the site of this new vibrancy.

Printing, as an activity, might best be defined at its core as the process that transforms surfaces. Originally, it was understood as "any indentation made in a surface, preserving the form left by the pressure of some object coming into contact with it." Printing left "a mark" or a "spot" on whatever surface was pressed. Such a process was the intentional altering of the surface of the body. The impressions made were a controlled means of transformation. The type (from Latin *typus*, a borrowed form of the Greek τύπος) could regularly recreate the same impression over and over again. These repeated impressions were reproductions. The invention of the printing press in the fifteenth century allowed for the reproduction of impressions upon materials at a regular and—by comparison to the copyist's hand anyway—vastly elevated rate.[12]

The act of printing reveals a fading asymptote between production and reproduction. At one time, the printing of a text was the creation—the generation—of the printed material. The impression made becomes the word itself. And yet the activity of printing is also the *re*-production of that text already authored; printing is the making of text again.[13] To produce (*pro*—forward, before, in front of / *ducere*—to draw, to lead, to calculate) is literally to bring something into being. To reproduce is to bring it into being *again*. The reproduction of printing is also always a production. The printing press allowed for the production and reproduction of texts on a mass scale. The transformations that resulted were, from the very multiplication of production of texts, both increasing access to texts (where otherwise such printings would have been too limited or impossible), and increasing the plurality of texts available to a literate population as well.

But the early invention of the technology of the printing press did not last long, and the culture of public discourse, both in the print shop itself and as produced through the pamphlets circulated from these shops, was quickly replaced by capitalist mechanisms of manufactured printing, that themselves distorted the subjectivity of those readers it began to depend on. As Jürgen Habermas reminds us,

> already in 1814 the *Times* was being printed on a new high-speed printing machine that after four and a half centuries replaced

---

[12] See Eisenstein, *The Printing Press as an Agent of Change*, 3–42.

[13] The classical Latin root of production highlights this tension. *Productio* from the verb *producere*—is an "extension or lengthening in time," also the "action of bringing or leading out," and event of "creation." But production also has a legal definition—"the presentation of a document or article before a court," including the "presentation of witnesses."

Gutenberg's wooden press. A generation later the invention of the telegraph revolutionized the organization of the whole news network. Not
only the private economic interests of the individual enterprise gained
in importance; the newspaper, as it developed into a capitalist undertaking, became enmeshed in a web of interests extraneous to business
that sought to exercise influence upon it.[14]

That web of interests was unique to this new form of printing. Just as the early
press had opened up new markets to literatures that previously had been unavail-
able, new technologies of printing began to rely on the logic of advertisement to
fund a more regular subscription service of news and information. Habermas
elaborates:

> The history of the big daily papers in the second half of the nineteenth
> century proves that the press itself became manipulable to the extent
> that it became commercialized. Ever since the marketing of the edito-
> rial section became interdependent with that of the advertising section,
> the press (until then an institution of private people insofar as they
> constituted a public) became an institution of certain participants in
> the public sphere in their capacity as private individuals; that is, it be-
> came the gate through which privileged private interests invaded the
> public sphere.[15]

Crucial here is the link between the press itself as a material object capable
of transforming society, and its transition to a logic that, subject to capitalist
paradigms, became itself a regulation on the public sphere. That "public sphere"
was an influence on the political subjectivities that could manifest themselves
therein, as well as the technologies that could accompany them.

As the press became more mechanized, there was a subsequent transformation in labor and society to match. It is Marx, in a passage echoing Rousseau, that
makes the costs of this transformation clear:

> No sooner does labour undergo the least development, than it requires
> specially prepared instruments. Thus in the oldest caves we find stone
> implements and weapons. In the earliest period of human history do-
> mesticated animals, *i.e.*, animals which have been bred for the purpose,
> and have undergone modifications by means of labour, play the chief

[14] Jürgen Habermas, *The Structural Transformation of the Public Sphere: An Inquiry into a Category of Bourgeois Society* (Cambridge: MIT Press, 1989), 184.
[15] Ibid., 184–185.

part as instruments of labour along with specially prepared stones, wood, bones, and shells. The use and fabrication of instruments of labour, although existing in the germ among certain species of animals, is specifically characteristic of the human labour-process, and Franklin therefore defines man as a tool-making animal. Relics of bygone instruments of labour possess the same importance for the investigation of extinct economic forms of society, as do fossil bones for the determination of extinct species of animals. It is not the articles made, but how they are made, and by what instruments, that enables us to distinguish different economic epochs.[16]

In the very instruments themselves we see evidence of the political subjectivity of the time. If the printing press evinces one modality of political subjectivity, and the mechanized press another, then the 3D press demonstrates yet another.

The contrast between modes of labor and modes of subjectivity makes the technology distinction between societies clear. Marx uses the example of the changing landscape of labor in the print trade to illustrate this point. As Marx explains,

the antagonism between the manufacturing division of labour and the methods of modern industry makes itself forcibly felt. It manifests itself, amongst other ways, in the frightful fact that a great part of the children employed in modern factories and manufactures, are from their earliest years riveted to the most simple manipulations, and exploited for years, without being taught a single sort of work that would afterwards make them of use, even in the same manufactory or factory. In the English letter-press printing trade, for example, there existed formerly a system, corresponding to that in the old manufactures and handicrafts, of advancing the apprentices from easy to more and more difficult work. They went through a course of teaching till they were finished printers. To be able to read and write was for every one of them a requirement of their trade. All this was changed by the printing machine.[17]

The once vibrant space of intellectual exchange described in Hornschuch's *Orthotypographia* becomes a more mechanized and more violent space, at least as Marx described it. It is his summary observation that labor takes on a new form according to the technologies present. Marx's analysis highlights the

---

[16] Karl Marx, Ben Fowkes, and David Fernbach, *Capital: A Critique of Political Economy*, Vol. 1 (London and New York: Penguin, in association with *New Left Review*, 1981), 285–286.

[17] Ibid., 614–615.

effects of manufacturing, and especially the printing press, on labor and the society of laborers it produced. What began as a vibrant intellectual activity, by
Hornschuch's accounting, slowly transformed into an oppressed and alienated
collective.

Fast-forward to the 3D printer, and the supposed utopian fantasies that
underlie it.

Simply defined, 3D printing—or additive manufacturing as it is sometimes
called—is the production of solid, three-dimensional objects through a repro-
ducible process. As early as 1981, researchers conceived of the possibility of
such print technologies. As Hideo Kodama explains, it was once the case that "to
show three-dimensional shapes such as those stored in the memory of a computer or imaged in the mind, one must normally substitute two-dimensional
displays (on paper or television), since no good method has been developed to
show three dimensions easily."[18] Kodama set out to explain a means by which
a solid model of such images could be constructed through photo-hardening
polymers. While some solid molds could be produced using CAD technology,
Kodama found such fabrications costly and time consuming. Instead, Kodama
envisioned and designed a device that could construct such objects using layers.

As we might understand the process today, 3D printing is the production of
these layers to "print" solid 3D renderings of images. The process itself can be
traced back to the increased technologies associated with photography and map
making.[19] David Bourell, from the Laboratory for Freeform Fabrication at UT
Austin, and his collaborators, argue that "as early as 1890, Blanther suggested a
layered method for making a mold for topographical relief maps."[20] As Bourell
elaborates, "The method consisted of impressing topographical contour lines on
a series of wax plates and cutting these wax plates on these lines. After stacking
and smoothing these wax sections, one obtains both a positive and negative
three-dimensional surface that corresponds to the terrain indicated by the
contour lines."[21] Here the utility of three-dimensional production incentivizes
techniques for reproducing solid image structures.

Equally significant was the earlier process of photosculpture. As Bourell
describes it, the process of photosculpture was such that "a subject or object was

[18] Hideo Kodama, "Automatic Method for Fabricating a Three-Dimensional Plastic Model
with Photo Hardening Polymer," *Review of Scientific Instruments* 52, no. 11 (1981), 1770–1773,
https: doi: 10.1063/1.1136492.

[19] See Duc Pham and S. S. Dimov, *Rapid Manufacturing: The Technologies and Applications of
Rapid Prototyping and Rapid Tooling* (New York: Springer, 2012), 2–6.

[20] J. E. Blanther, "Manufacture of Contour Relief Maps," U.S. Patent No. 473,901, 1892, in David
Bourell et al., "A Brief History of Additive Manufacturing and the 2009 Roadmap for Additive
Manufacturing," presented at the Workshop on Rapid Technologies, September 2009, 1.

[21] Ibid.

placed in a circular room and simultaneously photographed by 24 cameras placed equally about the circumference of the room."[22] This process allowed for simultaneous imaging of the same object from a multiplicity of perspectives. Bourell suggests, "Photosculpture arose in the 19th century as an attempt to create exact three-dimensional replicas of any object, including human forms." The project of replication—copying, or quite literally re-placing, a folding back—satisfied a desire for sameness and reproducibility. To have an exact double of one's own image would be the new form of portraitur—a capturing of the self.

While historically, the process of photosculpture and topography carved pathways for future additive technologies, the most significant breakthrough came in Charles Hull's operationalization of the process of stereolithography. Hull found a means of adding polymer together that seemed itself to be a form of solid stone writing. As Hull describes it,

> a system for generating three-dimensional objects by creating a cross-sectional pattern of the object to be formed at a selected surface of a fluid medium capable of altering its physical state in response to appropriate synergistic stimulation by impinging radiation, particle bombardment or chemical reaction, successive adjacent laminae, representing corresponding successive adjacent cross-sections of the object, being automatically formed and integrated together to provide a step-wise laminar buildup of the desired object, whereby a three dimensional object is formed and drawn from a substantially planar surface of the fluid medium during the forming process.[23]

Just as the printing press accomplished the reproduction of many words on many pages at one time, the 3D printer allowed for the reproduction, through additive composition, of material objects—many material objects. This includes the gun. From the production of one improvised gun at a time, now the printer could produce many guns at a time.

But 3D printing could be deployed to construct a whole host of objects. To what end would one use such technology to print a gun?[24] Here Cody

---

[22] Ibid.

[23] Charles Hull's original US patent for the Apparatus for Production of Three-Dimensional Objects by Stereolithography, patent No. 4,575,330, from March 11th, 1986; on recent innovations in 3D printing, and especially the use of such technologies in medical practices, see, for example, C. Schubert, M. C. van Langeveld, and L. A. Donoso, "Innovations in 3D Printing: A 3D Overview from Optics to Organs," *British Journal of Ophthalmology* 98, no. 2 (February 2014): 159–161.

[24] See, for example, Peter Jensen-Haxel, "3D Printers, Obsolete Firearm Supply Controls, and the Right to Build Self-defense Weapons under Heller," *Golden Gate Law Review* 42, no. 3 (June 2012); and the summary statement, "First Amendment—Technology, Defense Distributed v. United States

Wilson's narrative of Defense Distributed and the use of additive technologies for firearms manufacturing is particularly illuminating: "The political opportunity wasn't in manufacturing then (for anyone could produce a weapon with the right tools). It was in publishing . . . We could produce a gun with the most widely available 3D-printing technologies and then freely distribute the plans over the internet. We'd share the designs as open source software."[25] Wilson's aim was to multiply the means of production of firearms, disrupting the very structure of control that federal licensing produced. As Wilson argued, "We will have the reality of a weapons system that can be printed out from your desk. Anywhere there is a computer, there is a weapon."[26] It wasn't simply that anyone could make their own gun. What made the 3D printing of firearms so attractive as a project was the possibility of the multiplicative effects of being able to print a gun from anywhere, and many guns.[27] Increased access, and increased quantity of firearms, were now possible, and without direct government interference (as long as the plans for such printing were available). From Cody's perspective, the 3D printing of guns "is what access to the means of production was always going to look like."[28]

One key project at the core of Defense Distributed's use of 3D-printed technologies was the "Liberator" pistol.[29] Modeled after the US military initiative in WWII to drop single shot weapons over Germany in an effort to arm resistance fighters, this second "Liberator" would be available to anyone who could access the plans to print it. Access to a 3D printer would thus, by Wilson's reading, transform the subject from one who might have been a consumer of guns, to one who was now always capable of making guns—if only he wished. As Wilson explained, "You could have printed anything. Something helpful: a prosthetic. Why didn't you print a prosthetic? The God-damned printer was the prosthetic."[30] The printer itself was not just transforming society, but was

Department of State, Fifth Circuit Declines to Enjoin Regulation of Online Publication of 3D Printing Files, Recent Case: 838 F3d 451 (5th Cir. 2016)," *Harvard Law Review* 130, no. 6 (April 7, 2017).

[25] Cody Wilson, *Come and Take It: The Gun Printer's Guide to Thinking Free* (New York: Gallery Books, 2016), 7–8.

[26] Ibid., 64.

[27] Danton L. Bryans, "Unlocked and Loaded: Government Censorship of 3D-Printed Firearms and a Proposal for More Reasonable Regulation of 3D Printed Goods," *Indiana Law Journal* 90, no. 2 (Spring 2015), esp. 910–920.

[28] Wilson, *Come and Take It*, 8.

[29] On the history of the US Army plans for the Liberator pistol in WWII, see, for example, Charles Chandler, "Gun-Making as a Cottage Industry," *Journal on Firearms and Public Policy* 155 (1990), 156.

[30] Wilson, *Come and Take It*, 77.

transforming the political subject itself, making possible the complete, total, and universal access to firearms—so long as there was a printer to print them.

While 3D printers come in a variety of sizes, most can fit on a desktop. What characterizes them most is their sound. The gentle whirl of the rotating extruder head echoes softly, followed by the sound of gears that allow the head to move according to the assigned programing. No doubt the mechanized chorus is incomparable to the scene of the printer's shop Hornschuch described.

Part 2: Re-Enchanted

That printed guns could transform power relations in a parallel manner to the social transformations brought about by the printed word poses a fundamental paradox: The printing press itself produced a fundamental social change in the character of modern life, eliciting a mode of rationalization that led precisely to—as many have argued—the disenchantment of the material world. Wilson himself hopes "just as the technology of printing altered and reduced the power of medieval guilds and the social power structure, so too will cryptologic methods fundamentally alter the nature of corporations and of government interference in economic transactions."[31] Put differently, exactly what Wilson and others hope to accomplish through the 3D printing of guns is a re-enchantment of force. No longer a tool for use, a source of protection, or a good for purchase, the 3D-printed gun is available in a way that no other firearm could have been before. Increased access and availability transforms what the gun is, making it disposable, and readily available beyond territorial and governmental limits (assuming one has a printer at hand). But does increased access mean that the disenchanted political subject has transformed? This is the focus of this section of this chapter.

Western conceptions of modernity—alienated, secular, rationalized, bureaucratized—have famously traced back to the transition away from a magical imagination, and the prescientific rationality that supposedly accompanied this viewpoint.[32] The most famous narration of this transition presents itself in Max Weber's important lecture, "Science as a Vocation."[33] Delivered in the late

---

[31] From Tim May's "Crypto Anarchist Manifesto" (November 22, 1992); cf Wilson, *Come and Take It*, 85.

[32] Jason A. Josephson-Storm, *The Myth of Disenchantment: Magic, Modernity, and the Birth of the Human* Sciences (Chicago: University of Chicago Press, 2017), 4.

[33] Peter Lassman and Irving Velody's essay, "Max Weber on Science, Disenchantment, and the Search of Meaning," in *Max Weber's "Science as a Vocation,"* eds. Lassman and Velody, 159–204, which contains an excellent discussion of Weber's remarks on this topic; Richard Jenkins, "Disenchantment, Enchantment and Re-Enchantment: Max Weber at the Millennium," *Max Weber Studies* 1, no. 1

part of what was then known as the "Great War," Weber worried about what it meant to "think" (morally/politically/rationally) in a moment of such vast human-made catastrophe. At issue for Weber was a fundamental shift in the modern urban psyche. Exactly the mindset that had allowed World War I to come about was also the psyche that sought rationalization of all aspects of life. As Weber explained, "Unless we happen to be physicists, those of us who travel by streetcar have not the faintest idea how that streetcar works. Nor have we any need to know it. It is enough for us to know that we can 'count on' the behavior of the streetcar. We can base our own behavior on it. But we have no idea how to build a streetcar so that it will move."[34] Here the modern subjects reveal themselves in a unique form of ignorance. So long as the world continues to operate—so long as made things continue to be of use (or at least useable)—there is no need to actually know how such things operate. The modern bourgeois subjects become defined by what they use, and what they can use (what they have access to use), and not by their knowledge. When a subject takes on a view of reason that incorporates wish, such a subject becomes—famously—disenchanted. As Weber claimed, "The growing process of intellectualization and rationalization does *not* imply a growing understanding of the conditions under which we live. It means something quite different. It is the knowledge or the conviction that if *only we wished* to understand them we *could* do so at any time."[35] The logic of "if only we wished" has profound implications for how the human subject understands itself and its own rationality.[36] Under this logic, human reason becomes omnipotent, or at least so powerful that, if only we wished, such reason could solve the puzzle of usability. If only . . .

The admixture of reason and wish, though, is not without consequence. Weber continues, "(I)n principle, then, we are not ruled by mysterious, unpredictable forces, but that, on the contrary, we can in principle *control everything by means of calculation. That in turn means the disenchantment of the world.*"[37] The human subjects who believe themselves to be able, if only they wished, to reason out the mechanization of the world, become the human beings that believe, if only they

---

(2000), 11–32; Josh Landy and Michael Saler, eds., *The Re-Enchantment of the World: Secular Magic in a Rational Age* (Redwood City, CA: Stanford University Press, 2009); Ludger Honnefelder, "Rationalization and Natural Law: Max Weber's and Ernst Troeltsch's Interpretation of the Medieval Doctrine of Natural Law," *Review of Metaphysics* 49, no. 2 (December 1995): 275–294.

[34] Honnefelder, "Rationalization and Natural Law," 12–13.

[35] Ibid., 13.

[36] Horowitz, Asher. "The Comedy of Enlightenment: Weber, Habermas, and the Critique of Reification," in *The Barbarism of Reason,* eds. Asher Horowitz and Terry Maley (Toronto: University of Toronto Press, 1994), 195–222.

[37] Max Weber, *The Vocation Lectures: "Science as a Vocation"; "Politics as a Vocation"* (Cambridge, MA: Hackett, 2004), 13.

wished, they could control that world through calculation. Weber claims this is a disenchantment because previous subjectivities that eschewed or lacked access to such fantasies of calculation were open to superstition, or at least the possibility of a spirit that was beyond their own control and understanding. Where once persons were subject to spirit, now they are merely subject to wish.

Whether human beings have fully or partially transformed into such subjects through modernization may be beside the point. More crucial for this diagnosis is if they could, what consequences would they face, and what incentives would exist to resists it. As Jane Bennett reflects, "An intrinsically meaningless world also brings new opportunities for freedom."[38]

A re-enchantment of this world would mean a new relationship with things. No longer would subjects think of made things as spiritless. Nor would they imagine made things as subject to calculation. A re-enchanted world is one that eschews such an antithesis. As Bennett argues, "Modern scientific practices first induce the expectation of a telos and then flatly refuse to fulfill it; science first whets our appetite for completion of purpose and then insists that no final satisfaction is attainable and that is why a disenchanted materialism carries with it a psychology of disappointment and an affect of meaninglessness. Disenchantment names both this subjective state and the impersonal historical condition of the flight of the gods."[39] The crisis that the modern subject faces in the disenchanted condition they take on through mixing reason and wish is the continual refusal of the wish fulfillment. The subject takes on the internal grammar of "if only," constantly differing commitment and action. The hypothetical continuality of such a logic leaves the subject continually decentered, and absent any possibility of meaningful interaction. Exactly what was supposed to supply meaning—the scientific rationalization of the world that surrounds us—resulted in a lost spiritualized materiality, and a disaffected subject unable to actualize that spirit anew.

It is this decentered and disaffected spirit that Wilson seems to hope to resurrect. And yet the very process of this resurrection is the seeming fulfilment of exactly that process that everted it. Here Bennett is useful again, when she claims,

> Rationalization encompasses a variety of related processes, each of which opts for the precise, regular, constant, and reliable over the wild, spectacular, idiosyncratic, and surprising. In addition to eschewing magic as a strategy of will (i.e., "schematizing" desire), rationalization also systematizes knowledge (i.e., pursues "increasing

---

[38] Jane Bennett. *The Enchantment of Modern Life: Attachments, Crossings, and Ethics* (Princeton, NJ: Princeton University Press, 2001), 60.

[39] Ibid., 61.

theoretical mastery of reality by means of increasingly precise and abstract concepts"); instrumentalizes thinking (i.e., methodically attains a "radical end by means of increasingly precise calculation of adequate means"); secularizes metaphysical traditional bonds as the basis of social order with those founded on the natural reason of men.[40]

The very instrumentalized thinking that follows from the 3D printing of weapons seems the solution to Wilson's disenchantment subject. But how can he untie this knot?

It is worth speculating that the press itself is crucial to this procedure—the very mechanization of information becomes the origin of disenchantment. Bernard Stiegler argues that enchantment and disenchantment may not be so easily untangled. He sees the new religious spirits of capitalism originating in the "appearance of a 'techno-ology' of spirit." For example, Stiegler claims, "the printing press, which opened access to books for everyone (and in particular the faithful). . . will also be at the origin of the republic of letters and finally of modern, industrial democracy."[41] The social action of the printing press is such that it accomplished the production of new sources of social change, finally eliciting both the democratic sprit as well as the disenchanted one. Are these synonymous, or can the democracy spirit break from the disenchanted? This, it seems, may be what lurks beneath Wilson's argument.

For such a rupture in spirit to occur, the process of production and consumption require clear analysis. Stiegler worries that at issue here are competing notions of society. As he elaborates,

> The generalization of informational technologies and the redefinition of the forms of knowledge in which they consist, constitutes an epoch of this process of grammatization as the passage from the age of mnemotechnical societies to that of mnemotechnological societies— that is, to a stage where exteriorization takes the form of devices to which it is possible to delegate new cognitive functions. Now, it is also the passage from a society in which the clerks are separated from production, to a society in which production rests upon forms of knowledge and has absorbed the clerks—or has eliminated them to the extent that they formed a sphere separated from production.[42]

---

[40] Ibid., 58.

[41] Bernard Stiegler, *The Re-Enchantment of the World: The Value of Spirit against Industrial Populism* (London: Bloomsbury Academic, 2014), 5.

[42] Ibid., 87–88.

How far can society move away from production? It would seem that the disenchanted subject has defined itself by the wish and the separation of that production. There is a distinction between the subject that claims "I could make that . . . understand that . . . construct that . . . produce that . . . if only I wanted to . . ." and the subject that commits such action.

Production itself, and the means of production, seem tied to the pathways of disenchantment. But are these pathways political? For Weber, the political consequences of disenchantment are profound. If politics is the continual questioning of "What should we do? How should we live?" than the disenchantment self may risk a depoliticization. ("What might we wish for?" is not the same question.)[43] The shift seems to be in the question and logic of judgment. The subject, as the wishing self, has no impetus to cast judgment, no reason to determine for oneself why one should live one way as opposed to another, why we should do one act as opposed to another. In this way, science is not politics, for politics aims to answer the question who should we be, how should we live. As Weber reflects, "The simplest reply was given by Tolstoy with his statement, "Science is meaningless because it has no answer to the only questions that matter to us: 'What should we do? How shall we live?' "[44]

But if science is meaningless in regard to such questions, meaningless in regard to how we answer political questions, *things* may not be. The contrast is apparent in how Weber understands what counts as politics, and the relationship between violence and the state (which is itself, by Weber's own account, the site of pure politics).[45] Central to the sociological definition of politics is the means that are specific to it. We understand politics as distinct from economics, for example, because force is not an accepted practice of economic behavior. Famously, Weber argues that what is unique to politics is that it is defined by its capacity to legitimate the means of violent force. As he explains, "The modern state can be defined only sociologically by the specific *means* that are peculiar to it, as to every political organization: namely, physical violence . . . If there existed only societies in which violence was unknown as a means, *then* the concept of the 'state' would disappear; *in that event,* what would have emerged is what, in this specific meaning of the word, we might call 'anarchy.' "[46] The state is of course a specific site of politics, but it also the site which, by Weber's read,

---

[43] Weber, *Vocation Lectures: "Science,"* 18. For further discussion on this point, see Tracy B. Strong, *Politics without Vision: Thinking without a Banister in the Twentieth Century* (Chicago: University of Chicago Press, 2013), esp. the section "Max Weber, Magic, and the Politics of Social Scientific Objectivity."

[44] Weber, *Vocation Lectures: "Science,"* 17.

[45] Dallmayr, Fred, "Max Weber and the Modern State," in *The Barbarism of Reason,* eds. Asher Horowitz and Terry Maley (Toronto: University of Toronto Press, 1994), 44–63.

[46] Weber, *Vocation Lectures: "Politics,"* 33.

best illustrates for us what politics entails. For not only is the state licensed to use violence, it is that entity which has legitimate control over the very right to use violence. As Weber elaborates,

> We must say that the state is the form of human community that (suc-cessfully) lays claim to the *monopoly of legitimate physical violence* within a particular territory—and this idea of "territory" is an essential de-fining feature. For what is specific to the present is that all other or-ganizations or individuals can assert the right to use physical violence only insofar as the *state* permits them to do so. The state is regarded as the sole source of the "right" to use violence. Hence, what "politics" means for us is to strive for a share of power or to influence the distribu-tion of power, whether between states or between the groups of people contained within a state.[47]

Any violence that is legitimate falls within the preview of the state.

From licensure, to law and constitution, the state is that entity which legitimates violence. One contemporary mechanism for such licensure is the control of the means of production. Only through granting limited licenses to firearms manufacturers, and through clear documentation of the numbers of firearm produced, can a state exercise its claim to monopoly over force. What 3D printing of firearms might likely produce is the rupture of this very concept of monopoly, by creating a material barrier to the very monitoring of firearm production.

The threat to the monopoly of force usually takes the form of actors who replace legitimate force with that which is illegitimate. Contestation for the le-gitimate monopoly of force would thus be located in actors, not in things. As Weber elaborates, "Like the political organizations that preceded it historically, the state represents a relationship in which people *rule over* other people. This relationship is based on the legitimate use of force (that is to say, force that is perceived as legitimate). If the state is to survive, those who are ruled over must always *acquiesce* in the authority that is claimed by the rulers of the day."[48] What 3D printing of guns may allow is the transfer of that agency to things. Especially crucial here is that these things are temporary (known to not last very long, or not to shoot very well). Temporary things are not identical with "private things." What makes the 3D gun the site of this complicated agentic sovereignty is that it

---

[47] Ibid.
[48] Ibid., 34.

is meant to be disposed of—meant to be one of many, meant to not last. It is also meant to contain within it the threat of lethal force.

The link between the severity of force and the fugitive quality of the printed gun may transform that monopoly of violence itself. If it does, the question then becomes what happens to other modes of agency in this transformation. What happens to agents who might aim to defend the monopoly of force as a private good, even if framed by a public good (the right to keep and bear arms)?

Part 3: Things and the Fantasies of Equality They Might Produce

If the printing of guns poses a threat to the legitimate monopoly of violent force that the state relies on for its own security, at what level does that threat manifest itself? Is it simply the challenge to the monopoly itself, or is there a new form of subjectivity that manifests itself as undermining the monopoly? How does the gun change what the political subjects imagine themselves to be?

This line of questioning demands that we relate the thingness of the gun to the formation of political subjectivity. What kind of thing is a gun?[49] Does that thing change as its material changes? Certainly plastic guns have existed for a long time. From the Remington Nylon 66 to Glock Ges.m.b.H's polymer handgun, manufactured firearms composed over polymer plastics and stock and receivers combined and assembled through injection molding have been available since the 1950s.[50] The difference in 3D-printed guns is the direct access to the means of production. The gun itself transforms into a disposable, easily made, and easily used object of force. But how, if at all, does this new thing act on its user? How might it transform the subjectivity of the shooter, or the gunmaker? Here we might have imagined the gun again, as something new. Its very materiality, and the means of its production, may require that we reimagine the gun from its new possible effects. As Bill Brown argues, perhaps "objects are materialized by the (ap)perceiving subject, the anterior physicality of the physical world emerging, perhaps, as an after-effect of the mutual constitution of subject and object, a retro projection? (We) could imagine things... as what is excessive in objects, as what

---

[49] See, for example, Diana Coole and Samantha Frost, eds., *New Materialisms: Ontology, Agency, and Politics.* (Durham, NC: Duke University Press, 2010); and Jane Bennett, *Vibrant Matter: A Political Ecology of Things* (Durham, NC: Duke University Press, 2009). For a review of debates on New Materialism, see Andrew Poe, "Things-Beyond-Objects," *Journal of French and Francophone Philosophy* 19, no. 1 (2011), 153–164.

[50] See Roy Marcot's *History of Remington Firearms, The History of One of the World's Most Famous Gun Makers* (New York: Rowan and Littlefield, 2005), 86–88.

exceeds their mere materialization as objects, or their mere utilization as objects, their force as a sensuous presence or as a metaphysical presence, the magic by which objects become values, fetishes, idols, and totems."[51] If we can see a thing again, in all of itself—both its use and its consequences—we may begin to conceive that what the gun is and how it is made may have direct consequences on the subjectivity of those who use guns.

One line of theorization that may be especially useful here is that of Jean-Jacques Rousseau. While writing in the early enlightenment, and critical of social pathologies of inequality, Rousseau offers a framework in his *Second Discourse* on how things may affect political subjectivity. Rousseau intended his *Second Discourse* to be an entry into an essay contest held by the Academy of Arts and Science at Dijon. In response to the question, "What is the origin of inequality?" Rousseau wondered who would ask such a question, and the consequences for a society that legitimizes an authority that would ask such a question. Rousseau's response to this question is important, for it works to counter the malformations of a political imagination that desires equality, even as it establishes inequality (what we might call a pathological political subjectivity).

How can we imagine equality if we live in an unequal society? Rousseau asks the reader to reimagine humanity, as far back as possible, wherein they would still recognize the human they imagine as human. As he explains,

> If I strip this being, thus constituted, of all the supernatural gifts which he may have received, and of all the artificial faculties, which he could not have acquired but by slow degrees; if I consider him, in a word, such as he must have issued from the hands of nature; I see an animal less strong than some, and less agile than others, but, upon the whole, the most advantageously organized of any: I see him satisfying his hunger under an oak, and his thirst at the first brook; I see him laying himself down to sleep at the foot of the same tree that afforded him his meal; and there are all his wants completely supplied.[52]

This method of re-imagination is particularly useful, as it emphasizes the logic of wish within the contemporary enlightenment psychology, and the testing of the limits of that wish-filled logic. Rousseau asks his reader, and his contemporary society, to become self-critical. Imagine yourself as far as we can imagine ourselves. (How far is that, if we are malformed? If our imagination is malformed?)

---

[51] Bill Brown, "Thing Theory," *Critical Inquiry* 28, no. 1 (2001), 5.

[52] Jean-Jacques Rousseau, "The Second Discourse: Discourse on the Origin and Foundations of Inequality among Mankind," in *The Social Contract and the First and Second Discourses* (New Haven, CT: Yale University Press, 2002), 90.

The human we can imagine as part of our species is the human who is still equal to us as human. While Rousseau appears to narrate a primitive historical past, his theorization of inequality provides ample evidence that human beings are capable of imagining themselves as equal to one another. In this way, his theory of the origins of inequality uses the reader's own imagination to produce equality. And it is the loss of this equality which will prove the origins of inequality, at least as he hopes to explain it.

We are, it seems, a wishful species. The first human we can imagine who is still equal to us, according to Rousseau, is one who has all his wants satisfied—all his wishes fulfilled. Because we are a wanting species and we would imagine ourselves according to the frame of want, the human we could imagine who is still like us would be the self we would want to be. We want to be the person that has all our wants met. In that frame, what we would want would be to become one who does not want because all wants are already satisfied. This shows us the key pathology of the modern human, by Rousseau's accounting. This is not some odd nostalgia, or a passive fantasy of the human in some fictive primary nature. Rousseau is subtly toying with the narrative frames and his readers' anticipations. How much does what you want, and that you want, transform how you want?

Rousseau offers us an important contrast between the subject who wishes and the subject who does not. The first person described in this fictive world is the person without want, and in a nature which requires no tools. There is enough food and enough shelter. Everything is perfect, at least as far back as we—we wishful subjects—can imagine it (can want it). That contrast—between a wishful subject and a wish-fulfilled subject—closely parallels Weber's critique of the modern subject who thinks "if only." The contrast Rousseau offers us is one that relies on the desires of the present—the wishes of the contemporary subject—as a source of acceleration.[53] Here, in the competing temporalities of political subjectivities, we face the problem of progress. If we really believe in progress, how can we confront/oppose/unite/disrupt? How are we to confront injustices in our present experiences of political life—the emergency which we recognize as wrong, and yet is perfectly in conjunction with the development of things as usual? How we think of progress seems directly tied to how we understand the validity of various modes of historical time. To confront injustices in our present experiences of political life—the emergency which we recognize as wrong, and yet is perfectly in conjunction with the development of things as

---

[53] See, for example, Hartmut Rosa, *Social Acceleration: A New Theory of Modernity* (New York: Columbia University Press, 2013); see also William E. Connolly, *Neuropolitics: Thinking, Culture, Speed* (Minneapolis: University of Minnesota Press, 2002), esp. the section on "Democracy and Time."

usual—requires another view. Rousseau raises a serious anxiety here: Progress is demobilizing (if it always happens, why bother to act?).

So how might we respond to this demobilization, this alienation? Rousseau invites us to rethink history at its very bottom.[54] This rethinking is the logic of the hypothetical—what he calls his "experiments" in thinking. He asks the reader to consider, not how things are, but how they might be. What is the point of that? If we worry that something is wrong with how politics are, or how we want them to be, we need to practice rethinking—that means experimenting with our thoughts. Rousseau explains, "Let us begin, therefore, by laying aside facts, for they do not affect the question. The researches, in which we may engage on this occasion, are not to be taken for historical truths, but merely as hypothetical and conditional reasonings, fitter to illustrate the nature of things, then to show their true origin, like those systems, which our naturalists daily make of the formation of the world."[55] An investigation into equality, through a readership that has produced inequality through its own malformed imagination, requires some jolt, a reshifting of frame. The acceleration of the imagination is the method that Rousseau deploys, and in it we see both the costs of a wish-filled subjectivity as well as the political consequences—pertinent for our own rethinking of how things might condition contemporary political subjectivity.

The pathway of development that Rousseau traces for this political subjectivity is one of necessity. If the wishing subject is the contemporary subject, and that subject wishes itself to a place without want, a place where wants are all met, then this place is also that place where needs are satisfied. In this endemic condition, the subject lives without any experience of necessity. Under a tree that provides it shelter and food, near a stream where fresh water exists, this first human, as far as we can imagine, faces no obstacle to preservation.

The first subject only has the need to transform when it faces a threat to that preservation. This logic of preservation against threat appears through a particular mechanism of relation. Seeing other animals in harm's way, and noticing that danger exists, is an impetus for this first subject to change. As Rousseau argues the point, the human we imagine is not so strong as other animals, nor as fast, but particularly adept at comparisons. The fact of its subjectivity is set by its ability to engage in comparative relations. Rousseau observes, "These relations, which we express by the words, great, little, strong, weak, swift, slow,

[54] Frederick Neuhouser, "Rousseau's Critique of Economic Inequality," *Philosophy and Social Criticism* 41, no. 3 (2013); Richard Velkley, "The Measure of the Possible: Imagination in Rousseau's Philosophical Pedagogy," in *The Challenge of Rousseau*, eds. Eve Grace and Christopher Kelly (Cambridge: Cambridge University Press, 2013), esp. 223–226.

[55] Rousseau, "The Second Discourse," 88.

fearful, bold, and the like, compared occasionally, and almost without thinking of it, produced in him some kind of reflection, or rather a mechanical prudence, which pointed out to him the precautions most essential to his safety."[56] The subject who sees in relation to others finds the need to transform, through imitation, into these other entities. Seeing power elsewhere, the first human leaves behind the world as a pure object, and begins to experience accelerating necessities as a structure of survival. Rousseau explains,

> Nakedness, therefore, the want of houses, and of all these superfluities, which we consider as so very necessary, are not such mighty evils in respect to these primitive men, and much less still any obstacle to their preservation . . . In short, unless we admit those singular and fortuitous concurrences of circumstances, which I shall speak of hereafter, and which, it is very possible, may never have existed, it is evident, in any case, that the man who first made himself clothes and built himself a cabin supplied himself with things which he did not much need, since he had lived without them till then; and why should he not have been able to support, in his riper years, the same kind of life, which he had supported from his infancy?[57]

The new human becomes the person who creates needs. Central to this transformation of the subject is the prosthetics of things. Rousseau doesn't just imagine a human who once was unified with the world, and through comparative relations becomes disenchanted. Instead, Rousseau envisions a human who builds prosthetic extensions that allow him to become more than himself.

The example Rousseau returns to again and again is the hatchet. As he describes it, "The earth, left to its own natural fertility, and covered with immense woods that no hatchet ever disfigured, offers at every step food and shelter to every species of animals."[58] The first human world—a world without tools / that has not yet been disfigured by tools—is a world that provides for all in every way. As humans begin to disfigure it—as they become tool animals—that world becomes defined by necessity and scarcity, and can no longer provide what it once could. The costs for the human are especially destructive. For though the human may imagine itself as inventive, having managed to construct a hatchet which might allow it to build itself shelter, that prosthesis begins to affect the human's own self-conception and subjectivity. As Rousseau questions, "Had he

[56] Ibid., 115.
[57] Ibid., 94.
[58] Ibid., 90.

a hatchet, would his hand so easily snap off from an oak so stout a branch?"[59] The hatchet may make life in the wilderness appear easier, but that ease, over time, transforms the body of the human, making life without the prosthetic more difficult. Here the prosthetic of the hatchet, which appeared once as a means to provide better shelter, becomes a limitation on the psyche of the first human, accelerating the imagination, and making new needs, where before there were none. Rousseau explains, "At length, these first advances enabled man to make others at a greater rate. He became more industrious in proportion as his mind became more enlightened. Men, soon ceasing to fall asleep under the first tree, or take shelter in the first cave, hit upon several kinds of hatchets of hard and sharp stones, and employed them to dig the ground, cut down trees, and with the branches build huts, which they afterwards bethought themselves of plastering over with clay or mud."[60] The new human becomes more and more needy, more and more the human that the contemporary human knows itself to be.

The narrative of the human who was once free from need, but becomes wish-filled, and hampered by the tools he devises to satisfy his wishes, is often read as a nostalgic theodicy, a fantasy for what humans could have been.[61] Here I offer a counter reading. Rousseau defines the state of nature through a method which aims to dislodge the contemporary imagining of malformed subjectivities from their own instabilities. It isn't that Rousseau believes in or desires this originary condition. Rather, he imagines that the corrupted fantasies of the contemporary political subject may only ever be able to imagine such a world if asked to imagine the first human of their species. This is because even that desire is unstable. What Rousseau deploys then is a method of thinking that takes the imagining of the contemporary political subject as far back as it can imagine the species as still its own species, and then lets that imaginary narrative reveal itself into and past the present. What we might call an elastic temporality.

The acceleration of this history into the possible future becomes itself a hypothetical and mythic speculation on what might result if the malformed contemporary imagining was forced to focus on the pathway that would be constituent of its wishful thinking. Rousseau names this future as a second state of nature. As he explains, this accelerated state would eventually resolve itself as a despotism:

> Gradually rearing up her hideous head, and devouring in every part
> of the State all that still remained sound and untainted, would at last

---

[59] Ibid., 91.

[60] Ibid., 125.

[61] See, for example, Frederick Neuhouser, *Rousseau's Critique of Inequality: Reconstructing the Second Discourse* (Cambridge: Cambridge University Press, 2014); and Jimmy Casas Klausen, *Fugitive Rousseau: Slavery, Primitivism, and Political Freedom* (New York: Fordham University Press, 2014).

succeed in trampling upon the laws and the people, and establish itself upon the ruins of the republic. The times immediately preceding this last alteration would be times of calamity and trouble; but at last everything would be swallowed up by the monster; and the people would no longer have chiefs or laws, but only tyrants. From this fatal moment, all regard to virtue and manners would likewise disappear; for despotism, *cui ex honesto nulla est spes*, tolerates no other master, wherever it reigns; the moment it speaks, probity and duty lose all their influence, and the blindest obedience is the only virtue to slaves ... This is when everything returns to the sole law of the strongest, and of course to a new state of nature different from that with which we began, inasmuch as the first was the state of nature in its purity, and this one the consequence of excessive corruption.[62]

The subject that is wishful, defined by prosthetic things, will produce a politics of despotism, because they are inclined by the desire for things to become less and less equal with themselves. This increasing inequality is itself a form of enslavement.

How might we respond to such a dystopic future? How could our present political subjectivity resist this future deposit? What would need to change is our relation to inequality. As Rousseau argues,

Inequality, almost non-existent among men in the state of nature, derives its force and its growth from the development of our faculties and the progress of the human mind, and at last becomes permanent and lawful by the establishment of property and of laws. It likewise follows that moral inequality, authorized, solely by positive right, clashes with natural right, whenever it is not in proportion to physical inequality; a distinction which sufficiently determines what we are to think of that kind of inequality which obtains in all civilized nations, since it is evidently against the law of nature that children should command old men, and fools lead the wise, and that a handful should gorge themselves with superfluities, while the starving masses lack the barest necessities of life.[63]

Here Rousseau offers us a frame by which to respond. If we can reorient ourselves to a care of the species, and not the preservation of ourselves, if we can

---

[62] Rousseau, "The Second Discourse," 136.
[63] Ibid., 138.

bear witness to the violences of necessity that plague humanity, and deplore some—but not all—of the "necessities" of life. In short, if we can reorient ourselves to understand necessity as that which is and should be shared, rather than as that which is and should be felt by our individual selves, we can short-circuit the linear acceleration of the present wishful self from its ancient past where there were no necessities, to a despotic future of total slavery, becoming revolutionaries to the very logic of the necessary. For Rousseau, the break that is required is one with how we conceive necessity, and this entails a break with how we conceive of things (as these were the source of our pathological transformation into our wish-filled and prosthetic selves).

Rousseau is especially useful here for thinking through whether or how the 3D printing of guns—the making of things, and especially things capable of lethal force—might result in a kind of emancipated equality. The promise of Wilson's argument regarding 3D-printed firearms is that these weapons, and the means of producing them, begin a project of radical equality. The danger though, from a Rousseauian perspective, would be that these things have not yet changed our thinking on equality, and are likely to continue to reproduce the same dominations. What would be necessary for a truly radical equality would be the production of a thing that made things obsolete. Are 3D printers capable of such transformations?

Conclusion—Can a Gun Be a Public Thing?

The excess of made things—that incalculable element of the thing itself—seems to be a site of enchantment. But how can we attune ourselves to those excesses, rather than ignoring them? How can we orient ourselves to things in such a way that these things become sources of emancipation? In this chapter, I have explored the threat and the appeal of 3D-printed firearms. Those, like Cody Wilson, who advocate for their production, see such weapons as a material source of renewed equality. Critics, however, contend that such weapons pose a fundamental threat to the national security of the state. The recent ruling of the US 5th Circuit Court of Appeals sided with the latter. While Cody's own arguments may be flawed, is there any possibility for emancipation in 3D printing?

At issue here may be what sort of thing the gun becomes when it is printed using additive technologies. I have claimed before that what changes is the accessibility of the gun (as the means of production changes, so too does the increased access to the regular production of guns). But we might consider that in changing accessibility comes a new political subjectivity. It may matter if we consider such things as private or public things.

Guns are usually considered to be private things.[64] Held as private property, owned by private persons, protected by private right, the gun is, more than other things, defined by its subtraction from public space. Public things, by contrast, are those things which are shared. As Bonnie Honig has recently argued this point, "Democracy . . . postulates shared and common things such as public schools, hospitals, sewage systems, transportation systems, communications airwaves, prisons, town councils, local and national parks, public energy projects, and so on. Being shared or public means they are sites of confrontation and encounter, enjoyment and conflict, and that they are accessible to all."[65] But part of Wilson's lawsuit may highlight a need to change that thinking.

Could a printed arsenal become a shared public thing? Certainly the newest gun is not a public thing, for a shared love of some produced good for consumption would not transform the subject position of the consumer. As Bonnie Honig observes, "The public love of public objects is different from the mass consumerist need to all be in love with the same private object—the newest iPhone, say—and to have one, of which there are millions. That said, this contemporary consumer need may well be the ruin, the remnant, of the democratic need to constellate affectively around shared objects in their precommodified or noncommodified or more-than-commodified form. Sometimes, that is to say, the ruin speaks. But will we hear it?"[66] Can that need be directed to 3D-printed firearms? Should it be?

Judge Jones, the dissenting judge in Defense Distributed's appeal, offers a framework to begin to imagine anything printed as part of free speech, and thus as protected as a public good. Jones argues that the harm posed by the publication of the code for 3D-printed guns would not be sufficient to establish threat of harm to the State. As Jones claims, "the State Department turns freedom of speech on its head," and, he asserts, "the possibility that an Internet site could also be used to distribute the technical data domestically does not alter the analysis . . ." The Government bears the burden to show that its regulation is narrowly tailored to suit a compelling interest. It is not the public's burden to prove their right to discuss lawful, nonclassified, non-restricted technical data. As applied to Defense Distributed's online publication, these overinclusive regulations cannot be narrowly tailored and fail strict scrutiny.[67] A corollary line of inquiry

[64] See David Hemenway, *Private Guns, Public Health* (Ann Arbor: University of Michigan Press, 2006).

[65] Bonnie Honig, "Public Things: Jonathan Lear's Radical Hope, Lars von Trier's Melancholia, and the Democratic Need," *Political Research Quarterly* 68, no. 3 (2015): 623–636, 624.

[66] Ibid., 625.

[67] No. 15-50759 Doc. 00513686006, 1 (5th Cir. September 20, 2016), Defense Distributed; Second Amendment Foundation, Incorporated v US, 34.

to Jones's argument would be, does code count as speech?[68] Does data receive the same protections that other speech acts would receive? While it is unclear how expressive data can be, it certainly appears as information, and would seem to be due requisite protections. Again, as Jones argues, "None of the published information was illegal, classified for national security purposes, or subject to contractual or other distribution restrictions. In these respects the information was no different from technical data available through multiple Internet sources from widely diverse publishers. From scientific discussions, to popular mechanical publications, to personal blog sites, information about lethal devices of all sorts, or modifications to commercially manufactured firearms and explosives, is readily available on the Internet."[69]

The current standing on 3D-printed guns and the data used to construct them point to the threat these objects pose. And yet, there is a strong possibility that others may one day agree with Judge Jones, reading the data themselves as a speech act. If that shift begins to occur, the things produced by 3D printing could begin to take on the aura of additional rights. And then it will be up to democratic communities to decide if 3D-printed guns are best conceived of as private or as public things.

[68] See "First Amendment—Technology," *Harvard Law Review*; see also Ruth Miller, *Flourishing Thought: Democracy in an Age of Data Hoards* (Ann Arbor: University of Michigan Press, 2016).
[69] No. 15-50759 Doc. 00513686006, 1 (5th Cir. September 20, 2016), Defense Distributed; Second Amendment Foundation, Incorporated v US, 15.

3

Counting Up AR-15s

The Subject of Assault Rifles and the Assault Rifle as Subject

TIMOTHY W. LUKE

How to understand guns as not simply carriers of actions, but also as actors themselves is a challenging, but intriguing, assignment. Americans are often told, if not scolded, that they have a "gun culture." The ownership of guns, however, has been declining for decades, along with overall participation levels in outdoor sports, overall national crime levels, individual military service, and the popularity of hunting animals as recreation. In this context, where is the gun culture and what do guns mean?

To respond, this chapter reconsiders one type of firearm, namely the AR-15, along with its military M-16 and M-4 variants, which often are mistakenly labeled by the media as "assault rifles," to trace out the symbolic and material complexities associated with this type of gun. After this introduction, the first section maps some curious symbolic and material aspects of the gun culture tied to these weapons in the United States. The second section positions the AR platform within a material genealogy of battle rifles in Europe and the United States. It goes back to the beginnings of the original assault rifle during World War II, and follows the evolution of this weapon type after 1945 in the United States. Such firearms were developed as weapons of war. One set of American designs became the military-use M-16 and successor variants, while another morphed into the civilianized AR family of semi-automatic rifles. The third section situates the subject of assault-style rifles available for purchase by civilians around the United States, placing them within the context of a few recent high-profile mass shootings that have granted new emotive qualities and symbolic meanings to these guns. Given the weapons and their use in such crimes, the fourth section looks at the AR-15 as an agent, actor, or even a subject. This section is more speculative, but this approach draws upon the larger guiding thematic behind this collection of essays. One could say that a significant quality of these firearms is their capacity for generating new sub-jectivity from what is dismissed too often as inert thingness. To conclude, the fifth section ties together these themes by raising additional questions about the assault rifle as a cultural fixture in the public understanding of guns in the United States today.

Exploring these ideas is important. Guns are not always carriers of action. They signal actions, empower their carriers, and provide their owners with capacities that non-carriers do not have. Thinking through these possibilities of agency, as human actors carry guns brazenly in the open or furtively in concealed-carry rigs, is crucial. A few guns fire daily, but rarely all on their own. Some guns are used in forms of extremely violent interaction, but not always daily. Many guns in the minds of their owners and society are always at the ready for violent use at the drop of a hat. Concealed in carriers, strapped in open-carry holsters, slung over the shoulder, placed in a truck gun rack, or leaning in the corner by the front door, the gun is loaded. Still, most of these weapons are rarely, if ever, fired.

The Symbolic and the Material in Gun Culture

The meaning that any weapon conveys in the mind of its owner, and to the minds of others, determines how it is carried, displayed, or fired. Similarly, the actions that firearms perform in society condition their reception, presence, or circula-tion in everyday life. Deterrent displays of guns without actual discharge could be quite violent interactions, but frequent firings of other weapons might only be idle entertainments. Each of these gunplays, however, centrally feature firearms as actors. To ask what kind of symbol any gun is, in turn, becomes an intricate propo-sition. When, where, why, how, and to whom a gun becomes symbolically signifi-cant makes answering this question about material significance almost impossible to answer easily.

By the same token, what kinds of guns become symbols? In a country proud that it was, in part, made by Minutemen, the first American pioneers' flintlock musket undeniably is a national symbol. In 2000, a Cold War–era superstar, the actor Charlton Heston (aka "Moses" in *The Ten Commandments*, "Judah Ben-Hur" in *Ben-Hur*, and "Bright Eyes" in *The Planet of the Apes*) addressed the 129th National Rifle Association convention in Charlotte, North Carolina. Oddly enough, this Hollywood titan claimed he had only "ordinary hands," like anyone else. Then during an impassioned address, Heston raised up over his head a modern replica of muzzle-loading Kentucky long-rifle. Possessed by a look of reverent awe, he brandished it, like Moses's staff, Ben-Hur's spear, or Bright Eye's ape rifle. In an intense rebuke to then Vice President Al Gore's call for restricting the gun rights of Americans, Heston shouted, "From my cold, dead hands!"[1]

In material and symbolic terms, one wonders who or what is the actor here: does the musket carry Heston; are Heston and the Kentucky rifle head-liner co-stars celebrating the NRA; or is Heston, the human, brandishing a rifled musket, the thing, as an iconic token of the Constitution of the United States of America? The audience is a star-struck gun-rights pressure group, and this NRA plenary went supernova when Heston intoned "when ordinary hands can possess such an extraordinary instrument, that symbolizes the full measure of human dignity and liberty. That's why those five words issue an irresistible call to us all, and we muster."[2] For the NRA and its members, Heston declared its deepest principles, "To defeat the divisive forces that would take freedom away, I want to say those fighting words for everyone within the sound of my voice to hear and to heed—and especially for you, Mr. Gore: From my cold, dead hands!"[3]

This gun is an actor. It serves as a lead-spitting synecdoche for the United States of America, and Heston is the NRA's well-chosen big gun, firing for effect. One probably should begin by bearing in mind how such muzzle-loaders are nearly holy vessels in the Republic's civic religion. With their Minuteman shooters, for example, they appear all across the nation on public buildings, in history books, on official documents, in military insignia, on corporate signs, in business sta-tionery, and so on. These manifold material markers affirm that some sacred stuff for a mighty nation's citizens, in fact, is contained within such muskets. Indeed, there is an extraordinary anima/animus that "resides in that wooden stock and blue steel."[4] During this remarkable civic play of a national imaginary, the gun is a major player, and the actor is but an NRA gunhand espousing the interests of all in preserving their freedom to have and hold any type of firearm.

By the same token, this spirit cannot be separated from the development of the AR-15 and M-16 rifle platforms. These new rifles arrive during a water-shed moment in US history, namely, the years of intense Cold War tensions, the broadly opposed Vietnam War, and widespread resistance against routine mass conscription into the American military. Before 1973, most male citizens could expect to be drafted, and many were educated in the use of firearms before, during, and after their military service. Not simply the "armed citizens" that the

---

[1] Michael W. Chapman, "Flashback: From My Cold, Dead Hands," CNS News, January 14, 2013, http://www.cnsnews.com/news/article/flashback-charlton-heston-my-cold-dead-hands.

[2] Ibid.

[3] Ibid.

[4] Charlton Heston, "My Cold Dead Hands NRA Speech," YouTube, http://www.youtube.com/watch?v=rnXNowPnSQY.

NRA imagines should wander among twenty-first century America, serving as those "good guys" with a gun to take out some "bad guy" with a gun, the draft-age American citizen before 1973 was presumed to be a "citizen-at-arms," willing to serve in the regular forces, the reserves, or state guard units as a "sovereign," "citizen," "soldier." This symbolic cluster of intense civil engagement entailed important duties to the American body politic. Moreover, these civic roles were not strange fringe organization fantasies about state, county, or personal rights, but rather well-known obligations to the American nation reinforced in many rituals of citizenship.

Before Vietnam, American "gun culture" had a broad and deep civic tradition, which millions of Korean War, World War II, and World War I veterans affirmed in daily life. Over fifty years later, it is almost forgotten, purposely ignored, or not well understood. Nonetheless, it was real materially and symbolically. The loss of more capacious forms of civic agency for citizens, once embedded in the circuits of state war-making through the election of legislators empowered to declare war by the Constitution, made military service since World War II more telling as a meaningful civic duty during the Cold War. However, the last official declarations of war were passed by Congress against the minor Axis powers of Bulgaria, Hungary, and Romania on June 5, 1942. Thus, the elected national representatives of the voting public have broken the chain of responsibility with the rise of the Department of Defense, the threat of thermonuclear war, and the growth of a national security culture. These major political changes in citizen sovereignty haunt today's culture of gun ownership.

As a result, war making by the United States after the 1950s comes about grudgingly in strange "authorizations for use of military force" and "war resolution acts," which usually have unclear resolve, start fruitless wars, and then slip away from collective memory as tragically violent acts of Cold War and post–Cold War empire. After two generations of organizational change, America's armed forces have evolved into a professional volunteer military, and it is regarded now by most voters as another equal opportunity workplace for any able-bodied person, including foreign nationals, to build a respectable career without much real hazard in a high-tech workplace. Moreover, the American armed forces frequently outsource many of their more violent assignments to private military contractors—poor local allied nations and unmanned, remotely piloted weapons platforms "to defend the homeland." Still, at some point between the Iraq Wars of 1991 and 2003, the Department of Defense increasingly has come to call its soldiers, sailors, and airmen, both male and female, "warriors," in a nearly tribal, civilizational, or ethno-nationalist register. Before the 1970s, America's secular republican state rarely used this label. When citizens volunteered for the military, or were drafted into public service, Americans in uniform were regarded as citizens-at-arms rather than a special caste of warriors relatively isolated from the nation's general population. Consequently, the regular military was once staffed with far more active citizens, doing their first important civic duties as service men or service women, but these patterns no longer hold true.

These are subtle shifts, but their significance is not trivial. First, it should be noted that the US military, as President Trump has grumped, "does not win any-more" with these warriors from the all-volunteer forces. And, second, the people the United States has fought since 1949 typically are not armed with high-tech capital-intensive weapons equal to those fielded by the Pentagon. Third- or fourth-world enemy forces in the global south usually have only small arms or obsolete heavy weapons. They fight hard enough to not lose, but that level of intense popular armed resistance has stranded the United States in many geopolitical traps. And, these small wars leave Washington in uneasy armistices, forced strategic withdrawals, or unending tactical losses. Who the "good guys" and the "bad guys" are is not clear, or maybe not even determinable in these conflicts, but the poor opponents of the United States in the global south, who do not lose, always have guns.

It is against this backdrop that today's NRA has evolved into a power-house lobby for gun rights since the fall of Saigon in 1975. The National Rifle Association began in 1871, because Civil War veteran officers were dismayed with the shooting skills of their conscripts during the War between the States. The NRA has persisted through the decades as one of the largest firearms education organizations in the world, but its leaders also have become very effective advocates for gun and ammunition makers in the post–Cold War era.

A layered, close ethnographic assessment of the NRA might find that both Heston and his Kentucky long rifle were affirming the core symbolic values of the United States. They are coded, as many members of the NRA construct themselves, namely, as gun sellers and gun buyers who would only have their weapons pried out of their cold dead hands by some overweening government. They also believe every American should cherish the Constitution's Second Amendment principles. These legal rights affirm all Americans, according to this faith, as heirs of one of modernity's first wars of national liberation, armed popular revolutions, and militant settler civilizations, which all came to fulfillment in a historical play of Manifest Destiny through superior firepower. As subjects of the post–Cold War empire of bases engaged in a global war on terrorism, this mythos, of course, creates ambivalence, because it often seems quaint, brings a bad smell, and looks menacing at times. Yet, these mythic ideals also are very real, and they remain deeply entangled in the country's conflicted history.

Guns are symbols, but their materiality is loaded with civic signs, which highlight larger complexes of meaning. Recall for a moment images of John Rambo in Hope, Washington, with an M-60 machine gun; Detective "Dirty

Harry" Callahan in San Francisco with his Smith & Wesson N-frame Model 29 .44 Magnum; or Reuben J. "Rooster" Cogburn riding out in the Badlands firing his Model 92 Winchester carbine with a large loop lever.[5] Images of these three gunmen crackle with energy recurrently whipped up from America's rich folklore of armed violence. The guns convey divergent understandings of the gunman's effectiveness, while the actors trace different shades in the ethics of shooters: soldier, detective, cowboy, typically white, mostly male, but usually responsible for pursuing some larger symbolic collective good. Yet, the M-60, the S & W .44 Magnum, and the Winchester 92 also are historic headliner players filling key roles with their human costars.

Many experts assert "gun violence" amounts to a social tragedy, a national plague, a recurrent epidemic, or a male curse, but it is this simple. Must such reductive views of gun culture always find the significance of the gun in-and-of-itself mired in violent death and mayhem? Not many people confront the reality that lethal force sometimes is, in fact, unavoidable, necessary, or imperative. Beyond violence, are they fully aware of the multiple American subjectivities shaped by shooting, owning, handling, or appreciating guns? These questions are well worth bearing in mind as one examines "gun culture."

Unlike a specific new flu virus strain, however, there is not just one gun culture in America. There are many, not all involve shooting, and not all shooting is violent. These other American gun cultures, as the anthropologist Robert Redfield would suggest, have their own varied conventional understandings manifest in the acts and artifacts of certain human groups through time, but these nuances are rarely discussed. Few of them can be easily disentangled from the conflicted myths or shifting hatreds that churn at the civic core of the country's collective existence. But these psychic complexities and political contradictions also enable experts to naturalize gun use in the analytical *dispositifs* of the therapeutic state, cultures of securitization, and narratives of 24/7 police surveillance.

Counting Down AR-15s

At this conjuncture, it makes sense to survey the origins of the AR-15 in its development as a weapon of war, as well as its fate as just another semi-automatic rifle for sale to civilians. Given their space-age design configurations in the 1960s marketplace, such "black guns" or "black rifles" (due to the original colors of new light alloy materials used in the AR platform) have fascinated the shooting

---

[5] See Sylvester Stallone in *First Blood* (1982); Clint Eastwood in *Dirty Harry* (1971); and John Wayne in *True Grit* (1969).

and non-shooting public for decades.[6] This particular rifle came into service with the military during 1962 after multiple studies by the Pentagon.[7] In 1963, it was made available for sale to civilians, when ads in gun magazines showed the new futuristic Colt AR-15 "Sporter" for $189.50 in rustic hunting scenes that usually would feature at an old, beat-up .30-30 Winchester rifle or Mossberg pump shotgun. Colt claimed, "If you are a hunter, camper or collector, you'll want an AR-15 Sporter," calling it a "superb hunting partner."[8] In light of this long-standing market presence, AR black rifle images have circulated in many popular press outlets, new stories, and shooting circles since the Kennedy era.

A. DESIGN VARIATIONS

After the Korean War in the mid-1950s, American military planners rethought the nation's infantry weapons types. Virtually all existing rifle designs— developed from the mid-nineteenth to mid-twentieth century—were styled largely by embedded institutional inertia (prior-generation weapons had used large, heavy-barreled pieces with simple steel actions, wooden stocks, open sights, and bayonet mounts, not unlike early muskets), incrementalism (slow changes came mostly due to occasional new bullet types, projectile designs, propellant loadings, action designs, or cartridge capabilities, as well as limited defense budgets), and fixed investment (national armories and gun factories are capital-intensive plants that make objects with considerable endurance that can work well for decades).[9]

Most militaries around the world deployed battle rifles, even during the 1960s, which bear a fair resemblance to seventeenth-century muskets. Long guns still are made to be more than guns in war. Like combat four hundred years ago, when ammunition depletion, action failure, weather conditions, or hand-to-hand tactics required riflemen to remain in battle, soldiers still could fight with nonfunctioning rifles. When equipped with large bayonets, such guns could serve as sword-like, spear-like, or pike-like cutting/stabbing weapons, in

---

[6] C. J. Chivers, *The Gun* (New York: Simon & Schuster, 2010), 267–310.

[7] Department of War effectiveness studies of World War II American infantry units discovered perplexing patterns in their frequency of fire, the typical range of combat engagements, the number of rounds carried by individual soldiers into combat, and the need for high-caliber long-range cartridges on battlefields after 1945. Moreover, the US military during World War II fielded several types of battle rifles using different ammunition, requiring different shooting skills, and having varied battle-field effectiveness, especially in comparison to the weapons used by other Allied and Axis nations. All of these factors spoke to the merits of creating a new single type of battle rifle and ammunition.

[8] See Soldier Systems, "A 1963 Colt AR-15 advertisement," http://soldiersystems.net/2016/06/21/a-1963-colt-ar-15-advertisment/.

[9] Chivers, *The Gun*, 250–255.

addition to remaining lethal club-like blunt instruments for killing men and animals at close quarters with no bullets.

The first AR-15 rifle (AR stands for the Armalite Company, not "Assault Rifle") was designed by Eugene Stoner at the Fairchild Armalite company in competition for bids on a massive contract to sell a new multinational battle rifle in 7.2x51mm (.308) caliber for NATO and US use.[10] This original AR-10 design had promise, but suffered from several flaws due to its innovative use of aluminum, plastic composites, and modular construction when firing such high-powered ammunition. After it failed that competition, Armalite reconfigured it to fire smaller 5.56mm/.223 rounds, leading to greater success. Still, the firm won no American contracts, even though a few AR-10s were sold in Africa to newly independent countries willing to buy them. Armalite then sold the design and manufacturing rights to the Colt Company. Colt, in turn, re-engineered the design again as a selective-fire fully automatic weapon and marketed it to the Department of Defense for military use. The United States Air Force adopted it in 1962, and the other services eventually integrated it into their inventories as the M-16, and later the M-4 assault rifle, to replace their older M-14 7.62x51mm rifles, which basically were a redesigned, rechambered, and reconfigured variant of the successful M-1 Garand .30-06 semi-automatic rifle from World War II.[11]

B. AR-15S ARE NEITHER M-16S NOR THE FIRST ASSAULT RIFLE

The term "assault rifle" is, nonetheless, a complete misnomer for the AR-15 semi-automatic as it is sold on civilian markets in the United States. The AR-15 has been acquired by civilian buyers from its beginning as a "Sporter" or "Modern Sporting Rifle" with only one small-capacity (5-round) magazine. The first true assault rifle came into production during 1943 in Nazi Germany from the arms design bureau of Hugo Schmeisser in an essentially black program to respond to challenges from fighting on the Russian Front.[12] Schmeisser designed the iconic MP40 submachine gun, but its 9mm ammunition and limited range were handicaps in many battle situations.[13] Designated through various model runs as the MP43, MP44, or StG44, his new rifle putatively was named by Adolf Hitler himself as a "Sturmgewehr," or "assault rifle." Chambering a cut-down standard 7.92x57mm cartridge case used in Germany's K98 Mauser bolt action

---

[10] Ibid., 275–268.

[11] Ibid., 272.

[12] Ibid., 164–167.

[13] See Alejandro De Quesada, *MP38 and MP40 Submachine Guns* (Oxford, UK: Osprey Publishing, 2014), 15–33.

rifles, the StG44 could fire its 7.92x33mm rounds in fully automatic or semi-automatic modes. It, however, also usually had a wooden stock and could be fitted with a bayonet. Designed primarily to counter Red Army units equipped with PPS or PPSH-41 submachine guns (like the British STEN or American M-3 submachine guns of World War II), the StG44 gave German soldiers a new type of infantry weapon with high submachine gun rates of fire, but chambering ammunition with a range, bullet mass, and muzzle velocity closer to standard bolt-action infantry battle rifles.[14]

C. THE AK-47 AND THE RISE OF THE ASSAULT RIFLE IMAGINARY

The StG44 and its cartridge became better known around the end of hostilities in Europe to Mikhail Kalashnikov in the USSR, who designed today's most iconic assault rifle, namely, the AK-47. To produce a similar weapon, he endorsed cutting down the standard 7.62x54mm round used in the classic Russian Moisin-Nagant bolt-action rifle to 7.65x39mm.[15] Furthermore, the AK-47's general profile appears to slightly copy the StG44, even though the AK design much improved upon that German weapon as well as the American M-1 Garand and earlier Soviet Simonov SKS-45 fixed–box-magazine semi-automatic rifles.[16]

All of these military assault rifles have specific design characteristics integral to their roles: selective fire (semi-auto and full auto) switches, detachable box magazines with large capacities, an effective range around 350 to 400 yards, muzzle flash suppressors, and bayonet lugs.[17] The AR-15 semi-automatic rifle, on the other hand, was intentionally named a "Modern Sporting Rifle" for civilian sales. Even though it does have a detachable magazine receiver, its non-military variants are sold with only one very low capacity magazine. They also lack selective fire switches for fully automatic fire, bayonet lugs, and military-grade flash suppressors. These weapons can fire many rounds quickly, but they are not weapons of war. Nonetheless, alluring imaginaries of awesome power seeped into popular appraisals of any assault-style rifle. Even though the AR-15 did not fire like an M-16, or have all military features of M-16 weapons, it looked like an M-16 with its detachable magazines, similar shared butt stocks, and identical barrel shields. With these unorthodox looks, not unlike the AK-47, the AR therefore has been labeled inaccurately as "an assault rifle."[18]

[14] Chris McNab, *German Automatic Rifles 1941–45: Gew41, Gew43, FG42, and StG44* (Oxford, UK: Osprey Publishing, 2013), 8–31.

[15] Chivers, *The Gun*, 190–200.

[16] See McNab, *German Automatic Rifles*, 66–74; and De Quesada, *MP38 and MP40*, 31.

[17] McNab, *German Automatic Rifles*, 53–65.

[18] See Gordon L. Mottman, *The M16* (Oxford, UK: Osprey Publishing, 2011).

The condemnation of this particular gun as a weapon of war is perplexing. Most modern civilian rifle models from back into the 1800s came from military designs, or are actually military surplus weapons sold in civilian markets. Beginning with deadly rifled muskets, metal cartridge firing guns, or lever-action rifles from the American Civil War, average Americans could purchase late model firearms that had served as weapons of war. Compared to earlier smooth bore muskets, these guns could be regarded as the assault rifles of their day.[19] Unlike those once modern military rifles of 1860–1870, the AR-15 did not diffuse through civilian markets quickly due to corporate patent considerations, consumer preferences for traditional blue-steel wooden stock guns, and competitively priced .223 chambered conventional rifles.[20]

Many American hunters have taken big game since the 1870s with traditional rifles designed to kill with the maximum lethal efficiency of those earlier periods, but they also used these weapons against Native Americans, criminals, Mexicans, or anyone else who constituted a perceived threat to them. Elsewhere around the world in the nineteenth century, the Mauser bolt-action rifle was not unlike the M-16 or AK-47 of its day. Its bolt-action design was copied globally, including in America's M1903 Springfield rifle, and Mauser's rapidly loaded box magazines were the rapid repeaters deployed by armies in many conflicts.[21] Americans happily have acquired both civilian and military versions of Mauser rifles for decades, and they are found today in many US households despite their origins as weapons of war.

D. THE AMMUNITION OR THE RIFLE

To a large extent, whether to adopt the M-14 versus M-16 was a logistical rather than tactical question. At the point of the spear, as Pentagon briefings say in press briefings today, the purpose of either gun is to shoot heavy volley fire in massed or dispersed deployments of soldiers. Arguably, the rifle volley is the most decisive force materially and symbolically in modern battles. The clouds of bullets needed to fight and win wars in an age of intelligent machines are what make any army's rate, volume, and accuracy of rifle fire important, because these storms of metal must shred the opposing forces before they inflict comparable damage on friendly forces. It is effectiveness in keeping continuously and copiously firing bullets flying at the enemy that gives purpose to infantry weapons and soldiers.

---

[19] Pamela Haag, *The Gunning of America: Business and the Making of American Gun Culture* (New York: Basic Books, 2016), 65–107.

[20] See Chivers, *The Gun*; and Mottman, *The M16*, for more discussion.

[21] Neil Grant, *Mauser Military Rifles* (Oxford, UK: Osprey Publishing, 2015), 4–8, 77–78.

Both M-14s and M-16s are assault rifles, but the M-14 is the more traditional long-range weapon.[22] The M-14 could perform, and still does, this shooting task, but in most battlefield environments, such shooting situations are more extraordinary than normal.[23] Hence, the logistical trip-points of efficiency in military formations point to M-16 equipped forces, since the 5.56mm round, with its more unstable high-velocity bullet, trumps 7.62x51 rounds with much higher muzzle velocities and more stable bullets.[24] The M-16, then, is actually designed not as the deadliest, but rather the materially most efficient infantry weapon of war for military engagements.

Mass Shootings and Assault Rifles

To continue accounting for AR-15s, and situating the subject of assault rifles in contemporary America, one can recall several recent high-profile incidents in which AR platform weapons were used. Even though the vast majority of all gun crime in the United States is committed with pistols, not assault rifles, these shocking crimes serve as rhetorical range-finders in which one can sense why legally sold goods (AR-platform sporting rifles), frequently bought by ordinary consumers at big box outdoor stores, are decried by legislators, reporters, and victims as "weapons of war" let loose on civilians.

The deadliest attack to date in the United States unfolded in the evening of October 1, 2017, when a real estate investor and high-stakes gambler, Stephen Paddock, fired upon crowds at the Route 91 Harvest country music festival on the Las Vegas Strip from a suite on the thirty-second floor of the Mandalay Bay Hotel. During the ten-minute volley, Paddock fired over 1,100 rounds into the crowded concert venue, killing 59, while injuring or wounding another 548 people. Over twenty guns were discovered in his hotel room after Paddock

[22] At nearly 8.5 pounds with its 7.62x51mm cartridges in 20-round magazines, M-14 rifles fired more powerful cartridges through a larger weapon with a traditional wood stock, heavy steel action, and much longer barrel. The weight of the loaded rifle magazines and extra ammunition typically meant soldiers carried only half as many rounds as M-16 equipped troops. Unless well-supplied in fixed positions, like trenches, long-distance rifle volley fire also is much less common. At 6.5 pounds, 5.56mm rounds in 20 or 30 round clips, M-16 shooters could usually carry over twice as much ammunition as M-14 equipped forces. While its maximum effective range was around 430–450 yards, as opposed to 1000 for M-14s, the M-16 in closely ordered units did what it was meant to do, namely, deliver massive volley fire against dispersed enemy formations as opposed to allowing expert marksmen to shoot accurately out past 500 yards at individual opponents. See, for more discussion, Leroy Thompson, *The M14 Battle Rifle* (Oxford, UK: Osprey Publishing, 2014).
[23] Mottman, *The M16*, 4–6, 74–77.
[24] James Edwards Westheder, *The Vietnam War* (Westport, CT: Greenwood Press, 2007), 112.

died of a self-inflicted gun wound, and nearly a dozen of these weapons were different semi-automatic assault-style rifles. Three of them were outfitted with bump stocks to increase their rate of fire. This violent incident eclipsed the previous most-deadly attack a year earlier.[25] On June 12, 2016, Omar Maleen entered The Pulse, a gay nightclub in Orlando, Florida, with a SIG Sauer MCX semi-automatic rifle and a Glock 17 9mm semi-automatic pistol. Maleen fired around 110 rounds, killing forty-nine people, and wounding fifty-three others. US Senator Tammy Baldwin, Wisconsin (a Democrat), decried the massacre as an attack with "a weapon of war" on the LGBT community.[26]

On December 2, 2014, Syed Rizinan Farook and his wife, Tashfen Malik, entered the Inland Regional Center in San Bernardino, California, during a Christmas holiday party and unit training session for the San Bernardino Department of Public Safety. Armed with a Smith & Wesson MP 15 and a DPMS A-15 modern sporting rifle, both of which weapons had been modified by the shooters and other accomplices in violation of California law to accept high capacity magazines and "bullet buttons" to release them rapidly, they fired over 100 rounds, killing fourteen and wounding twenty-four. They then were both shot dead by police after a car chase. From their computer Web browser histories, police inferred that Internet jihadist videos motivated them to become martyrs.[27]

Many noticed an intense level of media coverage for this Islamic terrorist incident that stood in sharp contrast to another horrendous attack more lightly covered less than a week before by an American anti-abortion protestor turned domestic terrorist. On November 27, 2015, Robert Dear entered a Planned Parenthood Clinic in Colorado Springs, with an AK-47 semi-automatic rifle of unknown age, origin, and type, and killed three people (a University of Colorado-Colorado Springs police officer who responded at the scene, and two women at the clinic), and then wounded nine others, including five police officers and four civilians.[28] Dear's mental state was in disarray when apprehended, and his

[25] Rachel Crosby et al., "'It was a Horror Show': Mass Shooting Leaves at Least 59 Dead, 527 Wounded on Las Vegas Strip," *Las Vegas Review-Journal,* October 1, 2017, https://www.reviewjournalcom/local/the-strip/it-was-a-horror-show-mass-shooting-leaves-at-least-59-dead-527-wounded-on-las-vegas-strip/.

[26] Sarah Hauer, "Was Gun Used by Orlando Shooter a 'Weapon of War,'" Politifact, http://www.politifact.com/Wisconsin/statements/2016/jul/01/tammy-baldwin/was-gun-used-orlando-shooter-weapon-war/.

[27] See Byron Tau, "Grim Ritual, Barack Obama Again Calling for Stricter Gun Control after Mass Shooting," *Wall Street Journal,* December 2, 2015, http://blogs.wsj.com/washwire/2015/12/02/in-grim-ritual-barack-obama-again-calls-for-stricter-gun-control-after-mass-shooting/.

[28] See Julie Turkewitz and Jack Healy, "3 Are Dead in Colorado Springs Shootout at Planned Parenthood Center," November 27, 2015, https://www.nytimes.com/2015/11/28/us/colorado-planned-parenthood-shooting.html.

competence to stand trial was in question immediately. Nonetheless, some people's lives ended violently, several were injured, and the bad memories of other right-wing attacks on women's clinics across the United States during the 1990s spiked for a couple of days. The more complex origins of this home-grown event then were lost in the foreign-inspired terrorist gun smoke of the San Bernardino attack.

On December 14, 2012, Adam Lanza, a 20-year-old Connecticut suburban male, entered the Sandy Hook Elementary School in Newton, Connecticut, with a Bushmaster XM11-E2S semi-automatic rifle his mother gave him and a Glock 20SF 10mm semi-automatic pistol. Having fatally shot his sleeping mother in the head at their home, he killed twenty children, six and seven years old, as well as six adults working at the school. Two others were injured. Police arrived four minutes after the attack began; Lanza fatally shot himself in the head with his pistol about a minute later.[29]

President Obama, at an Interfaith Prayer Vigil on December 16, 2012, in Newton, exclaimed, "We can't tolerate this anymore. These tragedies must end. And to end them, we must change."[30]

Within a few weeks of Sandy Hook, New York passed its Secure Ammunition and Firearms Enforcement Act on January 16, 2013, while on April 4, 2016, Connecticut and Maryland also added new comparable restrictive provisions to their existing gun laws. But these varied measures only restricted gun magazine capacities, toughened existing background checks, and limited some ammunition sales. Senator Diane Feinstein, California (a Democrat), introduced the Assault Weapons Ban of 2013. It was styled on the restrictive 1994 ban that held in force for ten years with regard to certain types of weapons and magazines, but her bill did not get out of the Senate.[31]

On December 4, 2015, the *New York Times* published a front page editorial, "End the Gun Epidemic in America," asserting that "it is a moral outrage and national disgrace that civilians can legally purchase weapons designed specifically to kill people with brutal speed and efficiency. These are weapons of war, barely modified and deliberately marketed as tools of macho vigilantism and even

---

[29] See Tau, "Grim Ritual."

[30] See The White House, "Remarks by the President at Sandy Hook Interfaith Prayer Vigil," December 16, 2012, https://obamawhitehouse.archives.gov/the-press-office/2012/12/16/remarks-president-sandy-hook-interfaith-prayer-vigil.

[31] See National Shooting Sports Foundation, "Senator Feinstein Introduces Ban on Modern Sporting Rifles," January 25, 2013, https://www.nssf.org/senator-feinstein-introduces-ban-on-modern-sporting-rifles/; and Adam Gopnik, "One Person, One Gun," *New Yorker*, June 14, 2016.

insurrection."[32] This *New York Times* editorial captures many contradictions in gun control efforts aimed at assault rifle designs.

Acknowledging that "no law can unfailingly forestall a specific criminal," and "many with sincerity" talk "about the constitutional challenges to effective gun control," the *Times* editors opine that other countries at least try to regulate access to weapons, while the United States does not. Claiming, "it is not necessary to debate the peculiar wording of the Second Amendment," the editors then flatly declare, "No right is unlimited and immune from reasonable regulation." Their agenda was quite clear to gun owners: certain guns must be banned, the Constitution would be ignored, and the control of people as well as confiscation of their private property is the higher moral good behind gun control. That is, "certain kinds of weapons," like the slightly modified semi-automatic rifles used in San Bernardino, and "certain kinds of ammunition" must be outlawed for civilian ownership. Moreover, "it is possible to define those guns in a clear and effective way and, yes, it would require Americans who own those kinds of weapons to give them up for the good of their fellow citizens."[33] In his reactions to these incidents, President Obama concluded, "We have a pattern now of mass shootings in this country that has no parallel anywhere in the world."[34] This statement is not entirely true, since other countries have different patterns of mass shootings. Obama's remarks, however, stirred worries for many citizens inasmuch as such "gun control" equals "people control," which the Bill of Rights is meant to prevent.

The Materialities of Gun Culture

With respect to the control of firearms and people, and despite the views of the *New York Times* editors, something else is at play here. A person must be instructed in gun handling. Shooters must learn to take guns in hand, manipulate their actions, work with varied ammunition on the range, and fire both in different conditions. As with any type of autonomous agency, such skills are demanding. To know a gun will fire, remain ready for use, and hit where aimed in shooting is an elaborate set of complex skills that requires practice and focus. Actually, "thinking about manual engagement" with guns, ammunition, shooting, targets, and spent casings "seems to require nothing less than what

---

[32] "End the Gun Epidemic in America," *New York Times*, Editorial, December 4, 2015, https://www.nytimes.com/2015/12/05/opinion/end-the-gun-epidemic-in-america.html?_r=0.

[33] Ibid.

[34] See Tau, "Grim Ritual."

we consider what a human being is."[35] There is much more to guns, however, than just the shooting. The work of gunsmithing, weapon cleaning, ammunition loading, bullet casting, weapon maintenance, target placement, and gun firing are all crafts/skills with their own different demands and complicated challenges. All of these behaviors constitute regimes of discipline that constitute multiple layers of gun control.

The AR platform's modular architecture has triggered a great deal of customization and handicraft manufacture in entire cultures organized around different shooting types, OEM sources, and ammunition loadings. With regard to marketing, Bushmaster baldly asserts its rifles are "Freedom Built, American Made." This slogan says something about various AR-platform gun cultures, but not everything. With its complex readiness for modification, the AR is not like simpler automobiles of old, worked on by "shade tree mechanics." It is an open machine that invites new invention and operation directly by anyone with an interest. With AR platforms, it is possible to mix or match lower and upper receivers, different trigger and bolt assemblies, open fixed or varied optical sights, direct impingement or closed piston gas return systems, fixed or flexible stocks, ventilated or closed front barrel guards, light field-ready or heavy target-suited barrels, as well as many varied magazine types, capacities, and materials for different shooting needs.

This flexibility in the gun as implement makes the AR platform one of the most favored shooting technologies—for the shooters and for craftspeople.[36] Scores of suppliers make many of these parts and pieces, even if they appear first as the roughest of casting or most jumbled of pieces.[37] Nonetheless, there are entire do-it-yourself gun cultures tied to making, maintaining, and minding this machine at home with concentration and care in mental and manual labor. Creating and maintaining such rifles through such craft, the user often is dropped into "diagnosing and fixing things made by others," whether it is rifle bolts, barrel assemblies, or cartridge specifications, leaving one "confronted

[35] Matthew Crawford, *Shop Class as Soul-Craft: An Inquiry into the Value of Work* (New York: Penguin, 2010), 82.

[36] See Steven Gregersen, *The Gun Guide for People Who Know Nothing about Firearms* (Lexington, KY: Amazon POD, 2017); as implements, they call forth multiple subject positions, and anchor power/knowledge dispositions in this "implementality"; also see Timothy W. Luke, "Gunplay and Governmentality," in *Gun Violence and Public Life*, eds. Ben Agger and Timothy W. Luke (Boulder, CO: Paradigm, 2014), 1–24; and Jennifer Carlson, "States, Subjects, and Sovereign Power: Lessons from Global Gun Cultures," *Theoretical Criminology* 18, no. 3 (2013): 335–383.

[37] For example, see David Hänks, *The Workbench AR-15 Project: A Step-by-Step Guide to Building Your Own Legal AR-15 without Paperwork* (Boulder, CO: Paladin Press, 2004); or The Second Amendment, *Ghost Gun Build: 9mm AR-15 Project* (Lexington, KY: Ghost Gun Build.com/Amazon).

with obscurities" and requiring the user to "remain constantly open to the signs by which they reveal themselves."[38]

Speaking in such terms seems odd, but shooting is one of many activities, as Crawford might affirm, "that truly engages us," and "the best way to proceed is by *looking* at it, and taking note of its characteristic activity. That activity represents the 'end' . . . its purpose. In Greek, its *telos*."[39] The purpose of guns is to shoot; and, to perfect that purpose in all respects before, during, and after the shot is "experienced as intrinsically good. They contain their end within themselves: they enact that end, in 'real time,' as we say now."[40]

This mindfulness can serve the good, because such control also rests upon being responsible, acting with virtue, and doing everything right. These individual actions also can be done badly for the wrong reasons. Still, in being done well enough to shape subjects, one can concede shooting, gun handling, or hunting in their full mix of mental and manual labor are a type of soul craft. As with archery, to go far in the armed practice of shooting, and for the skill to become "spiritual," then "a concentration of all physical and psychic forces is needed" and, in fact, "cannot under any circumstances be dispensed with."[41] With good materials and refined skill, the AR platform also enables a remarkable range of workmanship to thrive, including totally de novo fabrication with no preformed components. And, "unless workmanship comes to be understood and appreciated for the art it is, our environment will lose much of the quality it still retains."[42]

Nonetheless, the key symbolic and material construction of most guns in the United States originates with mass commercial marketing by gun manufacturers, which is continuous, elaborate, and sophisticated. It must be this way for the firms to survive. Unlike automobiles, guns are highly durable, and most remain serviceable for decades. Despite popular belief, however, fewer people today are gun enthusiasts. Four decades ago in 1977, gun ownership was common. Over 50% of the population had at least one gun in their home, while less than a third own a gun today. Many of these gun owners have more than one—on average they have eight guns.[43]

Guns can kill, but they have other uses and meanings in gun cultures as well. As Nick Leghorn asks, and then answers, "Why would anyone want to own

---

[38] Crawford, *Shop Class as Soul-Craft*, 82.

[39] Ibid., 192.

[40] Ibid., 193.

[41] Eugen Herrigel, *Zen in the Art of Archery* (New York: Vintage Books, 1989), 41.

[42] David Pye, *The Nature and Art of Workmanship* (New York: Bloomsbury Academic, 2015), 19.

[43] See Evan Osnos, "Making a Killing: The Business and Politics of Selling Guns," *The New Yorker* (June 27, 2016).

a gun?"[44] Posing the question like it is a question about individual consumer choice, he comes up with six reasons, each with a different culture of gunning:

(a) *Recreational Target Shooting*, given how "there's something magical about making a projectile hit a target," and "target shooting is a great way to relax" that can "be very similar to meditation" or a practice "that becomes addicting";

(b) *Competition Target Shooting*, linking back to "ever since that first caveman chucked a stone at a target, some jackass has been there to claim he can do it better";

(c) *Long Range Target Shooting*, which begins at 1,000 yards, or well over half of a mile, where "the appeal is not only bragging rights to the furthest shot but also the job of putting theoretical physics to practical tests";

(d) *Hunting*, which combines "the biggest challenges of competition shooting (specifically accuracy under pressure and firing from a less than ideal shooting positions) with the added challenge of finding your prey," not to mention "wild animals provide an excellent source of protein and are much less expensive than store bought meat, and eating locally grown food reduces pollution and is much greener for the environment";

(e) *Collecting & History*: "There's no denying that firearms have changed the world . . . helped create the United States, and stopped an evil dictator or two during World War II . . . some people find beauty in mechanical ingenuity and want to have functioning versions for their own collection . . . like works of art, to be admired and cherished," and not only delight in the aesthetics of collecting, but "use it as a way to invest their money without playing the stock market or other traditional methods";

(f) *Self-Defense*, "this last reason is the one that is gaining the most popularity" due to slow police response time, fear of invasion, societal collapse, crime, and other disasters, which makes "buying self-defense firearms like buying insurance, except if used properly they keep bad things from getting worse instead of trying to clean up the aftermath."[45]

Cultural distinctions, therefore, vary with different guns and their specific subcultures. Shotgun shooters with their cultures of skeet and trap contests,

---

[44] Nick Leghorn, *Getting Started with Firearms in the United States* (Lexington, KY: Amazon POD, 2017), 11. Shooting, in turn, is not exclusively a male preoccupation. Guns and their holsters are increasingly a female interest as well as manufacturers seek new markets; see Kathy Jackson, *The Cornered Cat: A Woman's Guide to Concealed Carry* (Lexington, KY: White Feather Press/Amazon POD, 2017).

[45] Leghorn, *Getting Started with Firearms*, 11–14.

six-gun shooters in quick draw contests for Wild West re-enactments, Olympic-level competitions in target rifle shooting, and "prepper" survivalist weapon-building circles all attract different people with diverse understandings of guns and themselves. These cultural variations, in turn, will differ regionally, nationally, and internationally. Consequently, caution is warranted before reducing all of these practices to "the gun culture," even in the United States of America with its deep connections to firearms.

The Assault Rifle as a Subject and Symbol

Beyond these object-oriented ontographies of assault rifles as things, how can subject-shifting biographies of assault rifles as actors be written? Can one detect how, why, and in what manner the weapon is, or can become, a subject? For the sake of argument, why not say "yes." The shooter and the gun are perhaps symbionts. Gun and gunner are co-constituting subjectivities, once readied, prepared, and joined by ownership, instruction, and use. Neither can really come to be fully without the other. As some suggest, weapons define subjects. So human subjects armed with different weapon objects gain varied capacities, powers, and identities, as well as diverse allies, deterrents, and targets by becoming spearmen, swordsmen, axemen, clubmen, bowmen, or gunmen. And, these valences also can reverse, once these weaponized subjects interact collectively with others humans as stabbers, cutters, choppers, bashers, archers, or shooters—both symbolically and concretely.[46] Becoming adept with one weapon is a craft, and it demands discipline and training to truly become expert enough to master each weapon's capabilities and vulnerabilities.

There are several roads into armed subjectivity for the more philosophically inclined to fully grasp the material and symbolic significance of "becoming armed and dangerous." One need not surrender to the allure of vitalism, whereby one simply strides into the rush of events, or life force, to announce with Whitehead, Bergson, or Lucretius, knowing alternative realities are always around remaking "us." One simply can assume that matter is not dead, things are never inert, and objects are essentially fictive. Such ontological premises, in turn, allow agency and subjectivity to things, including firearms.[47] Real things

---

[46] Evan Selinger, "The Philosophy of the Technology of the Gun," *Atlantic*, July 23, 2012, https://www.theatlantic.com/technology/archive/2012/07/the-philosophy-of-the-technology-of-the-gun/260220/.

[47] Ray Brassier, *Nihil Unbound: Enlightenment and Extinction* (London: Palgrave, 2007); and Graham Harman, *Towards Speculative Realism: Essays and Lectures* (New Airesford: Zero Books/John Hunt Publishing, 2010).

caught up in the machinic meshes of modernity with human beings gain agency in polymorphous actor networks. Gun objects thereby can be recognized as discharging plenipotentiary powers for companies, designers, marksmen, peoples, and states that must channel delegated choices, designated capacities, or deliverable constructs of action through such objects. In firing and not firing, action still unfolds, since almost any stuff can be treated as brimming with layers of symbiotic processes, conjoining living and nonliving things in zones of "vibrant matter."[48]

These premodern, amodern, postmodern, or ultramodern ontographies are nothing new. They simply have been suppressed in Enlightenment-era codes that normatively conjoin *Thoughts* narrowly to only very constrained sets of *Beings*. This twist ignores the multiplicity of epistemic possibilities to correlate thinking with only a routine existence exclusively rooted in always already accessible a priori actions.[49] Rejecting Kantian principles of rigid correlationism between Thing and Being in which nothing beyond these rigidly fixed correlates is knowable, one can follow Quentin Meillassoux to repudiate the exclusive/exhaustive links of sufficient reason. There can be, and undoubtedly is, much beyond such conventional normative ontographies. Things may very well be organized otherwise, far beyond the daily correlates of Thought and Being conventionally believed to be knowable. Hence, the structure of reality can be, and always is, otherwise in different facticities. The same cause can create many different outcomes that strict correlationism obscures, neglects, or ignores.[50]

Things can be actors symbolically and materially, but too few human beings think otherwise, mostly due to an unwillingness to concede anything outside of the naively self-evident relations between Thought and Being, Subject and Object, Cause and Effect relations. To forget naive self-evidence, ignore the brittle principles of correlation, and admit that complex causality can cascade out in hundreds of directions—rather than the few serialized routines recounted in time or repeatedly observed in constant conjunction—changes the grounds of subjectivity. These conceptual releases loosen what is reified in the usual principles of causality. Beyond these epistemic doubts, of course, guns can easily be regarded as subjects, actors, or agents. And, many already freely accept their active agency and subjectivity.[51]

[48] Jane Bennett, *Vibrant Matter: A Political Ecology of Things* (Durham, NC: Duke University Press, 2010).

[49] Quentin Meillassoux, *After Finitude: An Essay on the Necessity of Contingency* (London: Continuum, 2008).

[50] Levi Bryant, *Onto-Cartography: An Ontology of Machines and Media* (Edinburgh: Edinburgh University Press, 2014).

[51] Steve Shaviro, *Without Criteria: Kant, Whitehead, Deleuze, and Aesthetics* (Cambridge: Massachusetts Institute of Technology Press).

While many hear only a metaphor, it is perfectly plausible to say this or that "Gun won the West." To win is to triumph, and more than one gun model won the West for the United States with the deadly force that massive numbers delivered. As an article in *True West* magazine asserts:

> Was the so-called West-winning gun given this coveted title because of the great numbers in which it was produced, or for the work it accomplished? Or was it simply because of who used it during those tumultuous times known as the Wild West? Although some firearms manufacturers advertise their lead-dispensing products as having rightfully earned that distinguished title, such a claim is not to be taken as gospel. While some folks feel that a single model firearm was most responsible for taming our raw frontier in the late 19th century—such as the 1873 Winchester repeater, 1874 Sharps buffalo rifle, double-barreled shotgun, or perhaps The Peacemaker, the legendary 1873 Colt Single Action Army revolver—most serious students of the American West agree that it was not a single model gun or type of firearm that "won the West." Rather, they believe it was an assortment of rifles, shotguns and handguns, in the hands of a diverse and colorful crowd of men and women, which brought both violence and law and order to our Western territories.[52]

To unpack this historical account, invading crowds of settler men and women with a rich assortment of guns ruthlessly shot down indigenous bands of other men and women who had far fewer guns. As a result, these crowds of gun-firing settlers "made a peace," standing over the bodies of their dead native opponents with an array of Colt, Remington, Sharps, or Winchester firearms still smoking with victory in their triumphant hands.

The Old West, however, might not be enough evidence. One can look to the US armed forces for how they accept guns as actors. No less than the United States Marine Corps maintains that guns are subjects, as the rifle is the closest companion to each and every human Marine. The Corps has a credo that acknowledges this special subjectivity: "The Rifleman's Creed" from 1941:

THE RIFLEMAN'S CREED
This is my rifle. There are many like it, but this one is mine.
My rifle is my best friend. It is my life. I must master it as I must master my life.

---

[52] See Phil Spangenberger, "22 Guns That Won the West," *True West*, October 27, 2015, http://www.truewestmagazine.com/22-guns-that-won-the-west/.

Without me, my rifle is useless. Without my rifle, I am useless. I must fire my rifle
    true. I must shoot straighter than my enemy who is trying to kill me. I must
    shoot him before he shoots me. I will . . .
My rifle and I have love knowing that what counts in war is not the rounds we
    fire, the noise of our burst, nor the smoke we make. We know that it is the
    hits that count. We will hit... My rifle is human, even as I, because it is my life.
    Thus, I will learn it as a brother. I will learn its weaknesses, its strength, its
    parts, its accessories, its sights and its barrel.
I will keep my rifle clean and ready, even as I am clean and ready. We will become
    part of each other. We will . . .
Before God, I swear this creed. My rifle and myself are the defenders of my
    country. We are the masters of our enemy. We are the saviors of my life.
So be it, until there is no enemy, but peace. Amen.[53]

Upon receiving his or her new life in military service, then, every Marine must
pledge full recognition of this Other as a subject. It is regarded as part of his or her
human being, continuing life, and national service. Each human soldier takes the
rifle into possession, and the weapon then possesses the Marine with its symbolic
power, material capability, and active authority. The rifle becomes the Marine's
life, and a life master for their national service. The rifle gives genuine use to the
riflemen, and the Marine truly uses the rifle in a mutually constituted hybrid existence. To fire true as defenders of country, masters of any enemy, survivors of
life, makers of peace, shooters that hit, parts of each other, the Leatherneck and
rifle must become these oath takers before other Marines, God, and Country.
    All Marines declare, "my rifle is human," like he or she, and it is what gives
him or her, as humans, their lives. The gun is forever a brother with weaknesses
and strengths. All of its parts and accessories are parts and accessories of each
Marine, who guards his or her weapon as the weapon safeguards each of them.
By staying clean and ready as a firearm, brother and sister Marine become, by
this creed, ready to serve as compatriot subjects in battle as armed war machines
until victory is created by vanquishing all enemies, and thus creating peace.
    Some see these declarations as metaphorical or symbolic, but belief in these
symbols clearly creates new subjects with unique purpose, resolve, and utility.
With the Marine and the rifle hybrids, the Corps fields its gunners and shooters,
riflemen and riflewomen, who would not be what they are individually without
becoming what they are together through well-disciplined conduct. Collectively,
with other brother and sister Marines at arms, their shooting creates the capacity
to attain a shared mastery of enemies and defenders of country.

---

[53] See also United States Marine Corps, Camp Lejeune, http://www.lejeune.marines.mil.

Despite this vision of subjectivity for Marines and their rifles, the popularity of AR rifles as actors developed slowly over the years. The repeating rifles available to civilians after the Civil War also did not sell quickly in the United States as objects. Gun culture then was utilitarian, since firearms were regarded as basic ordinary tools to be bought like farm equipment. Americans often chose "less expensive, more durable muskets over new weapons that could fire multiple shots" from the late 1860s to 1880.[54] Colt, Remington, Smith & Wesson, and Winchester had to export newer modern products overseas to keep their factories open, but those sales sagged along with domestic markets as frontiers closed, cities grew, and other commodities attracted buyers.

Like other Gilded Age industrialists, gun executives had to evolve into "captains of consciousness,"[55] creating needs that often did not exist, or fanning their intensity when they did, by making guns into actors through massive publicity campaigns. Casting Winchester rifles as luxury goods, like diamonds or golf clubs, tying them to "the vigorous life" of outdoors culture celebrated by Theodore Roosevelt, and evangelizing at Wild West shows to attract women, children, and urbanites to shooting sports proved to be effective marketing techniques. That is, "gun marketing had moved from describing how guns work to describing how guns make their owners feel."[56] The selling of shooting to women in the Victorian era, and then to boys as a component of every "boy's life" is part and parcel of bureaucratically planned consumption in American society.

In the 1960s and 1970s, AR-platform weapons also were not popular. Many shooters openly regarded them as ugly, junky, and/or flimsy. They were not inexpensive, and they consumed costly ammunition quickly. Many veterans of the wars in Indochina kept alive the AR's bad reputation for jamming and fouling when returning home from Vietnam. Only after a few years, and some better product placement for these weapons in the movies and on TV, did the AR-15 design gain a fresher image of power, manageability, or flexibility.

This flexibility helped make the AR platform the most enduring firearm in the US military's history, exceeding the fifty-two years of service the .30-06 Springfield rifle gave as a bolt-action battle rifle. This enduring materiality also has made it a global star. To be fair and fully assay its importance as an actor, one can survey the placements of the AR-15 and M-16 in popular culture. It is hard to forget Al Pacino's introduction of his live-in companion as Tony Montana in *Scarface* (1983), to attackers from competing drug gangs assailing his mansion,

[54] Paula Haag, "The Commercial Origins of Our Love for Guns," *Wall Street Journal*, April 23–24, 2016, C3.

[55] See Stuart Ewen, *Captains of Consciousness* (New York: McGraw Hill, 1976); and, Haag, *Gunning of America*, 225–266.

[56] Haag, "The Commercial Origins," C3.

as he comes out firing an M-16 A with an M-203 40mm grenade launcher, and announces, "Say hello to my little friend."[57] Film moments like that have helped sell a lot of modern sporting rifles for over a generation.

Thanks to this marketing, AR-15 variants now typically account for "up to 1 in 4 of all new rifles sold in the U.S.A., the AR family is truly America's rifle, at home and abroad. This popularity is reflected on screen, as the gun's futuristic looks and real-world ubiquity guarantee a starring role in television and movies."[58] AR weapons in their M-16 configurations, as a result, have appeared prominently in Hollywood for over fifty years. Their acting career begins in the *Seven Days in May* (1964), as well as *Ice Station Zebra* (1968), but they circulate as menacing figures of crime, espionage, policing, warring stories, as well as in tales about alien invasion, dinosaur resurrection, mercenary work, and shape shifter attack from *Shaft's Big Secret* (1972), *Octopussy* (1983), *The Enforcer* (1976), *Operation Thunderbolt* (1977) to *Predator* (1987), *Jurassic Park* (1993), *The Expendables 2* (2012), and *Wolfen* (1981). Perhaps more importantly, M-16s also are cast as starring actors in many single person shooter computer games, like the "Matrix" (2003), "Grand Theft Auto: Vice City" (2006), and "Call of Duty: Black Ops" (2010). In all of these roles, AR variants are implements of endangerment and empowerment, but they also feature central casting co-stars, lending their lethal power to shooters for good, bad, and indifferent ends.[59]

To conclude, it makes sense to suggest "guns and ammo" are actors, both materially and symbolically. Materiality matters, especially when dealing with American gun cultures with their different firearms and many diverse uses. One can only begin to judge guns by looking down their sights, knowing they are locked and loaded, and recalling rapidly a montage of such mass mediated moments. Then and there, any gun credibly becomes a material force, symbolic power, and great actor. Plainly, the AR-15 is a major player in these terms, and it is no surprise that owners of this weapon will cling to them even unto the death, as pledged to the NRA by Charlton Heston years ago. And, its presence as a powerful subject and sophisticated object has circulated as another high-tech sign for the United States of America since the 1960s. If and when AR rifles are discharged in blockbuster movies, weekend hunting trips, police raids, mass shootings, terrorist attacks, military landings, or ordinary crimes, their shooters all are firing for this effect.

[57] See Peter Barrett, "The Black Rifle: The Film Career of the AR-15," Get Zone (originally published July 2015 in *GunUp*), http://getzone.com/the-black-rifle-the-film-career-of-the-ar-15/.

[58] See "M-16 Rifle Series," Internet Movie Firearms Database, http://www.imfdb.org/wiki/M16_rifle_series#Film.

[59] Ibid.

Part II

THE SOCIAL LIFE OF GUNS

4

The Thriving Life
of Racialized Weaponry

Violence and Sonic Capacities from the Drone to the Gun

HEATHER ASHLEY HAYES

In the 1993 jam "The Sound of da Police," rapper and Bronx native KRS-One belts out a thick hook describing the materiality of living in a Black community in the United States:

> After 400 years, I've got no choices
> The police them have a little gun
> So when I'm on the streets, I walk around with a bigger one
> (Woop-woop!) I hear it all day
> Just so they can run the light and be upon their way
>
> Woop-woop! That's the sound of da police
> Woop-woop! That's the sound of da beast
> Woop-woop! That's the sound of da police
> Woop-woop! That's the sound of da beast[1]

Reading the words on a page doesn't mimic the experience of listening to the track; KRS-One configures all the "woop-woops," which are laced throughout the beat's verses and created entirely with his voice, to sound almost exactly like police sirens. The lyrics describe the impact of living in communities where hearing sirens triggers an awareness of nearing police, with guns; as much a threat to any black man today as was the overseer of the plantation during slavery, according to "The Sound of da Police."

---

[1] Lawrence "Kris" Parker (aka KRS-One), "The Sound of da Police," *Return of the Boom Bap*, Jive Records, 1993, CD.

Hip hop is rife with these kinds of sonic references to an awareness of being policed. N.W.A (aka Niggaz Wit Attitudes) opens their 1999 hit "Gangsta Gangsta" with police sirens coupled with screeching tires and the jarring sound of gunshots before the first verse of the song begins. In fact, you can find gunshots or police sirens in Nas's "Ether" and "One Mic," 50 Cent's "Many Men," Nick Cannon's "Pray 4 My City," Bone Thugs N Harmony's "Ghetto Cowboy," Tech N9ine's "Melancholy Maze," and The Notorious B.I.G.'s "Gimme the Loot," to name a few. You can, not surprisingly, find a highly stylized version of gunfire on Nicki Minaj's "Gunshots." The list goes on and it is extensive. This attention in hip hop culture to the sounds emanating from policing Black communities isn't a coincidence. Considered the first real hip hop track to go down on vinyl, Grandmaster Flash and the Furious Five's 1982 song "The Message" ends with all the characters in the song sitting on street corner planning their evening before hearing screeching tires and police sirens. All the characters are then arrested and carried off by police in the song's final twenty seconds.

Fast forward to late 2016, when news of the shooting of eleven police officers in Dallas, Texas—just 90 miles from where I was born and raised—dominated the national public sphere. As part of this tragic event, early reports described a new tactic used by the Dallas Police Department against one of the suspects that didn't require a gun or a siren: "the bomb robot." On the Friday following the shootings, Dallas Police Chief David Brown described the unquestionable logic to use the robot: "We saw no other option but to use our bomb robot and place a device on its extension for it to detonate where the suspect was. Other options would have exposed our officers to grave danger . . . The suspect is deceased as a result of the detonating of the bomb."[2] In an interview with the *Dallas Morning News*, Professor of Criminology Alex del Carmen noted a frightening truth: "This marked a historical moment in the new methods that are used by law enforcement agencies."[3] In the interview, del Carmen's comments went on to state what appeared, in his remarks, to be obvious: "What's used in the field overseas becomes a tool for domestic law enforcement."[4] The sounds of the police reverberate across screeching tires and wailing sirens to the popping sound of gunshots . . . and now, to the exploding sound of the bomb robot when it kills a suspect (who happened, at least in the Dallas case, to never have been found guilty of a crime via the US criminal justice system).

[2] David Brown quoted in Jeffrey Weiss, "Dallas Police May Be First U.S. Law Enforcement Agency to Use a Robot to Kill a Bomb Suspect," *Dallas Morning News*, July 8, 2016, para. 4.

[3] Alex del Carmen, quoted in Jeffrey Weiss, "Dallas Police May Be First," para. 2.

[4] Ibid., para. 6.

This introduces a potentially new set of troubling connections between the ten-year escalation of armed drone use by the United States as part of the terror wars against brown bodies abroad and the amplification of weapons used in domestic policing against black bodies. Not only do the sets of connections around this technological parallel lead to deadly logic deployed against Arabs and/or Muslims around the world via the terror wars, now there's the possibility that personless weapons logic used in supposed war zones will move "home," facilitating new iterations of violence against black and brown bodies in domestic policing. The nonhuman logic used in drone attacks (and the deployment of bomb robots) becomes self-fulfilling, and, as a result of the captivating lure of a personless weapon that can absolve an officer or soldier of agency, that logic crosses into our social understanding of guns.

Perhaps most revealing of this point is the low yield of any significant public deliberation in the aftermath of the Dallas shootings about the use of the "bomb robot" by the Dallas police. Despite facing what would seem a complicated, ethical conundrum around our social understandings of weaponry used against black bodies, the event almost wholly evaporated from the news cycle within seven days. It seems personless weapons being authorized to kill black and brown bodies, at home and abroad, is the new and unquestioned norm. And as Judith Butler again reminds us, "It is to the stranger that we are bound, the one, or the ones, we never knew and never chose. To kill the other is to deny my life, not just mine alone, but that sense of my life which is, from the start, and invariably, social life."[5]

Since 2010, what the world has come to know as the US-led terror wars have been dominated by new developments in weaponry. War fighting's history is rife with changes to help distance a weapon from the "authorized" user of that weapon, from bayonets to tanks to piloted aerial assault capabilities. Yet the arrival of personless aerial vehicles in the form of armed Predator and Reaper drones embarking on targeted killing missions throughout the majority Muslim world amplifies this effort to new levels. The deployment of a weapon with terminal consequences alongside its ability to surveil, track, and ultimately, target human beings outside of declared war zones without the immediate presence of a human operator poses a number of questions. Much of the focus on armed drone use, however, has come in the form of assessments about efficacy of the weapon, accuracy of its targeting mechanisms, or the legality of its very use. Despite prolific use of the technology throughout the Middle East and North Africa beginning in 2008, the Obama administration's

---

[5] Judith Butler, *Frames of War: When Is Life Grievable?* (London: Verso Books, 2009), xxvi.

near complete silence on the armed drone program was not broken until July of 2016 when death tolls from the weapon's use by the United States in non-declared war zones were finally released alongside an executive order attempting to curb civilian deaths brought about by the weapon's use. However, little scholarship has explored the life of the drone itself, the way the weapon, as an actor, functions. In addition, few connections have been made to the way the life of the drone may inform, guide, and expand the life of guns. This chapter will confront some of these questions, examining the personless weapons known as armed drones, used by the United States against almost entirely Arab and/or Muslim populations as part of their efforts in the terror wars. This work also prompts us to think about the drone's ontology as it relates to the way that guns are deployed, used, and come to have a life of their own—often in Black communities.

Specifically, I analyze one component of armed drones currently used as part of the US terror wars that is shared with guns: sonic capacity (that buzzing sound), alongside their capacity to generate fear in their targets. The drone itself, like the gun of KRS-One's music, is a living being in this sense, with the ability to speak and the ability to act, often with terminal consequences for those whom it acts upon (and sometimes those who may or may not direct it to act). Understanding the drone as having its own self-fulfilling logic, with the ability to speak via its generation of sound, will allow us access to think about the expansion of personless weapons programs within both war-fighting projects and domestic policing spheres. This understanding gives us unique insight into gun proliferation and the trajectory of gun use and exchange; we can reconsider the social life of the gun and the ability it has to speak (through its piercing aural punctuations when in use). The rush with which both the US military and domestic police forces are developing these technologies exhibits ways that all weapons systems threaten to take on lives of their own.

With the Dallas "bomb robot" case as but one example of a seamless stitch made to join distinct and different deadly governing technologies interacting upon black and brown bodies, the imperative to understand this trajectory is more pressing than ever. In short: what is the body of the drone able to do, seemingly absent human logic, and how does it access its power? How do its capacities to impact the sonic landscape facilitate its proliferation and power as a preferred technology of policing and war? How does this personless weapon's arc of circulation inform our understandings about the social life of guns? And ultimately, how does this exploration point us toward what discourses have been shielded from debate as a result of any weapon gaining self-fulfilling logic in our social life as an efficient way to police and govern populations?

The Dawn of the Drone and the Circulation of Gun/Drone Violence: A Racialized History

In many ways, the term "drone" has lost its referent. A quick search of the term "drone" via Google in mid-2017 reveals that drone rhetoric exists in a multitude of references: small quadcopters with high-resolution cameras clearly designed for personal use, personless logistics systems designed for city planning and large-scale industry use, films like the 2017 thriller (aptly titled "Drone") whose content deals with questions around military weapons use, personless armed aerial vehicles that resemble airplanes and are used in military operations; the list goes on. In the same way that Herbert Hoover promised a chicken in every pot and a car in every garage during the presidential campaign of 1928, today's mantra might be, "A drone in every backyard."

Consider the discourse of Matternet, a Silicon Valley drone startup company whose CEO Andreas Raptopoulos delivered a stirring TED Talk in June of 2013 titled, "No Roads? There's a Drone for That." The talk has received almost 1 million views. In Matternet's language, when asked "why we're here," the company responds:

> Our mission is to make access to goods as frictionless and universal as access to information. Our products will enable people, companies and organizations around the world to build and operate drone logistics networks for transporting goods on demand, through the air, at a fraction of the time, cost and energy of any other transportation method used today.[6]

Thus, the drone is ubiquitous, a technology ready to be adopted at a massive scale to serve everyone on the planet. Drones may take photographs, they may help make your car driverless, they may deliver vaccines to a rural village in Africa, they may deliver your Amazon book order, they may map watering patterns in agricultural areas of the Midwestern United States. They are everywhere and they can do everything.

In its proliferation, the term itself has lost its ability to refer to a stable sign. This understanding functions to occlude the geopolitical networks of death and trauma stemming from the (largely US) military use of the armed, unmanned aerial vehicles (UAVs, in most intelligence and military speak),[7] which in fact

---

[6] "Our Mission," Matternet, http://www.mttr.net/company.html.

[7] "Unmanned" is the most commonly used term by US military and intelligence communities when discussing armed drones. Specifically, they often use the term "unmanned aerial vehicle" or the

have a very specific and well-defined history and definition. Contrary to most understandings of the unmanned aerial vehicle as a "new" phenomenon in military technology, Medea Benjamin (2012) and Nick Turse (2012) trace the technology for flying remotely to the United States' military arsenal as early as World War I. Drawing from these historical accounts, I have noted:

> By the time the conflicts in World War II and Korea escalated, unmanned aerial crafts were being used as guided missiles, including the most infamous case largely forgotten by history: a deadly World War II experimental mission in which President Kennedy's older brother Joe was killed at age 29 in a secret operation over Germany. Termed Operation Aphrodite, Kennedy was a test pilot in the program where explosive laden B-17 Flying Fortress bombers attempted to deliberately crash into German targets by remote control. However, since the planes were not equipped to take off remotely, a pilot would fly the plane above 2000 feet, aim missiles toward the specified target, then parachute to safety from the aircraft before it catapulted into its target below. The operation was a massive failure, killing over 70% of the pilots who undertook Aphrodite missions, and was halted by the U.S. Air Force in early 1945.

> It was Abraham Karem, chief designer for the Israeli Air Force in the 1970s, who made, and continues to make, the most significant strides in drone technology. The Economist's Technological Quarterly of December 2012, profiling Karem as the "dronefather," noted that his aerial unmanned planes "transformed the way modern warfare is waged—and continue to pioneer other airborne innovations."[8] After almost ten years building technologies for the Israeli Air Force, Karem moved to the United States, taking his technology to the free market. Aided by sizeable grants from the United States Military's Defense Advanced Research Projects Agency and the Central Intelligence Agency, Karem unveiled a powerful new flight-controlled computer called the Gnat 750 in his Southern California garage. Disappointed with the early financial gains from his labor, Karem sold his company, along with the Gnat 750 technology, to Hughes Aircraft and then in turn to General Atomics, a private nuclear physics and defense contractor. As far as we know, they

shortened acronym "UAV." Here, I want to note the gendered language of this iteration of the term, which I do not endorse and which opens space for future critical gender work on this technology and its accompanying discourse.

[8] "The Dronefather," Economist: Technology Quarterly, December 1, 2012, https://www.economist.com/taxonomy/term/90/0?page=52.

currently retain Karem, and a number of Israeli engineers who worked on Karem's original technology, as consultants.[9]

The hundreds of billions of dollars authorized for terror wars against Afghanistan, Iraq, and an amorphous al-Qaeda force in early 2002 commenced a massive expansion of armed drone production in the United States. New armed personless aircraft were commissioned including the powerful 40-foot long Reaper model. Production schedules were escalated for the two existing models deployed throughout the 2000s, the 38-inch long Raven and the 27-foot long Predator with Hellfire missile capacity. Former Chair of the Joint Chiefs Mike Mullen and, supposedly, even Secretary of Defense Robert Gates proclaimed that the newest generation of fighter jet, the F-35, would be the Pentagon's last manned fighter aircraft.[10] Even with this increased development, the prolific armed drone program of the Obama administration would not come to fruition until the 2008 election. Richard Clarke, White House counterterrorism adviser to three presidents, described the resistance met upon suggesting expansion of armed drone use for targeted killings in the early 2000s:

> We found bin Laden in October 2000 . . . There was, however, no such thing then as an armed Predator, so we saw him but could not kill him. . . . After that experience, orders were given to create an armed drone, quickly. When President George W. Bush came into office, the CIA and DOD refused to fly the armed Predator, including balking at a cabinet level meeting on Sept. 4, 2001. . . . Once in office, Obama had no such hesitation.[11]

Since 2008, the United States' use of drone operations has increased forty-fold, primarily targeting Pakistan, Yemen, and northern Afghanistan. In Pakistan alone, nearly 426 strikes have killed between 2,508 and 4,014 people in the region, an estimated 424 to 969 of which were civilians, 172 to 207 of which were children. The Bureau of Investigative Journalism maintains as extensive catalogue of US drone operations since 2004 and cites at least 6,377 people killed in US drone strikes across Pakistan, Afghanistan, Somalia, and Yemen. It should be noted this number is updated weekly and it is their *lowest* casualty estimate.[12] Since the inauguration of President Donald Trump, at the time of this

---

[9] Heather Ashley Hayes, *Violent Subjects and Rhetorical Cartography in the Age of the Terror Wars* (London: Palgrave MacMillan, 2016), 80–81.

[10] "The Last Manned Fighter," *Economist*, Business section, July 14, 2011, http://www.economist.com/node/18958487.

[11] Richard Clarke, "Give Drones a Medal," *New York Daily News*, December 2, 2012.

[12] Bureau of Investigative Journalism, "Drone Warfare," http://www.thebureauinvestigates.com/projects/drone-war.

work's publication, armed drone attacks have increased 432%. President Obama approved about 542 strikes in 2,920 days in office, about one every 5.4 days. Trump approved 36 strikes in his first 45 days in office, one every 1.25 days.[13] If the rate Trump is authorizing new strikes continues, in Yemen alone, 2017 will be almost five times deadlier than the deadliest drone strike year on record (2012) in that country. Armed drone strikes aimed at the Arab and/or Muslim world by US military and intelligence communities are not ceasing, or even waning, anytime soon.

The Israeli link to the origin of drone warfare is a significant piece of the weapon's circulation that reflects the history of targeting Arab and/or Muslim populations even before the weapon became a central piece of United States counterterrorism strategy in 2008. Some drone researchers have gone so far as to say, "if you scratch any drone you will likely find Israeli technology underneath."[14] Israeli drone use dates back to the 1970s, before their engineers (like Karem) brought the technology to countries like the United States. As one Israeli Defense Ministry official noted, the Israeli army was able to capitalize on, and expand, armed drone technology most effectively "since we're always in a conflict [with Palestinians] which allows us to perfect our systems."[15] The Israeli model is worth noting here because its intense secrecy has been deemed a barrier to public deliberation around the program. As the head of a United Nations investigation into the use of armed drones notes, "This technology is being used by three democracies and there needs to be a public debate. It would be extremely helpful if Israel cooperated and it would be remiss of me to ignore Israel in an investigation of technology used by three states, one of which is Israel."[16] One other of the three states using the technology in addition to Israel is obviously the United States, where administration officials across both the Obama and Trump administrations have maintained a comparably high level of secrecy around the program.

Just like the US use of armed drones in the wake of the terror wars, Israeli armed drones have one target: Muslims, or in this case, most often Palestinians.[17]

[13] Micah Zenko, "The (Not-So) Peaceful Transition of Power: Trump's Drone Strikes Outpace Obama," *Council on Foreign Relations*, March 2, 2017, https://www.cfr.org/blog-post/not-so-peaceful-transition-power-trumps-drone-strikes-outpace-obama.

[14] Mary Dobbing and Chris Cole, "Israel and the Drone Wars: Examining Israel's Production, Use, and Proliferation of UAVs," *Drone Wars UK* (January 2014), 2.

[15] Yaakov Katz, quoted in Dobbing and Cole, "Israel and the Drone Wars," 4.

[16] Ben Emmerson, quoted in Anshel Pfeffer, "UNHCR Drone-Strike Investigator: Israel Would be Wise to Cooperate," *Haaretz*, February 21, 2013.

[17] I should note here that some Palestinians who have been affected by Israeli drone use, in Gaza and other territories, may have been members of other religions including Palestinian Christian (or even some, Palestinian Jews). The death tolls of fighting between Palestinians and Israelis rarely catalogue diversity of religious practice among dead Palestinians. These death tolls are most often

In one independent investigation, Israeli drones are reported to have killed around one thousand Palestinians in Gaza alone in the time frame between the 2012 mass assault and the end of the detention of Israeli soldier Gilad Shalit in 2011.[18] Those numbers don't take into account additional Israeli use of drones in other Palestinian territories within the Israeli Defense Force's control since the dawn of the technology in the 1970s. In short, the history of the weapon known as an armed drone, the weapon used by the United States against Arab and/ or Muslim populations as part of its war on terror, originated as a tool against, and continues to be deployed against, Palestinian populations by Israeli Defense Forces. This link is critical in thinking about the racialized and colonizing implications of the armed drone as an actor, especially the body of the drone alongside the body of the gun in the United States. In all legible military, policing, and intelligence schemas, black and brown (most often Muslim) bodies exist almost solely as these weapons' targets.

According to the Centers for Disease Control, between the years of 2010 and 2015, homicide was the leading cause of death among black people ages 15–34. Firearms caused 90% of those homicides. By contrast, between the years of 2010 and 2015, homicide was the fifth leading cause of death for white individuals aged 15–34, behind unintentional injury, suicide, malignant neoplasms, and heart disease.[19] According to the Brookings Institute, drawing from CDC statistics, "The firearm homicide rate among black men aged 20–29 is about 89 per 100,000. To put that fact in some international perspective, in Honduras—the country with the highest recorded homicide rate [in the world]—there were 90.4 intentional murders per 100,000 people in 2012. That includes all means, not just firearm homicides."[20] The same Brookings Institute study found that among white Americans, 77% of gun deaths are suicides. Among black Americans, 82% of gun deaths are homicides. Black death at the barrel of a gun is almost always inflicted against a victim by a perpetrator, not by the victim against themselves. White death at the end of that same gun barrel is most often going to be self-inflicted. In fact, as Alice Goffman notes, "the sheer scope of policing and imprisonment in poor Black neighborhoods is transforming community life in ways that are deep

---

maintained by the Israeli government in their State Archives in Jerusalem, which I visited in June of 2016 with no success in getting complete data. However, I maintain that the Israeli use I refer to in this chapter is important insofar as it demonstrates that targets of armed drones have been, since the armed drone's invention, almost entirely a configuration of Arab/Palestinian/Muslim populations, and people of color, in almost all cases where the technology is deployed.

[18] Dobbing and Cole, "Israel and the Drone Wars," 14, 16.

[19] Centers for Disease Control, "Injury Prevention and Control," https://www.cdc.gov/injury/.

[20] Richard V. Reeves and Sarah Holmes. "Guns and Race: The Different Worlds of Black and White Americans," Brookings Institute, December 15, 2015, para. 6.

and enduring, not only for young men who are their targets but for their family members, partners, and neighbors."[21] The fact that US armed drone actions have affected next to no white, Western victims, when considered alongside the significant impact the program has had on everyday life in regions throughout the predominantly black and brown Muslim Middle East, demonstrates the relationship armed drone actions have to a transformation of Black life in the United States, as a result of increased proliferation of guns and militarization of police. The material reality of living under the armed drone, or under the gun, involves daily assault on bodies of color and the spaces in which they live.

Sonic Capacities: Reading the Social Life of Weapons through Sound

The armed drone functions around three prominent bodily zones: the aural (ears), the scopic (eyes), and the decision-making power for killing (for lack of another analogy, the brain). These characteristics reveal the armed drone as a body in and of itself. The Dallas bomb robot case—the use of a self-acting police weapon to kill a black suspect with officers safely removed from the deployment of that weapon—points to the molding of domestic policing weapons in the image of drones, facilitating an autonomous weapon circulation that points to weapons as actors in and of themselves, moving farther and farther away from any need for human interaction with the weapon. The weapon can stand and act on its own. This transformation shifts the ground for understanding the ontology of the gun and the drone as weapons. Guns operate on similar bodily zones: aurally (via their sound when they are fired), scopically (via the image of fear they induce when pointed at a potential target), and via the carrier of the gun who has the decision-making power to discharge it at another human being. The bomb robot eliminates the need for a human carrier of the gun, shifting deployment logic farther away from the weapon akin to the logic of drone deployment. Taking one of these capacities alone, the capacity of these weapons to generate sound—to speak, in essence—facilitates a way to understand weapons as having a social life of their own.

In "Living Under Drones," a joint study by the International Human Rights and Conflict Resolution Center at Stanford Law School and the Global Justice Clinic at NYU's School of Law, sonic capacities of the drone, or its ability to "speak," are explicitly described in narratives of those living in Pakistan as the drone program has grown. Most of these expressions are acknowledgments of

---

[21] Alice Goffman, *On the Run: Fugitive Life in an American City* (New York: Picador, 2014), 5.

the new truth of life under drones: a continued fear of, and trauma under, the sounds you hear that signal the possibility of a strike at any time. Consider the report of former *New York Times* journalist David Rohde, who was kidnapped by the Taliban and held for several months in the tribal lands of Pakistan before safely returning to the United States after being rescued: "The drones were terrifying. From the ground, it is impossible to determine who or what they are tracking as they circle overhead. The buzz of a distant propeller is a constant reminder of imminent death."[22]

Describing the experience of living under drones as "hell on earth," Rohde explained that even in the areas where strikes are less frequent, people still fear for their lives, standing on constant guard for the ominous sound emanating from the sky alerting them to the presence of a Predator drone overhead. Pakistani civilians describe the experience of living in the regions where drones fly and strike similarly to Rohde. In the words of one interviewee: "God knows whether they'll strike us again or not. But they're always surveying us, they're always over us, and you never know when they're going to strike and attack."[23] Another interviewee who lost both his legs in a drone attack said that "everyone is scared all the time. When we're sitting together to have a meeting, we're scared there might be a strike. When you can hear the drone circling in the sky, you think it might strike you. We're always scared. We always have this fear in our head."[24]

Still more interviews in the report point to effects of this continued exposure to the drone dominated airspaces of Pakistan on culture and life in these regions:

In addition to feeling fear, those who live under drones—and particularly interviewees who survived or witnessed strikes—described common symptoms of anticipatory anxiety and post-traumatic stress disorder. Interviewees described emotional breakdowns, running indoors or hiding when drones appear above, fainting, nightmares and other intrusive thoughts, hyper startled reactions to loud noises, outbursts of anger or irritability, and loss of appetite and other physical symptoms. Interviewees also reported suffering from insomnia and other sleep disturbances, which medical health professionals in

[22] David Rohde, "The Drone War," *Reuters,* January 26, 2012, http://www.reuters.com/article/us-david-rohde-drone-wars-idUSTRE80P11I20120126.

[23] Khalid Raheem (anonymized name), as quoted in International Human Rights and Conflict Resolution Clinic at Stanford Law School and Global Justice Clinic at NYU School of Law, "Living Under Drones: Death, Injury, and Trauma to Civilians from US Drone Practices in Pakistan," September 2012, 81, https://www-cdn.law.stanford.edu/wp-content/uploads/2015/07/Stanford-NYU-Living-Under-Drones.pdf.

[24] Dawood Ishaq (anonymized name), as quoted in Stanford Law School and NYU School of Law, "Living Under Drones," 81.

Pakistan stated were prevalent. A father of three said, "drones are always on my mind. It makes it difficult to sleep. They are like a mosquito. Even when you don't see them, you can hear them, you know they are there." According to a strike survivor, "When the drone is moving, people cannot sleep properly or can't rest properly. They are always scared of the drones."[25]

Saeed Yayha, a day laborer who was injured from flying shrapnel in a drone attack on March 17, 2011, described the sonic effects of the drones on her daily life: "I can't sleep at night because when the drones are there . . . I hear them making that sound, that noise. The drones are all over my brain, I can't sleep. When I hear the drones making that drone sound, I just turn on the light and sit there looking at the light. Whenever the drones are hovering over us, it just makes me so scared."[26]

In thinking about the tasks of this chapter in understanding weapons as having a nonhuman life of their own, the ideas of violence and subjectivity are at the heart of the body of knowledge we have about what living under drones in regions such as Pakistan, on a daily basis, is like. Here, I have argued that turning to Foucault is helpful:

> What defines a relationship of power is that *it is a mode of action which does not act directly and immediately on others.* Instead, it acts upon their actions: an action upon an action, on existing actions or on those which may arise in the present or the future. A relationship of violence acts upon a body or upon things; it forces, it bends, it breaks on the wheel, it destroys, or it closes the door on all possibilities. Its opposite pole can only be passivity, and if it comes up against any resistance, it has no other option but to try to minimize it. On the other hand, a power relationship can only be articulated on the basis of two elements which are each indispensable if it is really to be a power relationship: that "the other" (the one over whom power is exercised) be thoroughly recognized and maintained to the very end as a person who acts; and that, faced with a relationship of power, a whole field of responses, reactions, results, and possible inventions may open up.[27]

[25] Mohammed Kausar (anonymized name), as quoted in Stanford Law School and NYU School of Law, "Living Under Drones," 83–84.

[26] Saeed Yayha (anonymized name), as quoted in Stanford Law School and NYU School of Law, "Living Under Drones," 84.

[27] Michel Foucault, "Afterword: The Subject and Power," in *Michel Foucault: Beyond Structuralism and Hermeneutics* (2nd ed.), eds. Hubert L. Dreyfus and Paul Rabinow (Chicago: University of

I have argued elsewhere that these narratives of drone victims in regions of Pakistan help to map the ways that the Muslim other, living under the eye and buzz of the drone, is recognized and maintained as a subject of fear.[28] Subjects respond to the vocal capacity of a personless weapon hovering above them. In the way that a human speaking subject, using threats, would provoke fear, the buzzing of the drone provokes fear. Either way, despite different signs, the referent of the sound (a threat) is the same for a subject living under drones as it is for those who live in the wake of constant gunshots: *I will kill you.*

Fear, and vigilance in attention to even the smallest sound that may indicate a nearing drone overhead, continues to reconfigure the entire field of possible interventions available to the governing apparatus or to those who resist it. For example, strikes that lead to death, destruction, and dismemberment may become less of a vital technique in the US regime of the drone war when the Predator model of the drone flies overhead precisely because the speaking drone generates enough fear in humans targeted by its technology. In other words, actually killing the target may be unnecessary if the target can hear the drones and, as a result, lives in constant fear and changes patterns of their daily life into a more acceptable model for the colonizing force utilizing the drone against them. This system allows for greater use of a more powerful machine that creates the loud buzzing sound that many of the subjects living under the drones identify as being most influential in their psychological and physical spaces. This fact may help explain the US military's public decision, from the Department of Defense in 2017, to begin phasing out use of the RQ-1 Predator drone in favor of the larger, more powerful RQ-9 Reaper model.[29] Though, it is notable that we can't know what models the CIA will continue to use in their strikes, and CIA strikes are known to far outnumber Department of Defense (DoD) strikes, since information on those strikes is almost completely classified. Either way, it is possible that the technology of sound, found in the fiercely enhanced and powerful US Reaper drones' buzzing overhead, generates a more potent set of available techniques to police populations living under drones. The sonic impact of this technology is inextricably linked to the monitored population's knowledge and memory of the actual deaths and destruction that have occurred, and can occur, in a strike.

Chicago Press, 1982), 202 (emphasis mine); I have previously introduced this bit of Foucault's work and suggested it be read in relation to the sound of drones—see Hayes, *Violent Subjects,* 63–65.

[28] Hayes, *Violent Subjects,* 64–65.

[29] Christian Clausen, "Air Force to Retire MQ-1 Predator Drone, Transition to MQ-9 Reaper," *U.S. Department of Defense News,* February 27, 2017, https://www.defense.gov/News/Article/Article/1095612/air-force-to-retire-mq-1-predator-drone-transition-to-mq-9-reaper/.

The effect of the sonic landscape a drone creates for its subjects and targets doesn't function only to induce fear; that fear manifests in cultural shifts. As Ian Shaw argues, the drone program can in part be understood as "threatening *patterns of life* that are coded, catalogued, and eliminated."[30] As Shaw goes on to note, most people killed by US drones in Pakistan have not been al-Qaeda fighters; in fact, only about 8% of those documented dead from the strikes were al-Qaeda members.[31] As a result, the coding of all possible human life in the regions where drones fly as a vaguely defined "threat" enables what Shaw calls a future-oriented biopolitics, and I would add, a necropolitics. As a result, under the Predator Empire (Shaw's term), "dangerous signatures or patterns of life are assessed on their very potential to *become* dangerous."[32] The patterns of life that most often code as a possible threat in the areas where US drone attacks are most common are often practices associated with Islam (e.g., gathering for *iftar* at sunset during the days of Ramadan, or attendance in communal prayer spaces). As a result, the buzzing of drones has a unique ability to influence cultural, religious, and social practice. Individuals living under the buzzing drone cease or hide activities that may place them within a life pattern that is marked for surveillance and death.

These effects extend far beyond *iftar* dinners. Ismail Hussain, interviewed in 2012 about the presence and impact of drones on Pakistani culture, noted, "the children are crying and they don't go to school. They fear their schools will be targeted by drones."[33] In the same interview, Fahad Mirza said, "We can't go to the markets. We can't drive cars." Reporter Conor Friedersdorf notes funerals are sparsely attended in these regions and friends often no longer visit each other's homes. And, the cultural and material shifts made in these communities, in response to the buzzing of the drones, are also demonstrable in the everyday actions of Taliban and al-Qaeda leaders. Top Taliban leaders, often responsible for some of the most devastating violence across Pakistan, are savvy to the methods used by US drone "brains" and the National Security Agency to find targets. As Jeremy Scahill and Glenn Greenwald report, "Some top Taliban leaders, knowing of the NSA's targeting method, have purposely and randomly distributed SIM cards among their units in order to elude their trackers ... As a result, even when the agency correctly identifies and targets a SIM card belonging

---

[30] Ian G. R. Shaw, "Predator Empire: The Geopolitics of US Drone Warfare," *Geopolitics* 18, no. 3 (2013): 545.

[31] Ibid.

[32] Ibid., 548.

[33] Conor Friedersdorf, " 'Every Person is Afraid of the Drones': The Strikes' Effect on Life in Pakistan," *Atlantic*, September 25, 2012, https://www.theatlantic.com/international/archive/2012/09/every-person-is-afraid-of-the-drones-the-strikes-effect-on-life-in-pakistan/262814/.

to a terror suspect, the phone may actually be carried by someone else, who is then killed in a strike."[34] Learning that cell phone and SIM card signatures may be part of the technological grid of US-led surveillance used to authorize deadly drone attacks, even terror suspects alter their daily lives to avoid the drones.

The notion of biopower helps explain the ways that life is transformed by the sonic landscape of the US drone program in regions of Pakistan, Yemen, and other Arab, Middle East, and North African countries. As Foucault points out, biopower is associated with the "right to make live and let die."[35] Individuals living within the regions policed and targeted by US drones are reconfiguring practices of teaching, socializing, and even plotting violence in new ways as a result of the buzzing of the drone. However, following Achille Mbembe, I have argued that the case of US drone dynamics is more aptly understood as the right to control the living only in service of the right to force subjects to die, rather than *allowing* them to die. After all, "the fight against terror makes the murder of its enemy its primary and absolute objective."[36] The buzzing of the drone overhead sonically points to the ways in which a death sentence is forced upon subjects, often with no recourse to demonstrate their innocence or appeal for their life. The dronified empire of the US governing apparatus is one in which particular figures of sovereignty make central their commitment to "the material destruction of human bodies and populations."[37] Drone politics are the work of death and their aim at black and brown, often Muslim, bodies is consistent with the ways "race has been the ever present shadow in Western political thought and practice, especially when it comes to imagining the inhumanity of, or rule over, foreign peoples."[38]

It is here where the return to circulation of drone technologies, circuitously embedded in the formation of both the Israeli state and the US war on terror, is helpful. Colonial occupation entails the creation of vast, substantial infrastructure; in this case, the US drone program depends on technological pathways woven throughout the Southwest and Midwest United States to Germany and across the world.[39] Yet, Israel provides a telling model

---

[34] Jeremy Scahill and Glenn Greenwald, "The NSA's Secret Role in the U.S. Assassination Program," *The Intercept*, February 9, 2014, https://theintercept.com/2014/02/10/the-nsas-secret-role/.

[35] Michel Foucault, "Society Must Be Defended," *Lectures at the Collège de France, 1975–1976* (New York: Picador, 2003), 241.

[36] Achille Mbembe, "Necropolitics," *Public Culture* 15, no. 1 (2003): 12.

[37] Ibid., 14.

[38] Ibid., 17.

[39] The circuitous path of US drone technological support throughout the world, including Germany, is detailed in Jeremy Scahill, "Germany Is the Tell-Tale Heart of America's Drone War," *The Intercept*, April 17, 2015, https://theintercept.com/2015/04/17/ramstein/.

about the use of colonial infrastructure: "small dust roads are dug out to allow Palestinians to cross under the fast, wide highways on which Israeli vans and military vehicles rush between settlements."[40] The "caves" of Pakistan and Afghanistan, vivid in the American imaginary after news coverage about the hunt for Osama bin Laden often described the landscape of rural Afghanistan in these limiting terms, exist as these small dirt roads. It is a carved-out space for those living under the power of a colonial force to attempt movement, engage in cultural practice, or, ultimately, escape the biopolitical encroachments on their social being deployed by the colonizer. The forging of this new infrastructure, under the necropolitical orientations of a colonial regime, is no less than what Mbembe calls "infrastructural warfare." Drones not only kill people but demolish homes, schools, mosques, and meeting areas. They destroy not only human bodies but also the very spaces necessary for everyday Muslim and/or Arab life. The sovereign that depends on this dronification of empire (in this case, the United States and a few Western allies) relies on a perfect marriage of biopolitical control, necropolitical extermination, and disciplinary regimes of power with a hefty focus on the force of death brought against those who very much want to live yet are robbed of any political means to express it.

The link between understanding the buzzing of the drone and the popping of a gun or the wail of a police siren in Black communities in the United States is exhibited in part in accounts of modern terror, which as Mbembe argues, always must address slavery as central in the narrative. Specifically, the slave condition (which can cross-apply to the colonized condition) is a "triple loss: loss of a 'home,' loss of rights over his or her body, and loss of political status."[41] Drone strikes have generated a similar set of losses across the majority-Muslim world to the losses encountered by black bodies living under slavery in the United States: losing homes and loved ones, losing rights over one's body to be safe from strikes and the violence of policing, and losing political status and civil rights. This loss of status is such that a drone target (or a black body encountering police) is never offered the opportunity to prove themselves innocent of the crime to which they have been assigned before they face not only aural colonization via the buzzing of a drone, the pop of a gun, or the wail of a siren, but ultimately, extermination.

---

[40] Eyal Weizman, "Introduction to The Politics of Verticality," *openDemocracy* (website), April 23, 2002; this excerpt drawn from quoted material in Mbembe, "Necropolitics," 29.

[41] Mbembe, "Necropolitics," 21.

From the Buzzing of the Drones to the Pops of the Gun: Subjectivity, Weaponry, and the Militarization of the Police

Mirroring gaps in thinking about drones as having a life and circulation of their own, scholars and citizens who think about gun violence often focus on its effects rather than the significance of the gun in and of itself. This view assumes that the distribution of guns, their presence and physical form, has no independent effect on the opportunities and choices of human agents who deploy force. In other words, the public is still mostly preoccupied with the supposed human choice for action, not the actual relationship between the weapon (rather than the human) and that choice. With drone attacks, we know that the logic of drones deliberately shifts this preoccupation. If the drone, as a vocal body, can distance itself from a human, then the human factors less and less (if at all) into the logic and agency of the drone when it takes an action. The debate over military medals for drone operators is a terrific case study of this phenomenon.

The Distinguished Warfare Medal was announced by Secretary of Defense Leon Panetta in February of 2013. The medal was intended to recognize military achievement in combat drone operations. After significant criticism, the medal's production was halted in March of 2013 and cancelled in April of 2013. The Military Order of the Purple Heart offered perhaps the clearest objection to the new medal's creation, which was almost unanimous across veteran and active military communities. The group "strongly urged" the Secretary of Defense to "develop another way to recognize the achievements of those whose indirect actions contribute greatly to the accomplishment of the mission without diminishing the sacrifice of life and limb by those who confront the enemy first-hand on the battlefield."[42] The discourse is specific: drone pilots are engaging in "indirect action" that "contribute(s) to the accomplishment of the mission." The physical distance of drone pilot/operator to the drone body itself is now enhanced by the military's position that a drone operator only contributes one indirect part to a mission's success. This begs the question: who then is acting directly in drone attacks? The answer peeking out from under this discourse is fairly clear: the drone itself, functioning as its own actor, shielding the operator from harm or injury to "life and limb." The action of a drone operator is demarcated from the "real" sacrifice of those who confront the enemy first-hand on the battlefield. The drone is "who" is directly responsible for the accomplishment of

---

[42] Military Order of the Purple Heart press release via John Bircher, "Military Order of the Purple Heart Opposes Precedence of New Defense Medal," February 15, 2013, http://www.purpleheart. org/News.aspx?Identity=238.

the mission and, as a result, drone pilots or operators shouldn't be eligible for medals or awards for the work they perform.

As may be clear at this point, in this chapter I heed the call for a corrective to the missing conjuncture in scholarly discussion of drones and guns in part by illuminating the parallel between the drone and the gun. As the sonic capacities of the drone indicate, the symbolic and cultural construction of the drone and the ways in which the material culture of the weapon shapes avenues for violent interaction generates and frames the narratives in which US governing society understands the drone as an actor in and of itself, absent human logic. I argue that the sonic landscape of policing in Black communities, heard throughout those communities in both everyday reality as well as the art that reflects it (e.g., hip hop), also is home to myriad ways by which aural colonization of a people is possible. The drone and the gun "speak," as does the voice of the police car sirens whose presence assures us that guns are nearby. These voices mandate a shift in the conditions of social patterns of life, or else the subjects within that social pattern of life risk being forced into death.

In his 1982 essay "The Subject and Power," Foucault oriented his entire scope of work as a study in "the way a human being turns himself into a subject." Following from my earlier discussion of necropower as an additionally necessary frame through which to understand drone and gun culture, I reorient this goal toward the general idea of weaponry. Technologies of governance in the US tactics of the terror wars and domestic policing are directed almost unilaterally at Arab and/or Muslim, black, or brown populations, often with life-altering or life-ending results. We can see the emergence of the weapon as social actor not only in the continued attempts to distance the human from the operation of a weapon (the intelligence community and military's personless drone abroad as well as the police's bomb robot at home). We can also witness this emergence of the weapon as social actor when looking to the ways subjects interacting with these weapons shift themselves into new, revolutionary and re-sistive subject positions, committed to the task of refiguring their role in the apparatus of power: an attempt to seize, and save, one's life outside the hands of the necropolitical body that will extinguish it via force.

I would argue, as Foucault does, that, "power applies itself to immediate everyday life which categorizes the individual, marks him by his own individuality, attaches him to his own identity, imposes a law of truth on him which he must recognize and which others have to recognize in him. It is a form of power which makes individuals subjects."[43] This orientation helps map an understanding of subjectivity around the drone that can be applied to the social life of the gun;

---

[43] Michel Foucault, "The Subject and Power," *Critical Inquiry* 8, no. 4 (Summer 1982): 781.

subject positions that are available to resist the drone as a body are also available to resist the gun as a body and can reveal the way the weapons function as actors in social life with the capability to impose death. I once more draw from Foucault in generating this orientation to subjectivity and its relationship to violence:

> The exercise of power can produce as much acceptance as may be wished for: it can pile up the dead and shelter itself behind whatever threats it can imagine. In itself the exercise of power is not violence; nor is it a consent which, implicitly, is renewable. It is a total structure of actions brought to bear upon possible actions; it incites, it induces, it seduces, it makes easier or more difficult; in the extreme it constrains or forbids absolutely; it is nevertheless always a way of acting upon an acting subject or acting subjects by virtue of their acting or being capable of action. A set of actions upon other actions.[44]

As a result, governing "is to structure the possible field of action of others."[45] Mbembe becomes necessary as a supplement to Foucault's work here as a result of the added attention to colonization and the increased attentiveness to race as integral in understanding bodily driven forms of power. In the way that governing for Foucault is described as structuring the possible field of action for others, Mbembe may draw our attention to governing as a system of *eliminating* possible fields of action for those being governed. Foucault's insistence to occlude warlike modes of action in his consideration of power here makes him ill-suited, without the work of Mbembe, to speak to the conditions of possibility required for understanding weapons or the possibility of the kind of aural colonization that refigures daily life for those living under it.

Employing this foundation, we may return to the sonic landscape weapons like the drone and the gun generate. In the case of the drone, the buzzing voice it carries with it signals to subjects living under its presence that it may strike at any time, forcing loss and death. Those subjects then reconfigure their social selves differently to avoid the drone and the sound it produces. In the case of the gun, the popping voice it carries with it signals to subjects living around its presence that it is striking someone else, or that it is nearby and could strike anyone, forcing death or injury. Those subjects then reconfigure their social networks to painstakingly avoid policing weapons, and the sounds they produce. Consider an exchange between two of the "6th Street Boys" who populate the

---

[44] Foucault, "The Subject and Power," 790; I have previously theorized this bit of Foucault's work in relation to violence and the terror wars in Hayes, *Violent Subjects*, 64–66.

[45] Foucault, "The Subject and Power," 790.

pages of Alice Goffman's previously cited book *On the Run: Fugitive Life in an American City*:

> "What are you going to do when you hear the sirens?" Chuck asked.
> "I'm out," his little brother replied.
> "Where you running to?"
> "Here."
> "You can't run here—they know you live here."
> "I'ma hide in the back room in the basement."
> "You think they ain't tearing down that little door?"
> Tim shrugged.
> "You know Miss Tonya?"
> "Yeah."
> "You can go over there."
> "But I don't even know her like that."
> "Exactly."
> "Why can't I go to Uncle Jean's?"
> "Cause they know that's your uncle. You can't go to nobody that's connected to you."[46]

Sirens, permeating the sonic landscape of the neighborhood, are configured here as the sign that evokes action to avoid a life-ending interaction with a weapon; in this case, the gun. Just like those who live under the buzzing of the drones, those who live under the wail of the siren and the pop of the gun create new social networks to avoid the death the weapons bring with the sounds they speak. In her appendix, Goffman describes how, in order to do her research about "the experiences of poor Black young men and women,"[47] she learned "to distinguish between gunshots and other loud bangs; to run and hide when the police were coming . . ."[48]

This link between the drone and the gun, for me, is embedded not only in the parallel I'm drawing between the sonic landscapes the weapons generate. It is also reflected in the substantial militarization projects of US police forces from the 1960s forward. In a statistical analysis including over 800 SWAT deployments conducted by 20 law enforcement agencies across the country in 2011–2012, the American Civil Liberties Union notes, "American policing has become unnecessarily and dangerously militarized, in large part through federal programs that have armed state and local law enforcement agencies with the weapons and

---

[46] Goffman, *On the Run*, 9.
[47] Ibid., 8.
[48] Ibid., 244.

tactics of war, with almost no public discussion or oversight."[49] Researcher Peter Kraska defines police militarization simply as "the process whereby civilian police increasingly draw from, and pattern themselves around, the tenets of militarism and the military model."[50]

This type of militarization of civilian police forces is rooted in a few historical moments, as Kraska and the ACLU report note: (1) the significant erosion of the 1878 Posse Comitatus Act by the United States, an act which prior to the 1980s generally prohibited military involvement in police matters; (2) the emergence of an intensified cooperation between the US military and US police grounded in part by a close operational relationship in both drug control and terrorism control efforts; (3) the steep growth and normalization of SWAT (Special Weapons and Tactics) units, modeled after elite military teams; (4) a redefining of ideas of "criminality" as "insurgency"; and (5) the weakening of the Fourth Amendment protection to privacy in one's home by the US Supreme Court.[51] Once the militarization process of US civilian police organizations began, it has quickly expanded to unprecedented levels. The types of weapons accessible in civilian police departments across the country now include flashbang grenades, battering rams, Armored Personnel Carriers (APCs), Mine Resistant Ambush Protected (MRAP) vehicles, and much, much more. The Dallas bomb robot was modeled almost exactly after a military device deployed against insurgents in Afghanistan and Iraq. In August of 2017, President Donald Trump demonstrated an even more expansive future commitment to the distribution of military grade equipment to local police forces by issuing an executive order reversing Obama era restrictions placed on distributing military surplus technology to police in 2014. As a result, his administration paved the way for more and more military grade weaponry to flood into communities throughout the United States. Praising the action, Attorney General Jeff Sessions triumphantly stated, "We will not allow criminal activity, violence, and lawlessness to become the new normal."[52]

The effects of this militarization of policing have been devastating, particularly in communities of people of color. SWAT team deployments to search people's

---

[49] American Civil Liberties Union, "War Comes Home: The Excessive Militarization of American Policing," ACLU.org, June 2014, 2, https://www.aclu.org/issues/criminal-law-reform/reforming-police-practices/war-comes-home.

[50] Peter B. Kraska, "Militarization and Policing—Its Relevance to 21st Century Police," *Policing* 1, no. 4 (2007): 3.

[51] Ibid., 2.

[52] Tom Jackman, "Trump to Restore Program Sending Surplus Military Weapons, Equipment to Police," *Washington Post*, August 27, 2017, https://www.washingtonpost.com/news/true-crime/wp/2017/08/27/trump-restores-program-sending-surplus-military-weapons-equipment-to-police/?utm_term=.56d66f147337.

homes for drugs are routine in many US cities. In the ACLU study, 79% of the 800 incidents analyzed involved the use of a SWAT team to search a person's home and more than 60% of those cases involved searches for drugs only.[53] In these searches, the primary targets were people of color. Of all the people impacted by deployments of SWAT teams to serve warrants, 54% of those were people of color, and reports find overwhelming racial disparities in the use of SWAT locally, especially when search warrants are involved.

The burning effects of SWAT weapons like remote explosives that cut through doors as well as flashbang grenades that can be thrown into homes—notably designed specifically to function without the aid of a human nearby to detonate them—create conditions that are responsible for not only substantial property damages in Black and Brown communities but also a number of deaths of people of color. One of these people, seven-year-old Aiyana Stanley-Jones, was killed when a SWAT team threw a grenade in her house and burst in, setting the blanket she was sleeping under on fire before firing a shot that killed her. Today, more than 17,000 law enforcement agencies in the United States have received weapons or resources from the Department of Defense via the federal 1033 Program, the Defense Logistics Agency, and the Enforcement Support Office in the amount of more than $4.3 billion. A city council member in Keene, New Hampshire, whose police department has been the beneficiary of some of these DoD resources, offered a chilling motive for the increased police militarization initiatives: "Our application talked about the danger of domestic terrorism, but that's just something you put in the grant application to get the money. What red-blooded American cop isn't going to be excited about getting a toy like this? That's what it comes down to."[54]

This slippage between the domestic policing and military spheres is typically difficult for objects and/or subjects to traverse. Targets of US police forces or suspects on the kill list maintained by US intelligence agencies as part of the terror wars certainly can't find traction across these spheres. Individual US gun enthusiasts, as of 2017, still find it difficult to access and own a full range of military grade weapons and artillery. Yet, the drone and the gun themselves, as well as the subsequent iterations of these weapons, have recently found easy circulation through and between both spheres. Their subjectivity may shift as they move from one to another, but their governing capabilities, and necropolitical missions, remain the same: the surveillance and elimination of black and brown bodies under the banner of "red-blooded American" ideology. The work of the US military in the war on terror, no matter its destruction via dead Middle

---

[53] American Civil Liberties Union, "War Comes Home," 3.

[54] Callum Borchers, "Armored Truck Maker in Middle of Debate on Dollars and Safety" *Boston Globe*, January 4, 2013, para. 9.

Eastern subjects, can be civilianized only via importation into domestic police forces; the militarization project, and its weapons, find no easy translation into US civilian life otherwise.

Individuals within the US police community then adopt the subject position of warrior, encouraging police officers to "steel [their] battlemind," with a battlemind defined as the warrior's inner strength to face fear and adversity during combat.[55] Armed with the sights and sounds of the military apparatus, US police officers charge into homes, cars, and offices of people of color. The sonic landscape that police forces create with this havoc, like the aural colonization of drone empire, refigures domestically located bodies of color as ungrievable threats to be eliminated by a police force now reconfigured as a fighting force against an enemy, not a protective force for defense of a fellow citizen. It is now a fully necropolitical apparatus. Those bodies of color, unable to escape the loss of home, political rights, and body they face in this colonized landscape, parallel to the crushing confines of slavery and, consequently, of those living under drones, have no other choices available within their possible field of action: they are forced to yield and, to die.

So, What Happened to the Human?

At this point, one seeming difference may remain in thinking about the drone and the gun in the context of a work on the social life of weapons. The drone more clearly has relinquished its relationship to the human. Its physical distance from an operator and the clear acceptance by military and intelligence communities that humans play only an indirect role in its operation prove this. In addition, debates about the logic of the "disposition matrix" enhance this logic as well. The disposition matrix, while not declassified, is understood as "a database of terrorist suspects that became a key tool in combating al-Qaeda and associated terror groups."[56] There is then a rumored algorithm, as part of the disposition matrix, used to determine when conditions for a "successful" drone attack are ideal.

By some reports, the disposition matrix suggests strike opportunities, and the only human role in the process is the final authorization of the strike, sometimes done in a less than three-minute discussion between the president and the CIA director at the president's family dinner table (in the era of the Obama

---

[55] ACLU, "War Comes Home," 23.

[56] Dan Gettinger, "The Disposition Matrix," *Center for Study of the Drone at Bard College*, April 25, 2015, http://dronecenter.bard.edu/the-disposition-matrix/.

presidency).[57] Whether the disposition matrix is what it seems to be based on all the data known about it, a computer-generated military authorization made absent almost any critical human input regarding targets of deadly drone strikes throughout the Middle East, is yet to be seen. What we do know is that the drone itself operates, and kills, far from a human operator or pilot. And, we know that its logic is hidden from view of the public. Even former Joint Chiefs have criticized the program publically,[58] which indicates the human input from traditionally charged US military minds is limited.

Yet, the gun still appears to be inextricably bound to human action. Some will ask: how can the gun be understood as its own entity when it can't move, operate, or function without "direct" action (by the rhetorical standards set in the military discourse about drone operator medals) on the object (i.e., the gun)? Don't they require a human for direct operation? In this frame, understanding "the social life of weapons" as an entity of its own—a worthy thought exercise this book takes up—may seem a challenging set of understandings. In response to these important questions, I offer another set of inquiries. Our focus should instead be: what can we gain when understanding weapons (the drone or the gun) as having their own bodily functions (e.g., "speaking")? What new theorizing is facilitated if we read the drone and the gun as having lives of their own within the landscape of the human condition? And, what is lost if we limit our understanding of the drone or the gun to the only actions of the human who we believe is most closely tied to its deployment? It is in these questions where I find fruitful terrain to map some closing thoughts.

Conclusion

Do drones launch themselves? Most likely, no. However, the lack of public information about the program in addition to some of what we do know about its functions from leaked documents and substantial investigative reporting certainly doesn't rule out the possibility. Do guns fire themselves? No. Many who are reading this chapter and/or this book will limit the definitional work of the term "gun" to a referent that is an object held in the hand or on the arm of a human who directly engages its firing mechanism to produce its deadly action. And perhaps that's fair. But, the use of a bomb robot by police to kill a black

---

[57] Daniel Klaidman, *Kill or Capture: The War on Terror and the Soul of the Obama Presidency* (New York: First Mariner Books, 2013).

[58] Retired four-star Marine General and former Vice Chairman of the Joint Chiefs of Staff James Cartwright has made several public statements about the potential "blowback" from the negative effects of the drone program.

suspect in Dallas and the subsequent silence of any substantial public deliberation around the dawn of that kind of unprecedented policing tactic call into question our traditional understandings of what a "gun" can be. Enhanced militarization efforts by police in the US more generally point to a trend in which police officers are increasingly outfitted with not only more potent and military-grade weaponry but also weaponry that allows them to enjoy increased distance from the suspects they target as well as the weapons themselves. I am arguing that in the necropolitical logic that marks the social life of weapons, this distance mirrors the same distance found in the relationship of the drone operator from their insurgent targets and from the weapon itself. And, those targets, in both cases, are disproportionately people of color.

In addition, the necropower of these weapons oscillates between their killing capacity and their bodily capacities like the capability to colonize a sonic landscape (e.g., buzzing of drones, pops of gunfire, wailing of sirens). As with any form of colonization, the effects outside of physical death are substantial: alienation, acculturation, and infantilization. The alienation effects of this type of aural colonization alone are psycho-socio-political and are reflected in the shifts and changes in culture throughout both majority Muslim communities in the Middle East/North Africa living under drones and Black and Brown communities in the United States living under militarized police forces. If we are to take the work of Frantz Fanon seriously, and I believe we should, those effects birth the psyche of the colonized as one desperate to "make new skin," to free themselves from "inferiority complex[es] and [their] contemplative or hopeless attitudes." The rebirth of those colonized people "can only emerge from the decaying corpse of the colony,"[59] pitting the yet unleashed violent potential of colonized subjects (which for Fanon, is substantial) against the necropower and domination of the governing apparatus that colonizes them. This map makes violence the centerpiece of an ongoing struggle for liberation; it is a blood-soaked map, at that.

So, to answer the questions: what do we gain when understanding the social life of weapons as if they (the weapons) have their own bodily functions (e.g., the ability to "speak")? What theorizing can happen when the drone and the gun are understood as fused in the social life of weaponry and when both are understood as having their own "subjectivities"? In short, at the simplest levels, we gain a richer understanding of the ways these weapons live in the social world of those affected by them. For example, the sonic landscapes created by the drone abroad and the gun at home are ignored if we presume

---

[59] Frantz Fanon, *The Wretched of the Earth* (New York: Grove Press, 2004). Various translations of Fanon's work exist. I take "make new skin" from his original French "faire peau neuve" in context and the remainder of the quotes from a blend of the French from which the Grove Press edition was translated.

we can assess all aspects of weaponry's capacity by limiting our aperture of analysis to the humans we believe are most tied to these weapons' deployment. One can imagine extensions of this argument that take up a study of the scopic capacity of the drone (via its surveillance camera devices) and the gun (via the substantial efforts made at attachable technologies enabling a human using a gun to fire at their target from farther and farther away). In this framework, the discourses of the gun and the drone as well as understandings of their capacities to act avoid evacuation of agency, which, in turn, offers new landscapes through which we may venture in our quest to understand the social lives of these weapons.

In addition, and perhaps more importantly, in this framework we can generate fledgling avenues of resistance to the racialization of these weapons. According to the Mapping Police Violence project, unarmed black people were killed by police at five times the rate of whites in 2015.[60] Of the approximately 1,092 people killed by police in 2016, almost half were people of color.[61] These numbers are in addition to the already alarming statistics earlier in this chapter demonstrating the significant racial divide in all gun deaths across the United States (not just those at the hands of police), data extended by a group of New York based medical researchers.[62] Victims of US drone strikes, almost universally, are Arab and/or Muslim people, as well as other people of color living in the nations of Pakistan, Yemen, Afghanistan, and Somalia. In fact, to date, there have only been two victims of US drone strikes publically identified as white US Americans or Europeans and both (American Warren Weinstein and Italian Giovanni Lo Porto) were aid workers captured by al-Qaeda before being killed in a 2015 drone strike along the border of Pakistan and Afghanistan. As far as we know, a few other American citizens have been killed: Kemal Darwish, Anwar al-Awlaqi, Samir Khan, Abdulrahman al-Awlaqi (Anwar's son), Jude Kenan Mohammed, Ahmed Farouq, and Adam Gadahn. However, all of these victims were people of color and all were practicing Muslims. Among this group, the US government only admits to targeting the senior al-Awlaqi, claiming the rest of these deaths were inadvertent.

Whether black and brown bodies are targeted and killed inadvertently by a series of almost statistically impossible "accidents" or they are targeted and killed as part of a systemic global necropolitical apparatus that knows nothing

[60] Mapping Police Violence Project, https://mappingpoliceviolence.org/unarmed/.

[61] "The Counted: People Killed by Police in the US," *The Guardian*, https://www.theguardian.com/us-news/ng-interactive/2015/jun/01/the-counted-police-killings-us-database.

[62] Bindu Kalesan et al., "State-Specific, Racial and Ethnic Heterogeneity in Trends of Firearm Related Fatality Rates in the USA from 2000 to 2010," *BMJ Open*, 2014, http://bmjopen.bmj.com/content/4/9/e005628; ACLU, "War Comes Home.

else to do with them, their targeting and their deaths persist. Until the systemic discourses that authorize and strip these bodies of all possible choices in a field of political and social action other than the ability to die are confronted, the possibility of interrupting the logic of the system will be out of our reach. The experience of a person of color living under the buzzing of the drone or the pop of the gun and the wail of a siren is one of aural colonization; a psychological state in which warnings and signals marking the loss of your space, rights, and person are ubiquitous and unending. The social lives of these weapons must be traced, and understood as multiple heads of the same monster, as part of the struggle for Black and Brown lives and the material transformation of the conditions of possibility for their liberation.

5

Dum-Dum Bullets

Constructing and Deconstructing "The Human"

JOANNA BOURKE

Bullets have a social life, both in interaction with the gun and as independent fetishized objects. In this chapter, I explore the history of what is arguably the most symbolic of bullets: the dum-dum. Colloquially, the word "dum-dum" is still used to refer to bullets that are hollow pointed, soft-nosed, expansive, or semi-jacketed. Even people with no intrinsic interest in weapons know that a dum-dum bullet is an atrocious assassin. Although other bullets have attained a cult-like status among collectors (especially in recent decades),[1] nothing approaches the symbolic significance of the "dum-dum." The onomatopoeic nature of the word dum-dum still evokes energy, military prowess, and prestige (for its proponents), and racism, cowardice, and cruelty (for opponents). A close reading of the historical trajectory of dum-dum bullets reveals their role in the political project of defining "the human."

It was May 1899, and defenders of the British Empire were panicking. At the First Peace Conference in The Hague, representatives of twenty-six nations were debating whether or not to prohibit one of the munitions used by the British army. The central question was, Were bullets that had been designed to expand when striking their "target" barbarous and inhumane? The missiles under discussion were commonly known as "dum-dum" bullets. Although both the delegates and the press routinely used the term dum-dum during their debates, in reality the delegates were discussing bullets that could "easily

---

[1] Interesting examples can be found on the website of "The Cartridge Collector's Exchange," http://www.oldammo.com/november04.htm.

expand their form inside the human body," including "bullets with a hard covering" that did "not completely cover the core, or contain indentations." They were referring, therefore, to a range of different type of missiles. Because of the symbolic weight given to the word, I will follow their usage by using the shorthand term "dum-dum" as well.

Tsar Nicholas II of Russia had convened the First Peace Conference at The Hague in an attempt to seek "the most effective means of ensuring to all peoples the benefits of a real and lasting peace, and, above all, of limiting the progressive development of existing armaments." By the end of the Conference, delegates had ruled against the use of asphyxiating, poisonous gases and the "discharge of projectiles and explosives from balloons and other new analogous methods."[2] However, the decision to ban dum-dum bullets generated discord. Twenty-three nations voted in favor of the ban, with only the UK and America voting against and Portugal abstaining. It wasn't until 1907 that Britain finally agreed to adhere to the Hague Declaration. Their eventual agreement was largely due to the fact that they had developed projectiles at Woolwich as devastating as the dum-dum but which stuck to the "letter but not the spirit" of the law.[3] This was the round-nose, hollow-point bullet or .202 inch Mark III, modified as the Mark VII in 1912. These missiles "tumbled" inside the body, causing injuries as serious as those of the dum-dum.

For the British delegates in 1899, however, the international condemnation of the dum-dum bullet was an insult to their ambitions. They fumed that any prohibition would be grossly unfair to the "flower of British manhood," who were sacrificing their lives for the sake of the Empire. Their arguments were essentially about establishing and then maintaining a hierarchy of humanity: a great "chain of Being" was established, progressing from the inanimate, to the nonhuman animal and then to graduations of "full" humanity.[4] "Savages" had shown that they would not submit passively when British soldiers, traders, missionaries, and politicians stole their land. Indigenous peoples were fighting back, which was why imperial troops believed that dum-dum bullets were militarily necessary: ordinary missiles simply did have enough "stopping power"

---

[2] Agreement was reached on July 29, 1899, and the Convention came into force on September 4, 1900.

[3] This was what Sir John Ardagh had hoped in 1899 when he commented that "even though a complete and unperforated envelope were to be accepted as a binding condition, it should not be beyond the ingenuity of the inventor to design a projectile which, while it conformed to the letter of this condition, might nevertheless produce a wound sufficiently severe to satisfy practical requirements": Ardagh, "Memorandum Respecting Expanding Bullets," June 15, 1899, The National Archives (London), FO 412/65.

[4] For a discussion of the wider context of this "chain of being," see my *What It Means to be Human. Historical Reflections 1791 to the Present* (London and New York: Virago and Counterpoint, 2011).

against such formidable resistance.[5] They believed that the stability and continued expansion of the great British Empire required the shedding of blood—preferably that of "savages." As the Director-General of the Indian Medical Service concluded, it was a "false humanity to allow our own men to be killed rather than take means to effectually prevent this by disabling the enemy."[6] Was "humanity" only to be "exercised on the part of the ill-used savage, while the [European] soldier is to take his chance?" thundered the *Daily Mail*.[7] Were the "bodies of white men going to be flung aside as though they were nothing more than human sacrifices to some African Ju-ju, in some African city of blood?" asked another commentator writing in the *British Medical Journal*.[8] These were some of the questions preoccupying imperialists in fin de siècle Britain.

This furor about dum-dum bullets was puzzling. Why were European powers fixating on this weapon? Why was there little objection to the formidable escalation of other, even more deadly technologies? In the years prior to 1899, artillery shells had grown in size and explosive power. Maxim and Nordenfelt guns, mines, submarines, torpedoes, and Lyddite shells enhanced the wounding and killing capacities of all major armies. The new, small-bore weapons that had been introduced throughout Europe in the late-nineteenth century were lighter and traveled at much higher velocities than their predecessors, inflicting wounds that could be as severe as those caused by dum-dums. The development of these weapons "caused no shudder of dismay or thrill of horror to run through the world," commented one ballistics expert in 1899: he lamented that "from end to end of the globe not one voice was uplifted nor whisper breathed against the use of such awful implements by man against man."[9] Why the fuss about dum-dum bullets only?

This chapter argues that these questions can only be answered by exploring the symbolic and rhetorical power of this missile. In the age of Empire, dum-dum bullets "stood in" for British influence in the world. In a period that saw

[5] Gwilyn G. Davis, "The Effects of Small Calibre Bullets as Used in Military Arms," *Annals of Surgery* 25, no. 1 (January 1897), 46.

[6] Comment by the Surgeon-General Harvey (Director-General of the Indian Medical Service), in discussion after the lecture by William MacCormac, "Some Remarks, By Way of Contrast, On War Surgery, Old and New," *British Medical Journal* 2, no. 2121 (August 24, 1901), 462.

[7] Frederick G. Engelbach, "A Plea for the Dum-Dum," *Daily Mail*, June 12, 1899, 4; also see Malvern Lumsden, "New Military Technologies and the Erosion of International Law: The Case of the Dum-Dum Bullets Today," *Instant Research on Peace and Violence* 4, no. 1 (1974), 17.

[8] Alexander Ogston, "Continental Criticism of English Rifle Bullets," *British Medical Journal* (March 25, 1899), 756.

[9] Alexander Ogston, "The Peace Conference and the Dum-Dum Bullet," *British Medical Journal* (July 29, 1899), 278.

a terrifying expansion of weaponry, small arms fire harked back to a world of face-to-face encounters against a foe that seemed to many Britons to be self-evidently inferior, yet whose resources (lands, minerals, labor, to name just a few) were essential to British wealth. But, I will be arguing, although extremely important, imperial ambitions and the corollary construction of hierarchies of humanity alone cannot explain the power of the "dum-dum." For this, we have to turn to its function in social discourse. An analysis of the social history of this weapon tells us a great deal about the symbolic and phenomenological status of weapons.

Dum-dum bullets took their name from the town in which the bullet was manufactured. The British armory used to be around ten kilometers (six miles) from the center of Kolkata (Calcutta), but is now part of that city. Some claim that the name derives from the Persian word "damdama," meaning "raised platform." Others posit a more imperial origin, maintaining that the name originated in the "dham-dham" sound generated when British imperialist Lieutenant Colonel Robert Clive tested his guns there in the 1750s. Whatever the case, the British East India Company built an ammunition factory in Dum Dum in 1846. Fifty years later, Lieutenant Colonel Neville Sneyd Bertie-Clay invented and manufactured dum-dum bullets there.

Resembling a "slate pencil,"[10] the original dum-dum was a variation of the .303 Lee-Metford bullet. However, modifications to the Lee-Metford transformed the missile into a formidable weapon. The original dum-dum had a thinner nickel shield and a "soft point." On striking human targets, it "mushrooms," shattering bone and tissue with explosive force. It causes devastating wounds. At the time, its formidable destructive power was a cause of celebration. Winston Churchill was a fan. He waxed lyrically over this "wonderful and, from the technical point of view, . . . beautiful machine." "On striking a bone," he observed, the bullet would "set up" or "spread out." It "tears and splinters everything before it, causing wounds which, in the body, must generally be mortal, and in any limb necessitates amputation."[11]

It was no coincidence that such a devastating weapon was developed and manufactured in the empire. The British Empire had long been an important laboratory for experimenting with new military technologies, which would then

---

[10] Henry J. Davis, "Gunshot Injuries in the Late Greco-Turkish War with Remarks upon Modern Projectiles," *British Medical Journal* (December 19, 1897), 1790.

[11] Winston Churchill, *The Story of the Malakand Field Force: An Episode of Frontier War* (London: Longmans, Green, and Co., 1898), 287–288.

be exported to other countries and used against other enemies.[12] As we shall see, the immediate reason for the development of the weapon was concern that the bullets being used to conquer other peoples were not as "effective"—that is, not as mutilating or mortal—as required. In the Chitral campaign (in what is today the far North West Frontier Province of Pakistan) of 1895, the Lee-Metford bullet had proved inadequate in subduing the enemy.[13] In the lead-up to the Peace Conference of 1899, the claim that dum-dum bullets were an absolute necessity during British military campaigns was repeated time and again.

Concerns about the inefficacy of Lee-Metford bullets and the formidable wounding power of dum-dums had generated considerable debate in British military circles before the 1899 Conference. In 1898, the War Office's Departmental Committee on Small Arms reported that they were worried that dum-dum bullets might be in breach of the St. Petersburg Convention of 1868. According to this convention, "civilized nations" had a duty to alleviate "as much as possible the calamities of war" and were forbidden from "the employment of arms which uselessly aggravate the sufferings of disabled men, or render their death inevitable." Among other things, the 1868 Convention banned explosive projectiles under 400 grams in weight. Britain signed this Declaration (America had not been invited to attend because it was not considered a great nation at that time), thereby promising not to "uselessly aggravate the sufferings" of men at war.

The question for the Departmental Committee on Small Arms in 1898 was clear: Were British small arms in breach of this ban? And what criteria should be used to judge "how severe a wound was to be regarded as permissible?" asked the Director-General of Ordnance Factories. Since there was no obvious answer to this question, the Inspector-General of Ordnance proposed a pragmatic solution: they were looking for a bullet that was

> capable of stopping . . . a horse in a charge of Cavalry, or a man on foot, while retaining, as far as might be, accuracy at all ranges and power of penetration, and at the same time not infringing the spirit of the declaration of St. Petersburg.[14]

---

[12] Rashid Khalidi, *Resurrecting Empire. Western Footprints and America's Perilous Path in the Middle East* (London: I. B. Tauris, 2004), 27; and James Garner, "Proposed Rules for the Regulation of Aerial Warfare," *American Journal of International Law* 18 (1924), 56–81.

[13] Davis, "The Effects of Small Calibre Bullets," 48; and Ogston, "The Peace Conference and the Dum-Dum Bullet," 278.

[14] "Memorandum of Recent Proceedings in Regard to .303-inch Bullets of Increased 'Stopping Power,'" initialed by E. M. (I.G.O.), January 26, 1898, 2, in The National Archives (London) WO 32/7055; and E. Bainbridge, Col. R. A., President of the Departmental Committee on Small Arms, *Departmental Committee on Small Arms. Report No. 7. Further Trial of Dum Dum Bullets, and of Bullets to R. L. Designs Nos. 9063B and 9063B** (London: War Office, January 17, 1898), 4.

He acknowledged that it was "doubtful whether any bullet would meet the conditions required, which would not inflict a severe wound at short ranges," so the bullets' effectiveness was going to be judged "at moderate range."[15]

The scientific adjudicator was Surgeon-Colonel William Flack Stevenson, soon to publish a major textbook entitled *Wounds in War* (1898). He presented his conclusions in a paper entitled "Statement on the General Question of the 'Stopping Power' of Modern Small-Bore Bullets." Like his colleagues, he recognized that the main problem was the inadequate "stopping power" of the army's Lee-Metford bullet in India. The bullet produced "stiletto-like perforations of soft parts, which must be accompanied by only the most trivial degree of shock or impact."[16] If the bullet did not hit a bone, an "Asiatic fanatic" might be able to continue advancing even after being hit by a Lee-Metford bullet. More worryingly, this was also the case with the much more powerful Henry-Martini bullet. The crucial variable was whether a bone was "implicated," in which case all the bullets "stop" the enemy "effectively enough."

Stevenson noted, therefore, that soldiers needed to be issued with a bullet that, "on traversing soft tissue only," will "produce a wound which will cause such destruction of muscles, nerves, and blood vessels, as will have the same stopping effect as if a long bone was fractured," In order to accomplish this, they needed a bullet that,

> on account of its alteration at its point, will strip its envelope and un-
> dergo fragmentation of its core in the greatest possible degree. Slight
> "bulging at the shoulder" will not have the required effect; the bullet
> must break to pieces.

With this in mind, Stevenson reported on three trials that he had carried out at Woolwich in December 1895. In all three cases, he had tested "altered Lee-Metford bullets." One of these bullets had a "wide, shallow depression at the point," the second had a "cross-cut in the point," and on the third, its "point had been filed away so as to expose the core." All three bullets (but particularly the one with the depression at the point) "underwent extreme deformation and fragmentation against the soft tissues of a horse, and produced most extensive and severe lacerations."[17] However, what rendered these bullets "unfit for use as

---

[15] Bainbridge, *Departmental Committee on Small Arms*, 4.

[16] Surgeon-Colonel William Flack Stevenson, "Statement on the General Question of the 'Stopping Power' of Modern Small-Bore Bullets," 24, in The National Archives (London) WO 32/ 7055.

[17] Stevenson, "Statement on the General Question of the "Stopping Power," 24.

a Service projectile" was not the fact that the injuries they caused "were, perhaps, unnecessarily severe," but the fact that they were "erratic in flight."[18] Stevenson later tested the dum-dum bullet and found that although it did inflict more severe injuries than the other bullets, it "did not do so to the extent which the reputation it appears to bear in India would lead one to expect."[19] In choosing a bullet, he stressed that the primary consideration should be which one "causes the greatest destruction to soft parts," especially since all the bullets had a similar, devastating effect if they hit bone. He had no scruples about recommending the most powerful bullets when dealing with non-European enemies since

> the fanatical Asiatic knows nothing of [international] congresses, and would only laugh at the suggestion of waging war on such principles. All his efforts are directed towards causing the greatest possible injury to his enemy, and he fully expects his enemy to do likewise by him. No purely humanitarian sentiments, therefore, need interfere with the use of bullets of a destructive nature by civilised nations when at war with people of this class.

The same degree of force was unnecessary in European warfare because "civilised soldiers, as a rule, do not continue to advance after the receipt of a wound, although it may not incapacitate them from doing so."[20] In other words, the current army projectile was fine for "civilised" warfare, but for "savages" the bullet with the depression in the point had the greatest "stopping power," even though it was inaccurate.[21]

With the help of Stevenson's report, the War Office's Departmental Committee on Small Arms in 1898 recommended discontinuing the production of dum-dum bullets. They concluded that the injuries caused by dum-dum bullets "were similar to those which might be expected to result from the Service bullet [the Mark II] when soft parts are traversed."[22] In combination with the dum-dum bullets' inaccuracy and the fact that "at long ranges . . . an equal stopping effect can be obtained by a bullet which will shoot accurately," they decided that it was not "desirable to carry out any further experiments with the Dum Dum bullet."[23]

---

[18] Ibid., 24.

[19] Ibid., 25.

[20] Ibid., 25–26.

[21] Ibid., 26. Stevenson's report was favorably quoted in subsequent discussions: see "Memorandum of Recent Proceedings in Regard to .303-inch Bullets," 1.

[22] Bainbridge, *Departmental Committee on Small Arms*, 22.

[23] Ibid., 8.

The remarkable thing about this recommendation in 1898, which the British forces immediately set out to implement, was that it did not dampen the furious *defense* of dum-dum bullets by British representatives at The Hague. In other words, despite the fact that the British army had already stopped production of this missile, they continued to act as though the entire might of the British Empire would falter if dum-dums were prohibited by international law.

In part, their ire was geopolitical. They were acutely aware that the challenge to dum-dum missiles was not only coming from Russia (which was falling behind in the arms race) but also from an aggressively militaristic Germany. In 1898, a Congress for German surgeons railed against the threat posed to "civilized nations" by the production and use of semi-mantled bullets. In his presentation at the Congress, Professor Von Bruns of Tübingen reported on the effect of British dum-dum bullets when fired into the carcasses of animals. It caused an outcry.[24] As a result, eminent surgeon Professor Friedrich von Esmarch of Kiel (writing in the *German Review* on December 10, 1898) appealed to representatives who were shortly to be attending the Peace Conference to ban these new bullets. He admitted that "no one ... expects or hopes that there is any immediate prospect of wars being put an end to," but insisted that "the philanthropist must remain content to be for ever striving to diminish, as far as may be ... the barbarities of warfare." It was the duty, he continued, of medical men to "protest in the name of humanity" when projectiles were introduced that "go beyond their necessary object of disabling a foe, and mutilate him as well." Von Esmarch admitted that such missiles were "perhaps, excusable in a war with fanatical barbarians, who, ignorant of the rules of international law, give and take no quarter," but were unjustifiable in wars with European enemies. He pleaded with the delegates at the Peace Conference to follow the lead of their predecessors in 1868 who had banned explosive missiles weighing under 400 grams of weight, to do so with these new missiles as well.[25]

This was the geopolitical context facing British delegates at The Hague in May 1899. They felt compelled to leap to the defense of semi-jacketed bullets. Six defenses were put forward. The first was to simply deny the evidence produced by the bullet's critics. British commentators argued that the experiments that drew the world's approbation to dum-dum bullets were flawed. They claimed that Professor Von Bruns had assumed that the British dum-dum bullets were identical to the "half-naked bullets" used in the German small-bore army rifle (the Maüser) and commonly employed by big game hunters in East Africa. This was not the case: the Maüser bullets had a "long point of soft lead, while the

---

[24] Ogston, "The Peace Conference and the Dum-Dum Bullet," 278.
[25] Ogston, "Continental Criticism of English Rifle Bullets," 754–755.

Dum-dum bullet had its leaden core barely visible at the apex."[26] The Maüser bullets were less tapered, had a greater diameter, and exposed 5mm of lead at the top while the dum-dums exposed 1mm or less.[27] General Sir John Ardagh, Britain's representative at the Peace Conference, insisted that as a consequence of such misleading evidence, the "gruesome illustrations of shattered bones and torn flesh" that the Germans claimed "needlessly aggravates the suffering of men when *hors de combat*" was incorrect. British tests had used "genuine" dum-dum bullets and showed that the "track of the Dum-dum and the wound itself are not more terrible than those of the Snider, the Martini-Henry, or fully-mantled bullets."[28]

Even if the correct semi-mantled bullets *had* been tested by the Germans, British defenders pointed out that the "mantle" was only one of the factors that resulted in particularly cruel wounding. Velocity and the weight of the projectile were other factors. This was their second argument. After all, bullets developed in Austria, Germany, France, Sweden, Portugal, Denmark, Japan, and Peru were larger than those in England, while those developed in Belgium, Turkey, Russia, the United States, Spain, and Italy were smaller. At short ranges, the English bullet was the slowest (574 meters velocity per second) compared to Germany, France, and Russia (640 fps), and Holland, Italy, Norway, and Romania (more than 700 fps).[29] Velocity and weight were crucial because these factors were "the main destroying forces; upon these depend its effects." It followed that if a "mantled bullet" struck a bone ("whether it breaks up or not"), it "communicates its force to a number of the fragments it produces and hurls them forward in a devastating shower, nearly as destructive of all that stands in their path as are fragments of the bullet itself."[30] Provocatively, Alexander Ogston (a surgeon from Aberdeen, writing in the *British Medical Journal*) charged that it might be

> a task of no very great difficulty to turn the tables on these Powers by formulating an indictment against them that theirs are the bullets which are really "inutilement [uselessly] cruel," as being beyond the requirements of warfare.[31]

---

[26] Ibid., 752.

[27] Alexander Ogston, "The Wounds Produced by Modern Small-Bore Bullets," *British Medical Journal* (September 17, 1898), 815.

[28] "The Peace Conference," *British Medical Journal* (June 10, 1899), 1420; the comparison between weapons was also made by "The Text-Book for Military Small Arms and Ammunition 1894," *Quarterly Review* 190 (July 1899), 174–175.

[29] Ogston, "The Peace Conference and the Dum-Dum Bullet," 278.

[30] Ibid., 280.

[31] Ibid., 278.

In other words, if dum-dum and hollow-point bullets were to be condemned, so too should *all* modern mantled bullets of small caliber, since they all produced terrible wounds. Logically, armies should "return to our former larger bores and black powder cartridges that gave a low initial velocity."[32]

The third argument made by proponents of semi-mantled bullets involved a kind of "cruelty accountancy." Comparing the degree of pain inflicted by specific weapons might have been morally contentious but was vigorously asserted nonetheless. Bizarrely, British and American spokesmen contended that using dum-dum bullets was actually an act of wartime *humanitarianism*: it reduced the total sum of suffering. This was argued by Surgeon-Major-General J. B. Hamilton. He explained that

> If the Dum-dum bullet be used, it, as a rule, will injure but one man, as when "set up," its power of penetration rapidly ceases; if, on the other hand, a projectile entirely covered with nickel be employed, it will possibly pass through two or three men, and gradually "setting up," inflict greater injuries on a fourth.[33]

Reiterating his argument, Hamilton maintained that there were worse ways to kill people anyway. Hamilton observed that an Admiral in command of a fleet would never "hesitate to 'ram' a battleship or blow her up with a torpedo, destroying perhaps 800 men in the operation." Indeed, he exclaimed, such an admiral would "gain renown for the action." In contrast, "if our War Office uses a projectile calculated to 'stop' individuals, it is condemned as 'inhumane!' "[34] As another author put it in an article entitled "Legitimate and Illegitimate Modes of Warfare," why was so much fuss being made about dum-dum bullets causing "superfluous injury?" Much more "hideous wounds" could be "inflicted by unexceptional implements of warfare" and it was impossible to conceive of a "fate more horrible than that of the engine-room complement when a battleship is going down."[35]

A similar debate flourished around the question of whether the wounds inflicted by dum-dum bullets actually *were* more agonizing than those caused by the Snide or Martini-Henry.[36] Ogston was particularly acerbic. He sneered at

---

[32] Ogston, "Continental Criticism of English Rifle Bullets," 756.

[33] Surgeon-Major-General J. B. Hamilton, "The Dum-Dum Bullet," *British Medical Journal* (June 11, 1898), 1559.

[34] Ibid., 1559.

[35] J. B. Atlay, "Legitimate and Illegitimate Modes of Warfare," *Journal of the Society of Comparative Legislation* 6, no. 1 (1905), 14.

[36] For an extended discussion, see Stevenson, "The Effects of the Dum-Dum Bullet from a Surgical Point of View," 1324–1325.

the other people's ignorance. People who "should know better" were giving the impression that

> the fully-mantled bullet used by most of the Powers is a missile which lets the life out of a man by the smallest opening possible and in the gentlest way—a utopian sort of bullet; while the Dum-dum and allied bullets are supposed to tear his nerves and sinews asunder, and leave a gigantic and painful rent through which the spirit issues in agony.

He accused such naïve commentators for being responsible for the misguided belief that a man who has been wounded by a fully-mantled bullet "has before him but a few weeks of pleasant sojourn in bed, while the open-fronted bullets will cost him his limb by amputation, if not worse."[37] Ogston extolled people to witness the shocking effects of *all* modern bullets: "the fearful rending of viscera, the cruel powdering and splintering of bones, the tearing of the flesh, and the lacerated, open deadspaces [*sic*] beneath the fasciæ and skin."[38] All rifles were "murderous" and it was "out of place to apply the term 'humane,' even in a relative sense, to any of them."[39] Furthermore, he added, it was ridiculous to pretend that other governments had adopted the *fully-mantled* bullet for any reason other than to "compel it to take the spin conferred upon it by the spiral grooves lining the interior of the barrel" and therefore be propelled with greater velocity. "Questions of humanity had nothing whatever to do with its introduction," he explained. "Quite the reverse. It was employed to make the bullet kill and wound more surely, more deeply, and at longer range."[40]

Even if it could be shown that the semi-mantled bullet was particularly cruel (a fact British spokesmen denied), the fourth defense of dum-dum bullets was based on the view that prohibitions against particular weapons always lagged behind technological developments. Attempts to stem the tide were doomed to failure. This was the argument of the author of "The Text-Book for Military Small Arms and Ammunition" (1899). He maintained that all weapons were viewed as morally repugnant when first utilized. Even stone throwing must have been regarded as an "innovation" when it was introduced in mortal combat and the "cross-bow was originally condemned in war between Christians." Most new weapons were "denounced as cowardly, brutal, and inhuman" until "its

[37] Ogston, "The Peace Conference and the Dum-Dum Bullet," 278.
[38] Ibid., 280.
[39] Ibid., 280.
[40] Ibid., 278.

advantages became recognised and its science was practised."[41] The same was true of the dum-dum.

The fifth defense accused the delegates of base motivations. Could the ban be the result of political shenanigans? Might it be a politically-inspired attempt by other powers to curb British imperial ambitions (for example, in the continent of Africa)? This was the view of the British even before the Congress. Again, Ogston made the most bullish defense along these lines. He believed that the decision of the Peace Conference was politically motivated. After all, prior to 1899, no one objected to European nations expanding their deathly arsenals, and there was no "expression of remorse by the great military Powers of civilisation."[42] Ogston accused the European Powers of seeking to place Britain at a disadvantage and "under the name of humanity" attempting to "coerce her into an undertaking to make no attempt to render her military rifle equal to theirs."[43] As he reminded readers,

> many of our campaigns are necessarily conducted under conditions so different from those which Germany, for example, are called upon to face, or can understand, that we must be careful lest we be led, by a false philanthropy, in such a matter to adopt suggestions that may prove most unjust and even inhumane to our own troops in their wars against desperate enemies devoid of all humanity.[44]

In other words, the enemy that British soldiers faced were not truly human.

However, the final, and extremely forceful, defense was pragmatic: only semi-jacketed or soft-jacketed bullets had the requisite "stopping power" when faced with "savages." Only dum-dum bullets would inflict wounds so horrific that they would instantly stop any "fanatic," Alfred Marks blandly noted in *The Westminster Review*.[45] Or, in the words of Ogston, it was ironic that it was legitimate to tear human beings apart using heavy artillery, but they were forbidden from employing missiles that had been designed to kill the "charging tiger, elephant, or buffalo" against a "fierce and tiger-like" human enemy.[46]

Writing from the Peace Conference, army surgeon Frederick George Engelbach made a similar argument. Soldiers in the French, Italian, Russian,

[41] "Text-Book for Military Small Arms," *Quarterly Review*, 153, 173.

[42] Ogston, "Continental Criticism of English Rifle Bullets," 752.

[43] Ogston, "The Peace Conference and the Dum-Dum Bullet," 278.

[44] Ogston, "Continental Criticism of English Rifle Bullets," 753.

[45] Alfred Marks, "Bullets—Expansive, Explosive, and Poisoned," *Westminster Review* (June 1902), 633.

[46] Ogston, "Continental Criticism of English Rifle Bullets," 752.

and German infantry typically fought other Europeans or "soft" indigenous people—groups who were easily rendered *hors de combat*. Engelbach claimed that "a European when struck in a vital part collapses utterly or else crawls from the fray with all his lust for fighting gone. Even the Abyssinian or the Shilock knows when he has had enough." In contrast, British soldiers were pitted against more formidable foes. The "Afridis, the bhang drunk Ghazi, and the howling dervish or Baqqara love to meet their deaths in action," he maintained. It was pointless to shoot such enemy with the nickel-coated bullet of the .303 Lee-Enfield magazine rifle since that bullet "drives with a velocity of 2,000 feet per second through four or five of them," rendering them "mortally hurt" yet still able to "gamely struggle on to strike one blow before they die." Death, for these enemies simply "opens Paradise." British soldiers would not gain any "satisfaction" in shooting "a shrieking fanatic" with a bullet that would "perforate" but take half an hour to actually *kill*. In that amount of time, British soldiers would be "lying dead one a-top of the other." What could be done, he concluded, "with a gallant fanatic who actually wriggles up the lance of his enemy to slay before his exhausted muscles give out?"[47] The Director-General of the Indian Medical Service put it more evocatively: a "fanatical Ghazi," he judged, "was not checked by the modern bullet, which went through him like a knitting needle through a pot of butter."[48]

It was a theme that defenders of dum-dum bullets returned to time and again. As *The Daily Mail* reported on June 28, 1898, the Lee-Metford bullet "does not disable an enemy as effectively as desirable." Indeed, in Khartoum, enemy combatants were "known to go on fighting after half a dozen Lee-Metford bullets have gone through them." They lauded the fact that dum-dum bullets "came into use for the purpose of stopping the rush of hordes of fanatics": its "advantage" was that it "spread[ ] out whenever it encountered resistance."[49]

Lurid tales were told of problems with other bullets. In one anecdote, a spy was hit by six regular bullets but managed to run "a quarter of a mile before he was overtaken by a mounted Sikh, who cut his head nearly off at a single blow with his sabre."[50] In other tales, hapless British troops armed with ineffective weapons were pitted against sturdy savages who "swarmed" toward them intent on murder. Captain Francis Younghusband's account was fairly typical. He was

[47] Engelbach, "A Plea for the Dum-Dum"; also see Sir John Ardagh, "Memorandum Respecting Expanding Bullets" (June 15, 1899), TNA FO 412/65.

[48] Comment by the Surgeon-General Harvey (Director-General of the Indian Medical Service), in discussion after the lecture by William MacCormac, "Some Remarks, By Way of Contrast, On War Surgery, Old and New," *British Medical Journal* 2, no. 2121 (August 24, 1901), 462.

[49] "A 'Man-Killing' Bullet," *Daily Mail*, June 28, 1898, 3.

[50] Davis, "The Effects of Small Calibre Bullets," 48–49.

appalled to observe that, while the Scottish Borderers were being attacked, a native drummer-boy was buoying up the spirits of their foe from a nearby roof. "Every now and then a bullet would find him out, and he would drop to dress his wounds," Younghusband claimed, but the drummer-boy would quickly recover and resume beating his drum. It wasn't until "a bullet got him through the heart, and he fell headlong . . . with his drum around his neck, and his arms ready to strike it" that the Scottish Borderers managed to eliminate this morale-booster for the enemy. Witnessing this scene convinced Younghusband that the "stopping power" of the Lee-Metford bullet was too poor to be of any use in battle.[51] Colonel Louis Antole La Garde echoed these sentiments, lamenting the "humane" character of weapons especially when dealing with "savage tribes," a "fanatical enemy," and "cavalry and artillery horses." The "stopping power" of ordinary bullets was "sufficient for all purposes of civilized warfare" only.[52]

British imperialists were profoundly anxious about the "excessive . . . vitality" of "savages"[53] who did not seem to *feel* physical pain as much as Europeans did.[54] If this wasn't bad enough, the enemy were believed to possess more "effective" weapons. As a Philadelphia surgeon complained in 1897, the Chitralis (Kho people) wielded a .45-caliber rifle, which "disabled or killed a man whenever they hit"—something that could not be said about the Lee-Metford.[55] Inadequate weapons dealt a severe blow to the status of British soldiers. Soldiers were taught to "distrust . . . his arms," a situation that inevitably would "diminish his prestige."[56] One commentator even lamented that "the natives expressed contempt for the bullet [Lee-Metford], saying it was not even good enough to steal."[57] How could British soldiers hold their head high when "the Pathans preferred to face European troops armed with the Lee-Metford, rather than native infantry armed with the Martini-Henry?"[58] *The Daily Mail*'s verdict was intended to be shocking: "the more expensive class of soldiers" (meaning, European ones) were "exposed to greater wear and tear" than native troops. This was

---

[51] W. Broadfoot, "The Lee-Mitford Rifle," *Blackwood's Edinburgh Magazine*, June 1898, 832; also see Henry J. Davis, "Gunshot Injuries in the Late Greco-Turkish War," 1789.

[52] Louis Anatole La Garde, *Gunshot Injuries: How They Are Inflicted, Their Complications, and Treatment* (New York: William Wood, 1914), 66.

[53] "The Doings of the Peace Conference," *Daily Mail*, June 2, 1899, 4.

[54] For a discussion, see Joanna Bourke, *The Story of Pain: From Prayer to Painkillers* (Oxford, UK: Oxford University Press, 2014).

[55] Davis, "The Effects of Small Calibre Bullets," 47–48.

[56] "The Lee-Metford Rifle," *Daily Mail*, May 31, 1898, 7; this was also cited by W. Broadfoot, "The Lee-Mitford Rifle," *Blackwood's Edinburgh Magazine*, June 1898, 832–833.

[57] "Terrors of the Dum-Dum," *Daily Mail*, July 13, 1899, 3.

[58] "The Lee-Metford Rifle," *Daily Mail*, 7.

"financially unsound."[59] In other words, "natives" were more expendable than white Europeans, yet the latter were being issued with the less powerful bullets.

Admittedly, they argued, it was not "pretty" to be cruel. But survival should trump all scruples. This was what the *Daily Mail* was alluding to on March 12, 1899, when it admitted that the dum-dum bullet was "not meant to be, and it cannot be, a humane weapon" but was nevertheless "absolutely efficacious."[60] The newspaper returned to the point three months later, asking whether the delegates at the Peace Conference "wish us to send our troops to the encounter with savage and barbarous tribes inefficiently armed?" If so, their "humanity is of a queer order."[61] In the words of another journalist in 1898, "We do not desire, nor is there any necessity to contravene even the spirit of the St. Petersburg declaration" (that is, the 1868 renunciation of explosive projectiles under 400 grams in weight), "but we do require from those responsible that the ammunition issued to our soldiers shall be serviceable, and such as to command their confidence." Of course, he continued, soldiers could simply ground down the "thick hard points of the bullets" themselves in order to increase their "stopping power." It was, however, "undesirable to allow soldiers to tamper with their ammunition"; therefore the army had a duty to supply such ammunition.[62] The author of "The Text-Book for Military Small Arms and Ammunition" (1899) was sarcastic, noting that it was "philanthropic" of authorities to say that the dum-dum bullet could be used against "savage" races but not against "white races." Whatever happened, he went on, "the enemy, whether civilised or savage, must be stopped in his charge." If the government listened to "seductive suggestions from abroad, backed by well-meaning but mischievous support at home," it would lead to devastating consequences for its soldiers in the field.[63] Because the British army was "fighting savage tribes to whom nothing short of a 'cripple stopper' is a deterrent," another commentator concluded in 1905, they could "never afford to fetter its action and sacrifice the lives of its soldiers" by adhering to international law.[64]

In the end, the international community at the 1899 Peace Conference at The Hague rejected these arguments, prohibiting (in certain circumstances) the use of bullets that "can easily expand their form inside the human body." Britain did not sign. They did, however, agree to use different bullets when fighting European

---

[59] Ibid.

[60] "For Fighting at Close Quarters," *Daily Mail*, March 13, 1900, 7.

[61] "The Doings of the Peace Conference," *Daily Mail*, 4.

[62] "The Lee-Metford Rifle," *Daily Mail*, 7; also see Atlay, "Legitimate and Illegitimate Modes of Warfare," 14.

[63] "Text-Book for Military Small Arms," *Quarterly Review*, 174–175; this was also quoted in "The Dum-Dum Bullet," *Review of Reviews* (August 1899), 179.

[64] Atlay, "Legitimate and Illegitimate Modes of Warfare," 14.

powers. In a War Office minute dated April 9, 1900, the Defence Committee decreed that the Mark II was to "be used whenever there is no risk of attack from savages," while the Mark V would be used against aggressive "savages" and "against Europeans who use an expanding bullet."[65] Time and again, British commentators reiterated their commitment to using the dum-dum bullet, but only against "fanatical" tribes.[66] The explosive bullets "were never intended to be used against white races," they insisted.[67] This argument was disingenuous, however, since implicit in their reasoning was the need for their use in *all* conflicts.

It is important to note that the delegates at the Peace Conference in 1899 shared the chauvinistic preoccupations of British commentators. In fact, they only partially banned dum-dum and soft-point bullets: the weapon was only prohibited *in wars conducted between the signatories.* Even this prohibition had its critics. More pugnacious voices could be heard asking why the ammunition should not be used more widely. "War cannot be made with rosewater," Hamilton reminded readers of the *British Medical Journal* in June 1899.[68] If dum-dums could be used against a savage foe, then why should it not be used to defeat a civilized one? It was absurd to bind ones' own hands. The idea that the British army would have to "arm our troops with a different weapon when engaged with savage races" was *"reductio ad absurdum,"* he concluded.[69]

Although these chauvinistic comments were particularly strident during the 1899 debates at The Hague, they reappeared whenever dum-dum bullets were discussed. One particular detailed exposition was attempted by Elbridge Colby, a captain in the US Army and literary scholar. At first glance, Colby was a passionate defender of international law. He argued that warring individuals and sovereign nations that failed to abide by regulations concerning the conduct of war should be severely punished. In 1925, he reminded readers that the laws of war had to be enforced in order to "insure decent morality, decent respect for persons and property, and the maintenance of modern standards of humanity and life" even in the throes of combat.[70]

However, it seems that Colby did not believe that international law was *universally* applicable. Just two years later, in the influential *American Journal of International Law*, Colby published an impassioned *defense* of combat-without-rules. For Colby, the need to insure "decent respect for persons" did not include

[65] War Office minute, initialed "G. W.," April 9, 1900, in The National Archives (London) WO 32/7059.

[66] "The Lee-Metford Rifle," *Daily Mail*, 7.

[67] Letter to the Editor from Mr. Doyle, *Daily News*, January 31, 1901, cited in Marks, "Bullets—Expansive, Explosive, and Poisoned," 626.

[68] Hamilton, "The Dum-Dum Bullet," *British Medical Journal*, 1559.

[69] Ibid.

[70] Elbridge Colby, "War Crimes," *Michigan Law Review* 23, no. 5 (March 1925), 483.

all people. It was only a requirement for *European* ones. In his article entitled "How to Fight Savage Tribes, " Colby resolutely excised "savages" from the category of "the human." When fighting "savages," he argued, European troops should have no compunction about the rules of warfare. He gave many reasons for this conclusion, including his belief that combatants and noncombatants were "practically identical" in "primitive" societies; "savage or semi-savage peoples take advantage of" European scruples to effect "ruses, surprises, and massacres"; and international law was fundamentally a "Christian doctrine" so could not be applied to pagans. He extolled readers to examine the "long list of Indian wars" in which American soldiers "defended and pushed westward the frontiers of America." In such conflicts, the "almost universal brutality of the red-skinned fighters" was indisputable. The only language "savages" understood was that of "devastation and annihilation." Anyone who promoted "excessive humanitarian ideas" or acted "overkind" to the enemy were actually being "unkind" to their "own people." In his words, "against such [an enemy] it is not only perfectly proper, it is even necessary, to take rigorous measures."

Colby admitted that it was "good to use proper discretion. It is good to observe the decencies of international law," but such niceties were wasted on uncivilized people. It was also possible to argue, Colby noted, that mass slaughter of these people was "actually humane," because it would shorten the conflict and thus prevent "the shedding of more excessive quantities of blood."[71]

Colby may sound particularly bloodthirsty, but his views were widely shared. In 1923, Professor Jesse S. Reeves of Williamstown, Massachusetts, also argued that international law was "not applicable" to uncivilized peoples and could have no influence upon them. It was "merely a body of rules and customs that have grown up among nations more or less similar for use among themselves."[72] In Britain, Colonel J. F. C. Fuller made a similar point. In his influential *The Reformation of War* (1923), Fuller stated that "uncivilized" societies were "like the organism of the lower animals"; they were "controlled by a series of nervous ganglia rather than centralized brain." As a consequence,

> in small wars against uncivilized nations, the form of warfare to be adopted must tone [*sic*] with the shade of culture existing in the land, by which I mean that against peoples possessing a low civilization, war must be more brutal in type (not necessarily in execution) than against

[71] Elbridge Colby, "How to Fight Savage Tribes," *American Journal of International Law* 21 (1927), 279–281, 284–285, 287.

[72] Professor Jesse S. Reeves of Williamstown in Massachusetts on August 2, 1923, cited in Colby, "How To Fight Savage Tribes," 280.

a highly civilized nation; consequently, physical blows are more likely to prove effective than nervous shocks.[73]

Even the official *Manual of Military Law* (1914) ruled that

> it must be emphasized that the rules of International Law Warfare apply only to the warfare between civilized nations, where both parties understand them and are prepared to carry them out. They do not apply in wars with uncivilized States and tribes, where their place is taken by the discretion of the commander and such rules of justice and humanity as recommend themselves in the particular circumstances of the case.[74]

There was one law for "us" and quite another for "them."

The furor over dum-dum bullets is important, in part because fears over their use arose in practically every conflict since 1899. Dum-dum bullets were the ultimate propaganda tool. They were symbolically potent. For example, during the Anglo-Boer war, there were widespread accusations of dastardly conduct using dum-dums. For the Field Marshall Commander in Chief of HM Forces in South Africa, the fact the Boers had breached "the recognized usages of war and of the Geneva Convention" by using expansive bullets was "a disgrace to any civilized power."[75] More emotionally, a soldier signing himself "Norm" in *The Saturday Review* in 1901 was appalled that, although both sides in the South African War had agreed that expansive ammunition was "unsuitable against civilised opponents of European descent," the Boer soldiers were using them. This made the Boers "just as much 'assassins' as the sword-duelist who murders his antagonist with a pistol." It was incredible, he lamented, that the War Office would send out "our poor fellows to fight with hard-nosed bullets against soft." It was a conflict of " 'Ten-per-Cent Killers' against 'Forty-per-Cent.' "[76] All Boer prisoners found with such bullets should "be promptly shot."[77]

Equally, British troops were also accused of using the "barbarous" weapon on fellow "white men." In mocking tones, a French journalist writing for *Journal des Débats* sneered about an England that "exports humanity, whisky, and cottons"

[73] Colonel J. F. C. Fuller, *The Reformation of War* (London: Hutchinson, 1923), 191.

[74] War Office, *Manual of Military Law* (London: HMSO, 1914), 251.

[75] Telegraph from the Field Marshall Commander in Chief, HM Forces S.A., in The National Archives (London) WO32/7873. Letter from Downing Street signed by F. Graham, to the Under Secretary of State, Foreign Office, December 16. 1899, refuted allegations that the British used dum-dum bullets in South Africa: in The National Archives (London) DO 119/382.

[76] Norm, "Boer Methods," *The Saturday Review*, December 21, 1901, 778.

[77] "Cruel Bullets," *Portsmouth Evening News*, October 5, 1900, 3.

but fails to "carry out her own humanitarian ideals." Why? Because (he sarcastically wrote) "England is very humble" and

> she does not wish to push herself forward. Do you know the genial, gentle, graceful Dum-Dum bullet? England has given the Hindus a taste of it. But their humanitarian zeal does not stop here. The excited Boers, who are white men, will also be pacified with it.

The British, "leads the world in civilization."[78]

In the absence of any major international military conflict involving the British army between 1902 and 1914, the furore over the ban on semi-jacketed bullets faded. This changed with the reintroduction of atrocious forms of warfare—including the use of poisonous gas—between 1914 and 1918. Once again, military and medical officers became aware that shifts in the technology of small arms (especially high-velocity projectiles) had changed the nature of the modern battlefield. Between the 1899 prohibition of dum-dum bullets and the start of the 1914 war, the velocity of bullets had increased from two thousand feet per second to four thousand feet per second. While the "explosive" effects of missiles were uncommon at velocities of less than two thousand feet per second, they were extremely common at muzzle velocities over twenty-five hundred feet per second.

Aghast by the extensive wounds they were seeing, officers and medical commentators on all sides began wondering whether dum-dum bullets had been reintroduced. Was it possible that dum-dum or other soft-nosed bullets were getting into the front lines? After all, such ammunition *had* been issued in training, primarily to reduce the likelihood of ricochet in some training camps.[79]

As early as October 1914, the British War Office issued a memorandum about British and German service ammunition, in which they claimed that the British service ammunition—the Mark VII, .030 ammunition, which was a pointed bullet—was very similar to that officially used by the Germans. They did state, however, that German troops in Togoland (a German protectorate in West Africa) and France had been using bullets with a "soft core and hard

[78] *Journal des Débats*, quoted in "Satirising England," *Daily Mail*, September 8, 1899, 4. There were also protests in November 1900 when forty soldiers in the 2nd Cheshire regiment were found with dum-dum bullets when policing a strike of quarrymen in Penrhyn: see "The Strike at Penrhyn," *Manchester Courier and Lancashire General Advertiser*, November 8, 1900, 5; "Dum-Dums for Rioters," *Daily Mail*, November 17, 1900, 3; *Morning Post*, November 17, 1900, 4; *Manchester Courier and Lancashire General Advertiser*, November 10, 1900, 15.

[79] Letter from M. de C. Findlay to the Right Hon. Sir Edward Gray, October 19, 1914, in The National Archives (London) WO 32/5085.

thin envelope, not entirely covering the core." They noted that the semi-official German journal *Lokal-Anzeiger* alleged that "flat-nosed revolver ammunition" had been found in the possession of some British POWs. This "can only refer to the Marks IV and V" revolver ammunition, the memo declared, and, contrary to the accusation that such bullets "can have no other purpose than to cause the most horrible wounds possible," it could be

> proved conclusively on irrefutable evidence that these bullets are as humane as any bullet can be.

These bullets did not have a "hard envelope" and a "soft core" and they could not be described as "soft-nosed." The bullet was "as humane as the ordinary conical bullet"; it "does not expand or flatten easily in the human body," and is not "calculated to cause unnecessary suffering." Indeed, the memo continued, they believed the only reason why the Germans were making these accusations was to justify the fact that they were issuing irregular projectiles to German troops.[80]

The "irrefutable evidence" they were referring to had been submitted by Sir Victor Horsley, in a memo he presented to the War Office in September 1914. Horsley noted that *any* projectile would have "explosive effects" if fired at close range. Such effects would also occur if the residual velocity exceeded fifteen hundred feet per second and the bullet passed through "a closed bony cavity," such as a person's skull or bone. The "disruptive effect" was due to the speed with which the bullet was traveling, rather than with "the occasional turning over of the projectile." He concluded that the British Service Rifle bullet, the Mark VII, was "probably the most humane projectile yet devised."[81]

Despite such proclamations, the Germans accused the British and Americans of violating the prohibition;[82] British and American spokesmen counter-accused

---

[80] "Memorandum Communicated by the War Office Respecting British and German Service Ammunition," October 7, 1914, 1–2, in The National Archives (London) WO 32/5187.

[81] Sir Victor Horsley, "Appendix I. Memorandum on the .303 (174 grains) Mark VII British Service Rifle Bullet in Reference to Explosive Effects," c.1914, 3, in The National Archives (London) WO 32/5187; for the original report, see Victor Horsley, "Memorandum on the .303 (174 Grain) Mark VII British Service Rifle Bullet in Reference to Explosive Effects," September 13, 1914, 3, in The National Archives (London) WO 32/5085; note that this quotation from Horsley was cited in "British and German Small Arm Ammunition," *British Medical Journal* (November 21, 1914), 893; also see Victor Horsley, "Note on the Flat-Nose Revolver Bullet, Mark VII, In Reference to the Provisions of the Hague Convention," September 15, 1914, 3, in The National Archives (London) WO 32/5085.

[82] "The Use and Action of Dum-Dum Bullets, translated from the Muenchener medizinische Wochenschrift from Jan 5th 1915," in The National Archives (London) WO 32/5085; letter from Frederic D. Harford to the Right Hon. Sir Edward Gray, November 23, 1914, in The National Archives (London) WO 32/5085; handwritten letter from J. Linton Shove Coft to the Secretary of

the Germans.[83] British officials argued that the spirit of the Hague Convention was being breached by inverting bullets[84] or designing them so that "centre of mass is far back," which meant that "on striking any tissue, soft or hard, it at once turns over and passes through backwards . . . mushrooming as it advances."[85] They speculated that German soldiers had been "methodically" converting bullets into dum-dums. They might even have been "furnished with a special tool for enabling this manipulation of the bullet to be performed quickly."[86] After all, British commentators noted, the bullets had been cut in ways that suggested considerable forethought and skill, not the "rough adaptation made in the trenches, by candle-light, by soldiers worn out with their long and dreary waiting."[87] As Ralph Glyn warned in "Austrian Explosive Small Arm Ammunition" (c.1915), it was "fairly common" to see the "whole of a man's back being blown out while the entrance of the bullet" was "of the normal size."[88] So feared were the "appalling wounds" caused by these bullets that Brigadier General George Macdonagh was advised that any German found reversing Mauser bullets should be executed immediately. This would "discourage the use of the reversed bullet."[89]

In the German press, the capture of two British officers—Colonel W. E. Gordon (V.C.) and Lieutenant-Colonel F. H. Neish, both of the Gordon Highlanders—caused an international, diplomatic incident after it was revealed

State for War, November 1, 1914, in The National Archives (London) WO 32/5085; "German Views on British Bullets," *British Medical Journal* 1, no. 2841 (June 12, 1915), 1023–1024; "The Second German Surgical War Congress," *British Medical Journal* 1, no. 2895 (June 24, 1916), 895; "Wounded in War," *Arms and the Man* 57, no. 2 (October 8, 1914), 24; "The Dum-Dum Charges," *British Medical Journal* (December 13, 1919), 792.

[83] For example, see "A British Surgeon in Belgium," *British Medical Journal* 1, no. 2829 (March 20, 1915), 504–505; "German Experience of Bullet Wounds," *British Medical Journal* 2, no. 2810 (November 7, 1914), 801; J. Hartnell Beavis and H. S. Souttar, "A Field Hospital in Belgium," *British Medical Journal* 1, no. 2819 (January 9, 1916), 64–66; "Dum-Dums Still Doubtful," *Arms and the Man* 57, no. 11 (December 10, 1914), 208.

[84] See Letter from W. Langley, the Secretary to the Army Council, March 18, 1915, in The National Archives (London) WO 32/5085; and H. E. Munroe, "Remarks on the Character and Treatment of Wounds in War," *Canadian Medical Journal* (1915), 963.

[85] Beavis and Souttar, "A Field Hospital in Belgium," 64–65; this was repeated in "A British Surgeon in Belgium," *British Medical Journal* (March 20, 1915), 504; and "An Epitome of Current Medical Literature," *British Medical Journal* (August 28, 1915), 17.

[86] Letter from Langley, March 18, 1915, The National Archives.

[87] M. Mayer de Stadelhofen, "Explosive and Dum-Dum Bullets" (London: Harrison and Sons, 1915), pamphlet republished from *Revue Militaire Suisse*, 5.

[88] Ralph Glyn, "Austrian Explosive Small Arm Ammunition" (c. April 1915), in The National Archives (London) WO32/5555.

[89] Memo signed by Captain Lefannerthorpe [sp?] to Brigadier General George Macdonagh, C.B., "Experiments with Reversed German Mauser Bullets," November 11, 1915, in The National Archives (London) WO 32/ 5085.

that they had signed affidavits admitting that they had been issued with soft-nosed bullets.[90] The Kaiser himself intervened, protesting that German officers had found thousands of dum-dum bullets. He wrote to President Wilson, as a representative of a (then) neutral country, complaining that

> you know what awful wounds and pain these bullets cause and that their use is strongly prohibited by the recognised principles of international rights. I, therefore, address you a solemn protest against this mode of waging war which, thanks to the methods of our opponents, has become one of the most barbarous known to history.

The Kaiser went even further, accusing the Belgium government of encouraging civilians to engage in guerrilla warfare, thus forcing his generals to

> take the strongest measures to punish the guilty, and to deter the blood-thirsty population from their murderous and infamous action. Some villages and even the old town of Louvain, with the exception of the beautiful Town Hall, had to be demolished in self defense and in order to protect my troops.

Rather disingenuously taking a line of "self-defence," he claimed that his

> heart bleeds, when I see, [*sic*] that such measures have become unavoidable, and when I think of the numberless unguilty people, who have lost their home and property on account of the barbarous conduct of those criminals.

He threatened to "repay like for like" and, when such ammunition was found to treat those possessing it "as bandits." For such "criminals,"

> there is nothing left but the gallows, and people who equip their soldiers with such weapons, which are only used against dangerous brutes, shall spare us for all times from their chatter . . . about culture, Christianity, and humanity.[91]

German surgeons joined in the accusations. They accused the British forces of "malignity," claiming that British soldiers had "a contrivance, fitted to the

---

[90] For a detailed discussion, see The National Archives (London) WO 32/4904.

[91] Telegram from the Kaiser to President Wilson, reprinted in a special edition of the *Leipziger Neueste Nachrichten*, September 12, 1914, in The National Archives (London) WO 32/4904.

butt of the rifle, enabling the soldier in the field to convert the service bullet into a soft-nosed dum-dum by amputation of its point."[92] Other "diabolical contrivances" allegedly used by the British included "an instrument like a cigar cutter, which shears off the tip of the bullet."[93] Even after it had been shown that the attachment that the Germans said was being used for "nipping off the point of the bullet" (called "nippers") was nothing more than a bracket for a telescopic sight, the Germans persisted in making the accusation as a way of appealing to the "civilized world against the barbarous methods of the Allies."[94]

These accusations led British commentators to fret about the effects of the German's "vigorous campaign" on the grounds that it was inciting hatred against the British in Germany, making peace even less likely. They claimed that one result of this "libellous campaign" was "the fomentation in the German mind of anger as great, though not as just, as that which is felt in this country in regard to poisonous gasses."[95]

It took the veteran Surgeon-General William Flack Stevenson (who in 1899 had defended using dum-dum bullets against "savages") to attempt to set the record straight. Writing in the *British Medical Journal*, Stevenson exclaimed that

> history again repeats itself! and surgeons at the front, and especially young civilian surgeons inexperienced in bullet wounds, on both sides, are accusing their enemies in this war of using "Dum-Dum" and explosive small-arm bullets.

He reminded British surgeons that the fact that bullets would break into fragments inside human bodies was no proof that they were dum-dums. Even the ordinary service bullet was "capable of causing more severe wounds in the limbs when they traverse compact bone at high rates of velocity." It "sometimes parts with its envelope, which may be torn into jagged and twisted strips of metal, while the leaden core is broken into slug-like pieces, with the result that the destructive effect on the soft parts of the limb is greatly increased."[96] Similarly, neither the British nor the Germans were using "explosive" bullets for the simple

[92] "German Views on British Bullets," *British Medical Journal* 1, no. 2841 (June 12, 1915), 1023–1024.

[93] Ibid., 1023–1024.

[94] "The Dum-Dum Charges," *British Medical Journal* (December 13, 1919), 792.

[95] "German Experiences of War Surgery," *British Medical Journal* 2, no. 2852 (August 28, 1915), 339.

[96] Surgeon-General William Flack Stevenson, "Note on the Use of 'Dum-Dum' and Explosive Bullets in War," *British Medical Journal* (October 24, 1914), 701.

reason that "it would be of no advantage to them, for solid small-bore bullets do all they desire of them"—in other words, cause horrific wounds.[97]

Stevenson wasn't alone in explaining to surgeons, politicians, and officers the effect of modern weaponry on human bodies. Time and again, military surgeons and other authorities reminded readers that there was no need to appeal to demonic "dum-dums" since ordinary bullets had a terrifying capacity to cause appalling wounds. For instance, on September 15, 1914, Major-General William Grant Macpherson of the Army Medical Service agreed with the Secretary of State that it would be possible to ask Medical Officers to "report all cases of wounds, which appear to have been caused by dum-dum bullets" but reminded him that even the "'humane' hard mantle, small calibre, high velocity bullet" possessed "extraordinary explosive wounding effects at short ranges." As a result, it was "practically impossible" to know whether a terrible wound had been due to "a man being hit by such a bullet at short range or by a dum-dum at any range."[98] On September 16, 1914, The *Times* even printed a letter to the editor from Frederick Courtney Selous (a celebrity hunter, imperial explorer, and military officer of the time) claiming that the accusations circulating about the use of dum-dum bullets were unfounded. He wrote,

> The serious, ragged wounds, supposed to have been caused by bullets which have been purposely tampered with have more likely been due to the fact, which I believe is not generally known, that the new pointed bullet—itself a German invention—now for the first time employed in warfare in Western Europe, inflicts at short ranges more grievous wounds than any form of soft-nosed expanding bullet.

He explained that when Theodore Roosevelt had gone game hunting with him in British East Africa in 1910, he also used the "solid, nickel-covered, pointed bullet" for all game except the heaviest. The bullet "never broke up on striking an animal" but they "inflicted more serious wounds than any kind of expanding bullet he had ever previously used for big game shooting." Selous's own experience shooting in Africa confirmed what Roosevelt told him—that is, "although the hole of entry is always small, round, and clean-cut, the skin is often torn open where they pass out on the other side." He predicted that "such accusations will be made on one side and the other in all future wars whenever the shooting is at fairly close quarters as long as pointed bullets

---

[97] Ibid., 701–702.
[98] Major-General William Grant Macpherson to the Secretary of State, September 19, 1914, The National Archives (London) WO 32/4904.

are used."[99] A man signing himself "Ballistica" in *Arms and the Man* in 1915, made this point to a wider audience. To explain the terrible wounds inflicted in modern warfare, there was no need to fear that dum-dum bullets had returned to the battlefield: after all, the wounds inflicted were merely "in the very nature of the modern high-velocity sharp-nosed" bullet.[100]

Similar observations were reportedly being made by German commentators. For instance, in January 1915, an article in *Muenchener Medizinnnnische Wochenshrift* included a report by Herr Braun on his examination of thousands of wounds caused by English bullets. Although some military surgeons disagreed with him, Braun noted that the dreadful wounds they were seeing were due to nothing more than ordinary "infantry ammunition," coupled with the "prox-imity of the trenches" and the fact that bullets frequently become "deformed" by "ricocheting off the ground." The *"Dum-Dum bullets of the English are mainly a product of fantasy,"* he emphasized.[101]

Although scares associated with the return of "dum-dum" ammunition were regularly dismissed by military surgeons and other authorities, anxieties about modern small-arms weaponry remained tied to this formidable concept: the dum-dum. It "stood in" for every kind of bullet. Ironically, modern armies no longer needed *actual* soft point bullets because *all* types had a similar effect when piercing human or animal flesh.

Before concluding, I want to include a brief coda about dum-dum bullets in the late-twentieth and early twenty-first centuries. From the 1970s, arguments in favor of using dum-dum or soft-nosed bullets have returned, particularly in the context of law enforcement, counter-terrorism, and non-conventional warfare. Arguments in their favor echo those made in the late 1890s and early 1900s.

Pragmatic, technological justifications for such armaments have been dom-inant, especially the argument that armies possess much worse weapons than semi-jacketed missiles and, therefore, prohibitions are disproportionate. As Irvin K. Owen, former special agent for the FBI, observed in 1974:

No one has paid much attention to the dum-dum ammunition issue in recent years when the use of claymore mines, fragmentation grenades,

[99] Letter to the editor of *The Times* from Frederick Courtney Selous, September 16, 1914, in The National Archives (London) WO 32/4904. He was killed in action in 1917. Selous inspired H. Rider Haggard to create the fictional character Allan Quatermain.

[100] Ballistica, "Questionable Bullets in Warfare," *Arms and the Man* 57, no. 19 (August 5, 1915), 374.

[101] Translation of "Report of an Evening Medical War Meeting in Lille on December 16th, 1914," *Muenchener Medizinnnnische Wochenshrift*, January 12, 1915, in The National Archives (London) WO 32/5085. It is unclear whether the underlining was in the original German or only the translation.

anti-personnel bombs, flame-throwers, and many other far more devastating warfare weapons than expanding bullets have been in common use.[102]

The second argument is historicist, claiming that contextual specificities of the original prohibitions had to be taken into account. After all, the 1899 and 1907 Hague prohibitions also prohibited the use of submarines and firing munitions from balloons. As Owen scoffed, these prohibitions were "a shallow justification for dismantling our air and submarine forces on whose might the safety of the free world has relied since World War Two."[103]

Third, was there ever a "humane" way to kill? As in the debates in 1899 and the early 1900s, these commentators argued that "greater suffering" was caused by "hitting" a foe repeatedly with standard ammunition than "striking him with a single bullet which does stop him."[104] Wounding a person *necessarily* causes suffering. As in the debates about the use of dum-dum bullets in wartime, proponents of soft-point bullets in civilian contexts sought to demonstrate that they did not cause *unnecessary* suffering. There was "no humane way of shooting an individual without causing pain and suffering."[105]

The fourth argument appealed to the need of law enforcement agents to self-protection. "As long as criminals have ready access to firearms," Collins explained, "police must be properly armed and trained."[106] As police officials in Washington, DC, noted when announcing the shift to hollow-point bullets, these not only had greater "stopping power" (meaning that they were "more likely to halt a criminal in his tracks and prevent him from firing back at a police officer"), but they were also less likely to ricochet and "less apt to pass through their intended victim's body and hit another person."[107] In the words of the Governor of Connecticut when defending suppling police with the new .357 Magnum pistol and hollow-nosed ammunition, it was pointless using "lollipops on gunmen."[108] In defending themselves against protests by groups such as the American Civil Liberties Union and other community groups, they responded

[102] Irvin K. Owen, "What about Dumdums?," *FBI Law Enforcement Bulletin* 44, no. 4, April 1975, 5; also see Charles G. Wilber, *Ballistic Science for the Law Enforcement Officer* (Springfield, IL.: Charles C. Thomas, 1977), 170.

[103] Owen, "What about Dumdums?," 5.

[104] Wilber, *Ballistic Science for the Law Enforcement Officer*, 177.

[105] Owen, "What about Dumdums?," 6.

[106] Ibid.

[107] Stephen J. Lynton and Alfred E. Lewis, "City Will Change Bullets for Police to Hollow-Points," *Washington Post*, November 27, 1976, B2.

[108] Cited in Dermot Purgavie, "Outlawed—But the Cops are Using Dum-Dum," *Daily Mail*, September 27, 1974, 2.

by instigating a public relations campaign designed to show that "hollow-points" were not "dum-dum" bullets.[109] The symbolic labor performed by the designation "dum-dum" was as powerful as ever.

The fifth defense evoked the need to maintain high officer morale. As one ballistic expert admitted, "using a dum-dum bullet makes cops think they have an edge. . . . It's now becoming a trendy thing, like owning a Porsche."[110] The debate became enmeshed with highly sensitive issues about the reform of the police force. For instance, the police chief in one unnamed Midwestern city chose to issue hollow-point bullets to law enforcement officers at least in part because it would "demonstrate his support for the rank and file" who were becoming increasingly concerned about changes in promotion policy and affirmative action initiatives among ethnic minorities. The city's mayor shared this police-chief's concerns. He also did not want to be seen to oppose the new ammunition (despite community disapproval of the ammunition after a robbery suspect was killed), because banning the hollow-point would "earn him the animosity of many police officers" and jeopardize plans to reform the force. In other words, "if the police do not win on this issue, a general demoralization will ensue which will result in increased opposition" to affirmative action programs.[111]

Finally, the debates were complicated by the changing nature of military conflict. As the armed forces were increasingly being called upon to deal with domestic riot control and law enforcement in "failed states," why should they be barred from using semi-jacketed bullets while policemen were authorized for their use? In "three block wars" (that is, wars in which soldiers were expected to fight insurgents, control riots, and spread peace within a three-block radius) were they allowed to use semi-jacketed bullets? In 2001, in his keynote address to the Third International Workshop on Wound Ballistics, Christopher Greenwood argued that in street warfare and in counter terrorists operations, it was wrong to

> regard suffering as unnecessary if it is inflicted for the purpose of protecting the civilian population. In other words, if the civilian population's protection is enhanced by the use of a particular weapon,

[109] Lynton and Lewis, "City Will Change Bullets for Police to Hollow-Points," B2; and Stephen J. Lynton and Alfred E. Lewis, "More Powerful Bullets Studied by DC Police," *Washington Post*, November 5, 1976, A1.

[110] Cited in Purgavie, "Outlawed," 2.

[111] James B. Brady, "The Justifiability of Hollow-Point Bullets," *Criminal Justice and Ethics* 9 (Summer/Fall 1983), 10–12.

then the adverse effects of that weapon on combatants cannot properly be regarded as unnecessary.[112]

In other words, in protecting civilian lives, using expanding bullets is legitimate.

Alfons Vanheusden, W. Hays Parks, and William H. Boothby discussed this in greater detail in their "The Use of Expanding Bullets in Military Operations: Examining the Kampala Consensus" (2011). Their intervention was provoked by the decision at the first Review Conference of the International Criminal Court, held in Kampala (Uganda) in June 2010. According to Resolution 10, it was agreed that employing bullets that expand or flatten easily in the human body (as well as using poison or poisoned weapons, and employing asphyxiating, poisonous, or other gases) were war crimes within the jurisdiction of the Court where such acts were committed in armed conflicts not of an international character. They decreed that using such bullets were a war crime "only if the perpetrator employs the bullets to uselessly aggravate suffering or the wounding effect upon the target of such bullets." For Vanheusden, Parks, and Boothby, the phrase "uselessly aggravates suffering or the wounding effect" was a "let out" clause. In their words, "one cannot regard the use of an expanding bullet in armed conflict as uselessly aggravating suffering or the wounding effect if this use enhances the protection of civilians." In other words, the "intent of the perpetrator" was important. If there was "a legitimate military utility attached to the additional injury or suffering . . . then the offence will not have been committed."[113]

This was also the point Kenneth Watkins was making in "Chemical Agents and 'Expanding' Bullets" (2006). He was interested in reigniting debate about the legitimacy (or otherwise) of using hollow-point ammunition and poisonous gas in the contexts of domestic riot control and "three block wars." Although he refused to categorically state that prohibitions of certain weapons ought to be removed, he warned that the "underlying rationale for these prohibitions, created more than half a century ago" needed to be critically analyzed. "Given the continuing complexity of 21st-century conflict," he pointed out, "the need to be flexible and to search out humane approaches to applying force, remains an important goal." Terrorism presented people with a "new challenge to the rule of law," forcing analysts to reinterrogate prohibitions of the use of chemical

---

[112] Christopher Greenwood, cited in Alfons Vanheusden, W. Hays Parks, and William H. Boothby, "The Use of Expanding Bullets in Military Operations: Examining the Kampala Consensus," *Military Law and the Law of War Review* 50, nos. 3‑4 (2011), 545; also see William H. Boothby, "Differences in the Law of Weaponry When Applied to Non-International Armed Conflicts," *International Law Studies* 88 (2012), 198–205.

[113] Vanheusden, Parks, and Boothby, "The Use of Expanding Bullets," 536, 540–545.

agents and explosive bullets "in order to ensure the protection for uninvolved civilians and other non-combatants is not unduly handcuffed by rules designed for large scale inter-state conflict."[114] It was a carefully-worded statement, but the presumption is the need for a relaxation, if not overturning, of the prohibition. Implicit in such arguments is that the "new challenge to the rule of law" comes not only from the terrorist but also from international law experts like himself.

To conclude: When the governmental representatives at The Hague in 1899 voted to prohibit the use of bullets that "can easily expand their form inside the human body," they had dum-dums and other semi-jacketed missiles in mind. Dum-dums were destructive because they transferred a greater amount of energy from the projectile to the tissues of the body. This results in wounds that were "explosive" in their effect on human tissue. Of course, similarly massive wounds could also be caused by increasing the velocity of the missile or making the bullet unstable in other ways. The furore over dum-dum bullets was linked to long-term anxieties about the increased wounding potency of small arms more generally at the *fin de siècle*. By reducing the diameter of bullets and charging them with greater explosive force, bullets were being produced that were able to travel at a much greater velocity. Since wounds are caused when kinetic energy is transferred from projectiles to bodily tissues, it follows that the seriousness of the injury soars with any increase in the transfer of energy. Velocity, as well as the nature of the bullet's jacket, its mass, and its stability in flight is crucial in producing wounds of greater or lesser severity. As a ballistic expert explained in 1898, the new bullets were "now encased in a hard mantle of nickel or nickel steel to prevent their losing their shape in passing through the rapid twists of the rifling of the barrel at their present high velocity." This meant that they had enormous penetrative capacity (they can "traverse three men or more in a row") and could kill at a range of up to two miles.[115] Reading the 1899 prohibition solely in terms of dum-dums allowed governments and militaries to continue inventing projectiles that adhered to the letter but not the spirit of the original proponents of the ban.

The precise construction of the bullets themselves, however, was less important than their symbolic life. This is why the nomenclature was so fluid: commentators had no hesitation in talking about hollow pointed, soft-nosed, expansive, explosive, or semi-jacketed bullets—all of which could be

---

[114] Kenneth Watkins, "Chemical Agents and 'Expanding' Bullets: Limited Law Enforcement Exceptions or Unwarranted Handcuffs?," *International Law Studies, US Naval War College* 82 (2006), 209–210.

[115] Ogston, "The Wounds Produced by Modern Small-Bore Bullets," 814.

"dum-dums." They were also routinely spoken about as agents. Although these bullets possessed no significant power outside of the gun (including barrels, armor systems, sights, muzzle attachments, systems technologies, and so on), and their "efficacy" as wounding agents was highly dependent on the effects of wind, velocity, gravity, and drag, nevertheless, they were conceived of as independent actors. This was also the case in the way they were represented socially. Although their status in international law was situated within debates about the military and imperial projects (including explicit ideological formulations about the "chain of being"), they were curiously abstracted from wider, political relations. Dum-dums were, in short, the legendary fetishized object.

6

The Death of the Unarmed Assailant

On Racial Fears, Ambiguous Movement,
and the Vulnerability of Armed Police

FRANKLIN E. ZIMRING

The shooting death of Michael Brown by Officer Darren Wilson in Ferguson, Missouri, in August of 2014 provoked not only a sustained protest in Ferguson but became a starting point for a national concern about police use of lethal force in cities and towns across the American nation. The place and the victim—Ferguson and Michael Brown—are now associated with a mass of civilian deaths, more than a thousand a year, and a great variety of different circumstances that provoke police shootings. In that important respect, the shooting in Ferguson now has a more general symbolic stature than the particular facts of the case.

But the particular facts of the Michael Brown shooting are also an important puzzle that may teach lessons about how and why police kill three citizens a day every day in the United States, why young men with dark skin die much more often than other citizens, and why clear administrative rules from police administrators are a more important and more promising method of reducing police killings than criminal prosecution.

The paradox at the heart of the killing of Michael Brown is this: For the generation since *Tennessee v. Garner* was decided by the US Supreme Court in 1985, the only justification for police use of deadly force is to prevent death or serious bodily injury. Making an arrest or stopping a fleeing felon is not a sufficient justification for lethal force. The prosecution in Ferguson found that the officer who fired the shots that killed Michael Brown had a subjective belief that Mr. Brown posed a threat to the officer's safety, which insulated the officer from criminal liability.

But Michael Brown was not carrying any weapon on his person during that fatal confrontation nor did Officer Wilson think Mr. Brown had either a gun or a knife. What, then, was the basis for the officer's fear? What made Mr. Brown a deadly threat in Officer Wilson's mind was the possibility that Michael Brown might seize Officer Wilson's gun and use it against him. No such intention was threatened verbally—it was the officer's interpretation of his adversary's physical movements that generated a fear of death or great bodily harm.

The foundation of Officer Wilson's worry is an inherent vulnerability of armed police officers in conflict. Half a million police carry guns into the community settings they patrol. As we shall see, more than forty thousand police a year are assaulted by unarmed civilians each year and about twelve thousand each year are reported by their departments as injured by the assault.[1] In an uncounted number of other cases, citizens make movements or statements that police officers regard as threatening. A very small proportion of these cases where the victim is not armed, ninety-four in 2015, result in a fatal shooting of the civilian by a police officer. Why? What can we do to reduce this death toll?

It has been reported that in 10% of all officer occupational homicides, the officer was killed with his own or another officer's gun.[2] There is no breakdown of whether it is the officer's gun or another officer's gun, or, if it is the officer's gun, whether it was self-inflicted. So there is some reality to the possibility that an unarmed assailant might seize a police officer's gun and use it in a life-threatening attack but no clear indication of the statistical risk of the lethal use of the weapon by an adversary.

But the specific and limited nature of the kind of danger from unarmed adversaries makes much that happened in Ferguson into an obvious case of excessive force. Firing multiple shots with a weapon that is now securely in the officer's possession is clearly not necessary to rescue the police officer from the danger of losing his weapon and being injured with it. Shooting at a person who is running away both from the police officer *and from the gun* cannot be necessary to save anyone from the assailant's use of that gun. Also, no matter what the usual rules about the duty to retreat, when the only life-threatening threat that an officer perceives is his own weapon, removing that weapon from the assailant's proximity is a complete removal of the danger and obviously a better result than using lethal force. When any retreat effectively terminates the danger to innocent lives, the officer should be under a duty to pursue it.

So the calculus of law officer justification when dealing with unarmed combatants should be much more restricted than the rules of engagement when the civilian combatants are armed with deadly weapons of their own. We need to create much more careful and more specific principles governing how police

---

[1] Franklin Zimring, *When Police Kill* (Cambridge, MA: Harvard University Press, 2017), 92–93.
[2] David I. Swedler et al., "Occupational Homicide of Law Enforcement Officers in the US, 1996–2010," *Injury Prevention* 20 (2014): 35–40.

Table 6.1 **Comparing the Concentration of African American Victims in Unarmed Victim versus All Other Cases,** *Washington Post,* **2015 Killings**

	Unarmed Victims	*All Other Victims*
African American	40.4%	24.5%
All Other Identities	59.6%	75.5%
	100%	100%
	(94)	(897)

officers can use deadly force to protect against the dangers that only their own weapons impose.

The demographic profile of the events that killed Michael Brown in Ferguson, Missouri, are typical for killings by police of unarmed adversaries and rather different from the distribution of victims who the police describe as armed with guns or other weapons. Young Michael Brown was tall, heavy, and African American, six foot four, and 292 pounds. The *Washington Post* collected crowdsourced data on all fatal shootings by the police during 2015 and reported that 26% of the almost one thousand fatality victims were African American. The *Post* also reported that about 40% of the ninety-four unarmed victims killed by police in 2015 were African American. The 26% concentration of African American victims is about twice the proportion of African Americans in the US population, so there is a significantly higher risk for African Americans for all killings by police. But the 40% estimate for unarmed African Americans is almost twice again the risk for this special category. Table 6.1 tells the statistical story.[3]

What Table 6.1 establishes is that while all sorts of confrontations between police and civilians kill African Americans at a rate twice as high as of other citizens, there is an even greater concentration of death risk for African American subjects when police kill an unarmed civilian. The 40.4% of unarmed civilian deaths is substantially more than three times the percentage of African Americans in the US population. And a statistical analysis of the difference between the 24.5% African American share of deaths when both the officer and civilian are armed and the 40.4% African American share of unarmed victim deaths shows the additional risk to African Americans in the unarmed cases is unlikely to be a random fluctuation from the 24.5% general African American death risk. The

---

[3] Table 6.1 source: Wesley Lowery, *Washington Post,* email to Franklin Zimring, December 23, 2016.

chi-square value for the distribution in Table 6.1 is 11.109, with a P value of 0.00083, indicating that the differential death rates for African Americans in the two groups of killings would happen by chance fewer than one time in one thousand trials.

This special vulnerability of African Americans to killing by police when they are *unarmed* seems relevant to one argument urged by skeptics of the "Black Lives Matter" protests that blame police for high race-specific death rates. The counterargument often made is that the reason for higher than population share risks for African Americans is that they are a greater danger to police. The only data suggested for this are the high rates of arrests for African Americans, although arrests for crime are not the major circumstance that creates killings of police or by police.[4] But finding that the largest differential risk of being killed relative to whites and others is when African Americans are unarmed is a major embarrassment to this "Blacks Are Dangerous" worldview. Why would the unarmed black man be four times as life-threatening to police as the unarmed white?

The analysis in this chapter concerns two linked questions. The first is why black men in particular are at special risk of being killed by police when they are not armed. The second question is what are the most effective and appropriate countermeasures that governments can employ to reduce the death toll from these troublesome cases.

I. Why the Super-Concentration of African American Victims?

The most likely explanation for why African Americans become 40% of the deaths of unarmed citizens from shootings by the police must start by putting the ninety-four fatal events involving unarmed civilians in a broader statistical perspective. Figure 6.1 compares the volume of unarmed adversaries killed in 2015 against the statistical categories which provide some count of the potential cases of unarmed assailants where police might feel threatened.[5]

Police departments report an average of forty thousand attacks using "personal force" by civilian against police officers each year. Even if this universe of assaults against police accounted for all of the killings of unarmed attackers, the ninety-four deaths would be fewer than one of every four hundred assaults

---

[4] Zimring, *When Police Kill,* chaps. 3 and 5.

[5] Figure 6.1 sources: Zimring, *When Police Kill,* 92–94 (personal force assaults and reported officer injuries), *Washington Post,* Database of Police Shootings (2015) (fatal shootings by police of unarmed civilians), https://www.washingtonpost.com/graphics/national/police-shootings/.

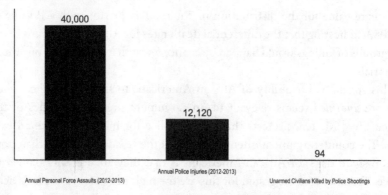

Figure 6.1. Assaults against police officers by persons who were not armed.

against an officer and less than one in every one hundred assaults that are reported to injure police. What this shows is that only a tiny fraction of personal force attacks against officers provoke a lethal response from the officer.

In fact, there are a wide variety of settings where police officers use lethal force when the provocation from the target fell far short of an attack against the officer. The media accounts of 2015 homicides by police we analyzed included over 14% of all killings where the suspect made a "sudden suspicious movement" (6%), "was combative with police" (4.9%), or ran away (3.4%).[6] What these non-assault provocations suggest is that the volume of incidents that produce the ninety-four killings of unarmed civilians in 2015 are probably closer to twice the number of reported assaults by personal force, so that the volume of potentially threatening incidents each year that produce ninety-four killings by police could well be eighty thousand unarmed provocations each year and the ratio of deadly responses to unarmed provocations could be smaller than once in each eight hundred cases.

There are three important lessons to be learned from just these aggregate statistics. The first statistical lesson is that the proportion of unarmed citizen interactions that lead to fatal shootings by police is tiny. The vast majority of hostile interactions with unarmed civilians do not provoke police to fire their weapons or fear for their lives. Even though hundreds of thousands of police officers are armed with weapons that might be used against them, this does not provoke the officer's use of deadly force in at least 99.8% of all cases.

One reason why most officers are not frightened by unarmed adversaries is that the risk to the officer's life is very small. In a typical year either no police or one officer nationwide is killed by personal force or blunt instruments. Only the officer's gun puts the officer at risk, and we don't know whether the

[6] Ibid., Table 3.8, 62.

appropriated weapon of a police officer produced any killings of officers in recent years. Further, there are a number of precautions that police can take to reduce the vulnerability of their weapons to expropriation and hostile use. So the first implication of the large gap between the volume of potential provocations and the number of lethal responses is that most police do not regard these recurrent incidents as life-threatening.

Yet the aggregate death toll from shooting unarmed adversaries in the United States is anything but tiny. The ninety-four deaths in 2015 from unarmed citizens being shot is at 2.9 per 10 million population, an annual risk three times as high as the average of *all* civilian killings by police in Germany[7] and more than ten times the annual death rate per 10 million from all shootings by police in England and Wales.[8] While shooting the unarmed is a small percentage of US killings by police and probably doesn't represent best practices by well-managed police forces, it is still a major public health cost of policing in the United States.

The third statistical lesson from determining that shootings of the unarmed are a police reaction in only a tiny fraction of the incidents that police officers confront is to warn observers that this very small segment of assaults or other hostile interactions are probably unrepresentative of the circumstances and personnel that account for most other cases. The one officer in 800 provocations who shoots and kills the unarmed sets himself apart from the other 799. This is a statistical warning to observers that they cannot use the behaviors in this small and unrepresentative sample of police conduct as a profile of what most police feel and do. Shooting unarmed civilians may not quite be deviant behavior for American police, but it is not representative behavior either.

Is this large overkill in the ninety-four unarmed victim cases conclusive evidence that most American police officers and most American police departments are racially biased? The answer is negative, and the reason why the pattern of racial bias cannot be attributed to all or most police is the highly unrepresentative character of the lethal force responses. Those who shoot may well be racially biased, but they are in no sense typical police. What is clear from the huge over-representation of deaths for unarmed people with dark skins is that one major risk factor for shooting unarmed adversaries is racial fears, and therefore screening to eliminate officers with pronounced *racial fears* can be justified as a public health necessity.

What are the distinguishing characteristics of these cases? The officer's feeling threatened, for one thing. These officers are more prone to interpret physical movements toward an officer or another person as threatening death or great

---

[7] Ibid., Figure 4.3, 78.
[8] Ibid., Table 4.2, 82.

bodily injury if the adversary is black. Even if the adversary has no weapon, if the officer thinks his or her weapon might be vulnerable, that is a fear of great bodily harm. Are more police officers likely to be afraid of men with dark complexions? The answer here is obviously yes since 40% of the unarmed people they kill are African American.

One further circumstance which provokes police to kill unarmed persons is when the officer is alone rather than with a partner or a group of police. In the sample of 551 deaths we analyzed, when police were alone, a full 37% of all cases where they killed involved unarmed adversaries, the proportion of unarmed citizen deaths was at least nine times greater than when more than one officer is present.[9] This is quite consistent with the thesis that the officer's subjective fears are a powerful influence on when, in the eighty thousand or so confrontations between unarmed citizens and armed police, the police end up using deadly force. And the almost fourfold increase in death risk when these subjective fears fall on African American targets does not appear to be based on any fault on the part of the victim. This is as close to a pure case of racial discrimination as any aspect of police use of deadly force in American life. But the moving parts in the minds and hearts of most of the police officers who produce this pattern of deadly discriminatory impact can often fall short of explicit racism. This is often the result of what social psychologists are coming to label "implicit bias," but it is implicit bias with devastating costs to its blameless victims.

While the dangers of death to police from assault are vastly greater in the United States than in other developed nations, the use of deadly force by police also produces about twenty times as many deaths as police suffer each year, and the operational controls on police use of deadly force are much too loose in the circumstances where deadly force is permitted and in lack of control on the number of shots fired once the police open fire.[10] Almost half the cases where police killed civilians in 2015 were confrontations where the police were not at any objective risk of a deadly attack. The ninety-four cases where an unarmed adversary was shot and killed by police are an important part of these overkill events, where the death toll from police could be eliminated without increasing the death risk for on-duty police. But a great variety of political, governmental, and labor relations complications must be considered and neutralized before effective controls on police use of deadly force can be subjected to reasonable controls which will cut the civilian death toll at least by half.[11] The next section details some of the governmental and political obstacles to preventing unnecessary killings using the unarmed adversary problem as a case study.

---

[9] Ibid., Table 3.6, 60; and Table 3.7, 61.
[10] Ibid., chap. 11.
[11] Ibid.

II. What's to Be Done?

The protests surrounding the shooting death of Michael Brown in Ferguson were fabulously successful in focusing attention on unnecessary and excessive police use of deadly force, but they produced no criminal charges against the officer who fired the shots that killed Michael Brown, no examination of or change in the rules governing use of deadly force in Ferguson or in the State of Missouri, and no changes in federal law to create more effective federal controls over excessive police use of deadly force. And these failures of the criminal process and the legislative process are not one-off failures in Ferguson County or in Missouri, but are typical of the failures to control police killings a thousand times a year.

One problem—again typical—is that the exclusive focus of the protesters was on the use of the criminal law to condemn and punish Officer Wilson's acts. But the obstacles to convicting a police officer of a crime on duty are formidable. Police officers have the legal right to protect themselves or others against the threat of death or great bodily harm from attackers. And the police officer's actual belief will be sufficient to preclude criminal liability if it is not clearly unreasonable. The standards for use of deadly force in Ferguson are as vague as they are in most police departments, and police officers have skills developed on the job to persuasively explain their concerns after using deadly force. Moreover, other police officers will support a shooting officer's story in most circumstances.[12]

The legal officer who decides whether and for what charges a police shooting will result in a criminal charge is the local district attorney, an elected local official who must depend on police cooperation in producing and presenting evidence in thousands of criminal cases. District attorneys and police share common attitudes toward crime and the criminal process. And the district attorneys' need for police cooperation provides a strong incentive to avoid conflict wherever possible.

The net effect of this mix of legitimate and problematic obstacles to prosecution are that more than a thousand killings a year produce a tiny trickle of criminal charges—ten or fewer per year prior to 2015 and a national total of actual convictions of officers in killing cases of one to three per year. The expansion of video camera recordings from police or commercial surveillance film or citizen cell phones may generate a somewhat larger volume of criminal charges,[13] but the volume of criminal charges and resulting convictions will stay quite small. If ninety-four cases per year of unarmed civilians being killed occur under current

---

[12] Ibid., chap. 9.
[13] Ibid., at chaps. 9 and 10.

police regulations that permit officer shootings, the number of criminal charges from those ninety-four cases can probably be counted on the fingers of one hand.

Under current law and practice, it is foolish for the primary focus of reformers to remain on the criminal prosecution of police. The criminal law must be used in extreme cases of police misconduct because the perception of impunity for shootings would undermine all sorts of legal controls of police conduct and would destroy the prospects for legitimacy of police in minority communities. But the primary efforts to reform the police use of lethal force should be the use of clear rules on police use of deadly force. The right kind of administrative rules generated by police departments can save hundreds of lives each year.

What sorts of rules can save substantial numbers of lives? Let's revisit the unarmed assailant situation to produce a list of five specific instructions that should govern the next edition of the conflict between Officer Wilson and Michael Brown on the streets of an American community.

Rule #1. An all but complete prohibition of officers shooting unarmed assailants. This is a simple rule, easy to understand, and dispositive for the vast majority of cases, but it is not unqualified. What might justify a police officer using deadly force? The one obvious exception is when the officer who shoots cannot otherwise limit the access of an assailant to another officer's gun, and the threat of the assailant to fire that weapon is immanent and unqualified. There are two points about this potential justification which limit its capacity to inspire mistakes. First, the combination of factors is quite rare, and the burden of persuasion should be on the officer. Second, this situation can only occur when there is more than one officer on the scene and when the non-shooting officer is in a position of extreme vulnerability. All other confrontations between unarmed citizens and officers require either retreat or non–life-threatening force.

Rule #2. Any confrontation between a civilian and an officer who is alone should end when the officer calls for assistance and withdraws until help arrives. This rule covers many more situations than just those involving an unarmed assailant, but it also would prohibit shots in a very substantial number of unarmed assailant confrontations that now kill.

Rule #3. An unconditional duty to retreat when the sole lethal threat is the officer's service weapon. If the only threat of lethal outcome is a gun within the control of the officer, that officer is under the duty to remove the weapon and himself from the confrontation.

Rule #4. An unconditional prohibition on the use of lethal force when an unarmed assailant is withdrawing from a confrontation or running away. When Michael Brown was running away from officer Wilson in Ferguson, he was also running away from the only weapon that had generated any potential lethal threat. Any justification for lethal force that had been based on his access to Wilson's service weapon disappears when he flees. So shots fired after withdrawal or flight can only be attempts to arrest, an insufficient foundation for killing.

Rule #5. A prohibition on continuing to fire shots after inflicting any wound on an unarmed assailant. When a police officer shoots and wounds an unarmed combatant, it is beyond unlikely that the former assailant can gain access to a firearm now within the officer's control. That part of the interaction between Officer Wilson and Michael Brown is an obvious violation of even the most generous statements of justified self-defense, but the explicit prohibition of any further wounding makes an obvious point crystal clear.

There are two characteristics of these five proposed rules worth noting. First, they are fact-based rather than simply general principles that deadly force is "necessary to prevent death or great bodily harm." Second, they are attempts to make an officer's duty quite clear in "shoot" or "don't shoot" terms.

The application of these rules to the sequence of events in Ferguson in August of 2014 is not a difficult task. Some or all of Officer Wilson's shots violate all five of the fact-based standards. But how is this clarity and specificity supposed to influence the behavior of police administrators, police, district attorneys, and juries? The major impact of such rules should be on preventing shootings rather than punishing them. Teaching clear fact-based rules and making it equally clear to police and to cadets that the department intends to enforce them uniformly will reduce shootings in prohibited circumstances a lot. The major benefit will be saving civilian lives through prevention.

But credible prevention depends on the willingness of police administrators to discipline police officers who violate lethal force guidelines. There are indications that sometimes the preventive effect of changes in policy can be immediate and substantial with little need to test the willingness of command staff.[14] If protests come, either in collective bargaining or in litigation or with noncompliant use of lethal force, they must be met with swift and firm administrative response. Both professional and financial sanctions of high magnitude can sustain the credibility of the administrative threat. Loss of status and loss of pay are powerful threats in police administration.

But the emphasis on creating and enforcing administrative standards also will provide support for the extreme cases that require criminal prosecution. If police have been taught clear rules that are ignored in a confrontation that kills, it is much easier to regard the officer's behavior as willful. Clear rules that are disobeyed provide much more substantial evidence of recklessness and manslaughter liability. And the willingness of police administrators to impose

---

[14] Ibid., "The Philadelphia Story," 235–238.

administrative sanctions also might reassure prosecuting attorneys that police department leaders would not feel betrayed if a criminal prosecution were launched in appropriate cases. So effective administrative enforcement against excessive use of deadly force will may enhance the prospects for criminal charges in extreme cases where warranted.

The five rules outlined in this chapter as relevant to the reduction of unarmed assailant cases are only some of the administrative regulations that can be based on existing knowledge to reduce unnecessary killings by police. There are a number of other fact-specific restrictions on deadly force that can reduce the death toll in cases where civilians carry some forms of weapons.[15] And three of the five rules just outlined (numbers 2, 4, and 5) also apply to many other types of police/civilian confrontations where deadly force is not required.

Outcomes in a Post-Rule Environment

The first and most important outcome when rules such as the five previously suggested are put in force is an immediate and very substantial decline in the number of shootings of unarmed civilians and an even more substantial decline in the deaths from such shootings. If rules are clearly communicated they can be immediately successful. The volume of total shootings by police officers in unarmed assailant cases is not known, but if the fatality rate from this kind of "critical incident" is the same as from the shootings by Chicago police over the seven years we analyzed, the ninety-four killings in 2015 would predict a total of between two hundred and three hundred police shootings of unarmed civilians.[16] Any well-implemented set of rules could immediately reduce the volume of shootings by 75% in unarmed civilian cases. There is no reason to suppose that there should be a significant lag time once new standards come into force. Administrative change could immediately reduce the ninety-four killings in 2015 to twenty-four in 2018.

There will, however, be some time lags between the announcement of new standards and their implementation in administrative disciplinary proceedings. There may be a substantial period in a police department before a critical incident violates the new standards and produces a substantial administrative and civil judicial process, during which both the rules and the consequences of their violation are challenged as violation of labor agreements or an overreach of administrative authority. So the full tests of the administrative process could take

---

[15] Ibid., chap. 11.
[16] Ibid., 65–69.

years in one of the first departments to implement new standards, but this delay would probably not postpone the preventive effectiveness of the new rules.

The impact of administrative standards on the volume of criminal prosecutions against police is difficult to guess and not critically important. When and if outrageous violations of don't-shoot rules happen, the clear standards will make the case for prosecution stronger and will also bolster the prosecutor's confidence that the police department will support a prosecution. So egregious cases of police violence will have a somewhat higher probability of prosecution and conviction. That said, more than an officer's failure to observe a don't-shoot rule will be necessary to support a criminal charge, and certainly to secure a conviction. Criminal prosecution of police officers will remain difficult, and conviction will continue as a low probability event. Moreover, if the volume of shootings of unarmed civilians drops substantially, the volume of criminal charges may also be reduced from levels that would otherwise occur. But that would be good news for police, for the people they shoot, and for the communities in which police killings all too often happen.

Part III

THE PRIVATE LIFE OF GUNS

7

The First Rule of Gunfighting Is
Have a Gun

Technologies of Concealed Carry in Gun Culture 2.0

DAVID YAMANE

In April 2016, the United States Concealed Carry Association (USCCA) held its second annual Concealed Carry Expo (CCX) at the Georgia International Conventional Center near Hartsfield International Airport in Atlanta. The USCCA bills the CCX as "the nation's only event dedicated to the CCW life-style." Here CCW is short for "concealed carry weapon," and although the idea of a "lifestyle" might seem to trivialize the practice of citizens carrying deadly weapons in public, the reality is quite the opposite. Over the course of three days, various seminars repeatedly stress the seriousness and importance of being a regular and responsible armed citizen.

A seminar on the laws governing the use of lethal force in self-defense by at-torney Andrew Branca is free and open to the public. Although it begins at eight a.m., the audience is, literally, standing room as the overflow spills out from the combined German 1 and 2 suites into the hallway. Branca later signs copies of the third edition of his book, *The Law of Self-Defense*, which the USCCA has licensed and is giving away free of charge to Expo attendees. Other seminars presented throughout the weekend cover concealed-carry basics for beginners, hand-to-hand techniques to employ before using a firearm, mental preparation for self-defense, weapon retention, and gunshot wound treatment.

Like the National Rifle Association's more well-known annual meeting, the heart of the CCX is the exhibition hall where vendors display and market their products and services. One might think a concealed-carry exposition would focus on guns, and guns are certainly present. Nine manufacturers have booths, including multinational giants Glock (Austria), Walther (Germany), and Taurus (Brazil), as well as American upstarts Bond Arms and Heizer Defense. In contrast to the NRA annual meeting, the CCX also allows attendees to live fire some of the guns on the show floor inside a semi-trailer retrofitted with armor and sound proofing.

But standing in the middle of the nearly thirty-eight-thousand-square-foot show floor, it becomes abundantly clear that there is more to gun culture than just guns. For every gun manufacturer there are six companies exhibiting other products— holsters, packs and purses, clothing—designed to help armed citizens solve the riddle of carrying a lethal weapon concealed on or about their person in public safely, accessibly, and comfortably. This is what is meant by the concealed-carry *lifestyle:* making carrying a concealed firearm part of one's *everyday life.*

One of those companies exhibiting products other than guns is Elite Survival Systems (ESS). ESS is displaying such a wide range of products that, in fact, it has purchased a double booth on the end of one row. The company is known for its nylon rifle carrying cases, but has branched out more and more into the civilian concealed-carry market. Scanning the booth, a new product being introduced to the public at the Concealed Carry Expo stands out. It is a "fanny pack" called the Marathon GunPack. At first glance, it looks very similar to the popular running brand Nathan's, with its ubiquitous hydration belts. Both are adjustable nylon belts with quick-release buckles featuring center storage pouches and holsters on either side to hold flasks of water. But the pouch on the Nathan can only accommodate an iPod Classic. The Marathon GunPack's pouch is large enough to hold a pocket pistol like the Ruger LCP or Kahr P380, and comes with a Velcro holster to keep the gun secure in the pouch.

When asked how the gun show is going, one of the Elite Survival Systems reps replied, "It's been good so far—interesting and different," compared to other more general gun shows that he usually works. In elaborating on his response, he gives the example of a customer who was at the booth looking at holsters. When the rep asked what gun he owned, the customer—a dues-paying member of the USCCA—said he did not own a gun yet. This seemed ass-backwards to the rep. Like many people contemplating "CCW"—carrying a concealed weapon—the rep thinks first about the *weapon* and only then proceeds to figuring out how to *conceal and carry* it. But the customer's approach reflects the reality that the concealed-carry lifestyle is as much about the "CC" as it is about the "W." In fact, according to some experts, the carrying component of the CCW equation is by far the most important. Tom Givens is one such expert.

Givens is well known in the gun training community in no small part because over sixty of his students—that he knows of—have used their firearms in self-defense.[1] In a June 2014 accounting, based on post-encounter interviews he conducts, Givens reports his students' outcomes as you would a sports team's

---

[1] Most of these students he trained at Rangemaster in Memphis, Tennessee. Givens opened

results. In terms of "wins" and "losses," his students had a record of 61-0-2 in their 63 incidents. "That's 61 clear victories, zero losses and 2 forfeits," he writes. Forfeits? How do you forfeit in a gun fight? Givens explains:

> The two forfeits were people who died as a result of not being armed on The Big Day. Both were killed in separate street robberies. Essentially, both were executed for the contents of their pockets. They were not able to defend themselves because they chose not to be armed that day. They made a poor choice. Of the 61 students who won, only 3 were injured, and all recovered from those injuries.[2]

What made the "clear victories" possible for so many of Givens' students? Although he makes his living as a gun trainer, like any good coach Givens doesn't take much credit for his students' wins. In his view, the most important factor in successful armed self-defense is *"having your damn gun on you when the event occurs."*

In saying this, Givens acknowledges that he is just paraphrasing gun writer Mark Moritz who observed that "The First Rule of gunfighting is *have a gun.*" Although this would seem to be a common sense starting point, it is in fact easier said than done, especially for civilian concealed carriers. As a precondition of having a gun, the concealed carrier has to answer a number of questions: How to carry the gun safely? How to keep the gun hidden? How to carry the gun so that it is accessible? How to carry the gun comfortably in everyday life? The answers to these questions can be in tension with each other or even in direct opposition. Safety is at odds with speed of access; speed of access is at odds with concealment; concealment is at odds with comfort. The gun itself has a role in this puzzle, as well. A larger gun is more lethal but harder to carry than a smaller gun, and vice versa. Clint Smith, founder and director of the gun training center Thunder Ranch, famously declared that "carrying a gun is not supposed to be *comfortable*; it's supposed to be *comforting.*" But countless Americans who are permitted to carry a handgun in public do not do so because they cannot comfortably fit the gun into their everyday lives. As a result, a large part of the business of concealed carry is developing products that help people reconcile these competing demands so they can live the concealed-carry lifestyle promoted by the USCCA at the CCX.

Rangemaster in 1996, after a twenty-five-year career in law enforcement, and ran the indoor range, store, and training center until August 2014. During that time, he and his staff taught hundreds of students in Tennessee concealed carry, combative pistol, defensive revolver and shotgun, and vehicle defense classes.

[2] Tom Givens, "Carry Your Darned Gun!" *Rangemaster Digest* email newsletter, June 3, 2014.

The very existence of the United States Concealed Carry Association and its Concealed Carry Expo reflects a profound change that has taken place in American gun culture over the past half century, from a culture rooted in hunting and recreational shooting to one centered on armed citizenship and personal defense. As shorthand, I describe this as an evolution from Gun Culture 1.0 to Gun Culture 2.0. In what follows, I begin by giving a brief history of the rise of Gun Culture 2.0. I then propose a cultural approach to studying gun culture, based on a working definition of culture that emphasizes the ways in which it helps us to understand the world by defining problems and prospects, and helps us to act in the world by suggesting recipes and providing tools for action in relation to those problems and prospects. Here, objects of material culture like guns and gun-related accessories play an important role. Far from being static entities, in addressing the problems associated with carrying concealed weapons in everyday life, these technologies respond to and facilitate the cultural practice of gun carrying which is central to Gun Culture 2.0.[3] I apply this cultural approach to studying gun culture using ethnographic observation at the CCX to explore some of the many technologies that have been developed to help those who want to be armed citizens reconcile the competing demands of carrying a concealed handgun in public. These material culture technologies include guns and holsters, as well as products designed to address women's specific carry needs.

The Rise of Gun Culture 2.0

In his 1970 essay, "America as a Gun Culture," historian Richard Hofstadter remarked on—or, more accurately, lamented—the uniqueness of the United States "as the only modern industrial urban nation that persists in maintaining a gun culture." In Hofstadter's account, US gun culture is rooted in the reality of widespread, lawful possession of firearms by a large segment of the population. He recognizes that guns as material objects are central to the construction of any gun culture. Without guns there is no gun culture. But in itself this is a trivial statement. What is crucial to explain is how people understand and use guns, as well as how guns themselves change over time, both responding to and facilitating different understandings and uses.[4]

---

[3] As I argue in my larger project on Gun Culture 2.0, these challenges are individually and collectively addressed in the developing culture of armed citizenship not only through the "hardware" of material culture like guns, accessories, and other products, but also through the "software" of ways of thinking, legal frameworks, and the development of relevant abilities.

[4] Richard Hofstadter, "America as a Gun Culture," *American Heritage* 21, no. 6 (October 1970), 7, http://www.americanheritage.com/content/america-gun-culture; in this section, I draw on my

"What began as a necessity of agriculture and the frontier," Hofstader observed, "took hold as a sport and as an ingredient in the American imagination." Hunting became not only a source of food but a dominant form of recreation for many, and casual target shooting competitions were commonplace on the frontier in the nineteenth century. Into the twentieth century, hunting continued to be an important part of US gun culture, particularly in rural areas, but also among urban-dwellers looking for some escape from city life. Especially as part of socialization into hunting, receiving a "real" rifle became seen as a rite of passage from boyhood into manhood. The gun industry also increasingly promoted guns as objects of (typically masculine) desire through the mass advertising that was increasingly embraced by corporate America to fuel consumer capitalism. Gun collecting as an avocation and a business arose in the early twentieth century in conjunction with this evolution away from a purely utilitarian view of guns.

Hunting, target shooting, and collecting continue to be important aspects of US gun culture today. Like Abigail Kohn in her book *Shooters,* Timothy Luke's contribution to this volume highlights the reality of these and other subcultures within American gun culture.[5] At the same time, the center of gravity of US gun culture has shifted over the course of the past half-century from various forms of recreational use of firearms to armed self-defense. To borrow terms from gun writer Michael Bane, we see an evolution from Gun Culture 1.0, America's historic gun culture, that Hofstadter described, to Gun Culture 2.0.[6]

Gun Culture 2.0 is centered on armed self-defense, or what I call the culture of armed citizenship. The concept of armed citizenship recognizes the large and growing number of people in the United States who are exercising their rights as citizens to carry firearms in public for self-defense. Although the motivations for gun ownership are complex, the majority of gun owners today—especially

article "The Sociology of U.S. Gun Culture." *Sociology Compass* 11, no. 7 (2017), https://doi.org/10.1111/soc4.12497.

[5] Abigail A. Kohn, *Shooters: Myths and Realities of America's Gun Cultures* (New York: Oxford University Press, 2004).

[6] In distinguishing between Gun Culture 1.0 and Gun Culture 2.0, Bane is drawing on the language of "versions" or "generations" of the World Wide Web shifting from Web 1.0 to Web 2.0 (and beyond). Just as Web 2.0 grew out of but did not simply replace Web 1.0, Gun Culture 2.0 developed out of and added new elements to the Gun Culture 1.0. Recognizing the centrality of the culture of armed citizenship today does not mean that self-defense was not a part of Gun Culture 1.0. Similarly, older elements of Gun Culture 1.0, like hunting and target shooting, survive, but they are less central to gun culture in general. Some individuals who were raised in Gun Culture 1.0 became leading figures in the development of Gun Culture 2.0, while others only partially transitioned (Gun Culture Version 1.5) or have remained steadfastly at home in Gun Culture 1.0. The newer gun culture even has a name for these throwbacks to the old gun culture: "Fudds," after the Looney Tunes cartoon character Elmer Fudd, the hapless hunter who can never bag his prey, Bugs Bunny.

new gun owners—point to self-defense as the primary reason for owning a gun. In a 1999 ABC News/*Washington Post* poll, 26% of respondents cited protection as the primary reason for owning a gun; by 2013, that proportion had grown to 48%. Hunting, target/sport shooting, and gun collecting together declined by a roughly equal amount. More recently, the 2015 National Firearms Survey found 63% of respondents indicated "protection against people" to be a primary reason for owning a firearm. Significantly, a 2013 *Washington Post*/ABC News poll found more Americans saying that having a gun in the house makes it a safer place to be (51%) than a more dangerous place to be (29%). This view extends outside the home, as well. A 2015 Gallup Poll found a majority of Americans (56%)—including 50% of women and 48% of non-gun owners—believe that if more Americans carried concealed weapons, the country would be safer.[7] These statistics are reflective of the changing legal structure governing the carrying and use of firearms for self-defense. This dramatic liberalization of gun laws over the past four decades reflects and facilitates the development of Gun Culture 2.0.

In the early republic, no special licensing was required to bear arms, either openly or concealed. But beginning with Kentucky in 1813, there was a movement in several southern states to ban the carrying of concealed weapons in public. In time, these prohibitions spread from the south to the rest of the United States. This "restricted era" of gun carry continued through the 1970s, but over the last four decades there has been dramatic shift toward the liberalization of concealed-carry laws. The dominant movement in concealed-carry legislation has been toward state passage of what have come to be known as "shall issue" laws.[8] From 1980 to 2013, thirty-eight states passed these laws that require state or local authorities to issue a permit to any applicant that meets the

---

[7] Pew Research Center, "Why Own a Gun? Protection Is Now Top Reason," 1999 ABC News/ *Washington Post* poll, March 12, 2013, http://www.people-press.org/2013/03/12/why-own-a-gun- protection-is-now-top-reason/; Deborah Azrael et al., "The Stock and Flow of US Firearms: Results from the 2015 National Firearms Survey," *Russell Sage Foundation Journal of the Social Sciences* 3, no. 5 (2017), 38-57, https://www.rsfjournal.org/doi/full/10.7758/RSF.2017.3.5.02; Scott Clement and Peyton Craighill, "Majority of Americans Say Guns Make Homes Safer," *The Washington Post*, 2013 *Washington Post*/ABC News poll, April 18, 2013, https://www.washingtonpost.com/news/the-fix/ wp/2013/04/18/majority-of-americans-say-guns-make-homes-safer/; Frank Newport, "Majority Say More Concealed Weapons Would Make U.S. Safer," 2015 Gallup Poll, October 20 2015, http:// www.gallup.com/poll/186263/majority-say-concealed-weapons-safer.aspx.

[8] On the early history of concealed weapon bans see Clayton Cramer, *Concealed Weapon Laws of the Early Republic: Dueling, Southern Violence, and Moral Reform* (Westport, CT: Praeger, 1999); on liberalization of carry laws, see Brian Anse Patrick, *Rise of the Anti-Media: In-Forming America's Concealed Weapon Carry Movement* (Lanham, MD: Lexington Books, 2010); on the spread of "shall issue" permitting, see Richard S. Grossman and Stephen A. Lee, "May Issue Versus Shall Issue: Explaining the Pattern of Concealed-Carry Handgun Laws, 1960–2001," *Contemporary Economic Policy* 26 (April 2008): 198–206.

objective statutory criteria if no statutory reasons for denial exist. The issuing authority's discretion over subjective criteria like the "good moral character" or "good cause" of the applicant is removed from the process. Two hundred years after Kentucky banned the carrying of concealed weapons in public, state or local governments in all fifty states must have (according to court decisions) some provision in place for issuing permits to citizens allowing them to carry concealed firearms in public. "Shall issue" laws prevail in forty of fifty states, and only nine states maintain more restrictive "may issue" laws. Vermont has never banned the practice of carrying a concealed weapon without a permit and so does not issue concealed-carry permits.[9]

As concealed-carry laws have been liberalized, the number of concealed-carry permit holders has grown considerably. Although there is no national database of concealed-carry permits, the Government Accountability Office estimated that there were at least 8 million active permits to carry concealed handguns in the United States at the end of 2011. This amounted to at least 3.5% of the eligible US population (adults who are legally allowed to possess guns). A report released in 2016 by John R. Lott, Jr. suggests the number of permits now exceeds 14.5 million, or some 6% of the total US adult population. The portion of individual state populations with a concealed-carry permit varies, but shall-issue states like Indiana (728,976 permits, 15% of the adult population), South Dakota (91,785 permits, 14.7%), and Alabama (513,209 permits, 14.1%) have the highest rates in the country. It would surely surprise many to know that one out of every seven adult citizens in these states is potentially legally armed in public, not to mention one out of every seventeen Americans overall.[10]

---

[9] The nine states in which the issuing authority is not required to grant a concealed-carry license but *may* issue one at its discretion are California, Connecticut, Delaware, Hawaii, Maryland, Massachusetts, New Jersey, New York, and Rhode Island. New Hampshire is difficult to classify because the term "shall issue" appears in its statute, but other language suggests discretion on the part of the issuing authority to determine that "the applicant is a suitable person to be licensed." It may be best classified as *de facto* shall issue. Sometimes called Vermont carry, freedom to carry, or Constitutional carry (because "the Second Amendment *is* my carry permit"), permitless carry represents the next phase of this liberalization of gun laws. Including Vermont, eleven states now allow individuals to carry a concealed weapon in public without a permit, with certain restrictions and exceptions: Alaska, Arizona, Idaho (residents only), Kansas, Maine, Mississippi, Missouri, New Hampshire, West Virginia, and Wyoming (residents only). Other than Vermont, these ten permitless carry states still issue concealed carry permits, which offer additional benefits depending on the state. For example, only permit holders in Arizona can carry concealed in businesses that service alcohol (provided the business allows firearms in the first place and the concealed carrier does not drink). Concealed carry permits from permitless carry states also allow the permit holder to carry in others states that have reciprocity agreements with the issuing state.

[10] Government Accountability Office, "Gun Control: States' Laws and Requirements for Concealed Carry Permits Vary across the Nation," GAO-12-717 (Washington, DC: United States Government Accountability Office, 2012), http://www.gao.gov/products/GAO-12-717;

This lawful carrying of firearms for legal purposes has received very little attention from sociologists, who have largely ceded the study of guns to criminologists and epidemiologists. Among the few who have seriously studied legal concealed carry is Jennifer Carlson. In her landmark book, *Citizen-Protectors: The Everyday Politics of Guns in an Age of Decline*, Carlson observes, "Guns solve problems for the people who bear them."[11] This problem-solving is facilitated by shall-issue permitting laws that have expanded the opportunity to carry guns concealed in public. In promoting the idea of a concealed-carry lifestyle, the USCCA's Concealed Carry Expo is targeted at the increasing number of people who seek to solve problems by carrying guns. At the same time, the practice of CCW poses new problems for the potential armed citizen, as noted at the start of this chapter: How to carry a lethal weapon safely, comfortably, concealed, and accessibly in public? The CCX, therefore, showcases a myriad of products designed to reconcile the competing demands of CCW so as to optimize the likelihood that a person will, as Tom Givens put it, "carry your damn gun." Thus understood, the CCX is both a response to the rise of Gun Culture 2.0 and a facilitator of its continued development.

A Cultural Approach to Gun Culture 2.0

This chapter illuminates one aspect of the negotiation of the opportunity and challenge of concealed carry by adopting a cultural approach to studying gun culture. As the discussion of Hofstadter's work makes clear, others have used the term "gun culture" to explain Americans' unique relationship to firearms, historically or today. But, as the historian Pamela Haag observes, "The phrase 'gun culture' is used more than it is defined."[12] Part of the reason gun culture often goes undefined is because culture itself can be difficult to define. In moving from a generic label to a specific definition of culture, we are immediately confronted with a problem: there are seemingly as many definitions of culture as there are people who study it.[13] Haag's definition of gun culture is, nonetheless, in line with the way many implicitly understand it:

John R. Lott, "Concealed Carry Permit Holders across the United States: 2016," July 26, 2016, http://dx.doi.org/10.2139/ssrn.2814691.

[11] Jennifer Carlson, *Citizen-Protectors: The Everyday Politics of Guns in an Age of Decline* (New York: Oxford University Press, 2015), 178.

[12] Pamela Haag, *The Gunning of America: Business and the Making of American Gun Culture* (New York: Basic Books, 2016), xvii.

[13] Marshall Battani, John R. Hall, and Mary Jo Neitz, *Sociology on Culture* (Hoboken, NJ: Taylor and Francis, 2004), 7; for summaries, see Wendy Griswold, "The Sociology of Culture," in *The Sage Handbook of Sociology*, eds. Craig Calhoun, Chris Rojek, and Bryan S. Turner (London: Sage, 2005),

A gun culture is a matter not only of quantity [i.e., the number of guns] but also of quality—in anthropologist Marshall Sahlins's terms, of how cultures "give significance to their objects"—and of the "social life" of a commodity. These qualitative dimensions are difficult to gauge or generalize . . . but they include the place that the gun occupies culturally as a whole and for different groups—the degree of gun affinity, love, symbolism, charisma, and totemic force and the political resonance of the gun.[14]

The dominant approach to studying gun culture follows Haag in emphasizing the "symbolic" nature of guns and the emotions they inspire. What does the gun stand for and how does it make people feel?

To mention just a few prominent examples, in *Gun Show Nation: Gun Culture and American Democracy*, Joan Burbick explains the American obsession with guns (and hence gun culture) as driven by political conservatism and nationalist sentiments. Guns in her view stand for and inspire a traditional vision of America. Scott Melzer's *Gun Crusaders: The NRA's Culture War* also sees gun culture reflecting traditional values, specifically the myth of frontier masculinity. Guns stand for a time that never was that gun owners wish could be again. In *Warrior Dreams: Violence and Manhood in Post-Vietnam America*, James William Gibson offers a Freudian psycho-sexual analysis of not only guns as phallic symbols but also of hollow point ammunition ("A perfectly expanded bullet bears some resemblance to an erect penis") and wound cavities in ballistic gelatin ("drawings of wound channels . . . look very much like vaginas"). Angela Stroud's *Good Guys with Guns: The Appeal and Consequences of Concealed Carry* highlights broader cultural ideals of what it means to be a man as driving gun culture, in addition to racialized cultural definitions of "good guys" and "bad guys."[15]

To be sure, all of these symbolic and emotional aspects of guns exist to some extent. Listening to any speech by National Rifle Association Executive Vice President Wayne LaPierre—for example, in the wake of the Sandy Hook Elementary School massacre—makes this abundantly clear. But there is more to

---

254–266; Wendy Griswold, *Cultures and Societies in a Changing World*, 4th ed. (Los Angeles: Sage, 2012); John R. Hall, Laura Grindstaff, and Ming-Cheng Lo, *Handbook of Cultural Sociology* (Hoboken, NJ: Taylor and Francis, 2010).

[14] Haag, *The Gunning of America*, xvii.

[15] Joan Burbick, *Gun Show Nation: Gun Culture and American Democracy* (New York: The New Press, 2007); Scott Melzer, *Gun Crusaders: The NRA's Culture War* (New York: New York University Press, 2012); James William Gibson, *Warrior Dreams: Violence and Manhood in Post-Vietnam America* (New York: Hill & Wang, 1994), 91–92; Angela Stroud, *Good Guys with Guns: The Appeal and Consequences of Concealed Carry* (Chapel Hill: University of North Carolina Press, 2016).

understanding gun culture than just figuring out the *symbolic meanings* of guns; to look at guns as only representing *something else* does not tell the whole story. Although suggesting scholars adopt a cultural approach to guns is not novel, adopting a cultural approach which goes beyond the symbolic dimension of culture is.

Recognizing that definitions are tools we use to advance understanding, and not simply mirrors of reality, I propose a working definition of culture to apply in this case study. To begin with, a good working definition recognizes that culture has both ideal and material dimensions.

With respect to the ideal dimension, culture encompasses both "ideas, knowledge (correct, wrong, or unverifiable belief), and recipes for doing things." Culture helps people to understand the world around them. But culture does more than simply help people interpret the world and their experiences in particular ways. As anthropologist Clifford Geertz famously phrased it, culture not only provides "models of reality" through which we render the world comprehensible; it provides "models for reality": guidelines and strategies of action according to which we act in the world. Culture also includes material objects such as "humanly fabricated tools (such as shovels, sewing machines, cameras, and computers)" and "the products of social action that may be drawn upon in the further conduct of social life" (such as food, clothing, photographs, and emails). Like the ideal dimension of culture, these tools and products are made, disseminated, and used by various collectivities—groups, movements, associations, organizations, businesses. [16]

The active language used here to describe culture is significant because it shifts our attention from what culture *is* to what culture *does*. Culture helps us to understand the world by defining problems and prospects. It helps us to act in the world by suggesting recipes and providing tools for action in relation to those problems and prospects. As a result of our actions in the world we create new cultural products and ideas—that is, a new cultural environment—which often suggests new problems and prospects to be addressed. In this way, the ideal and material dimensions of culture are made real and dynamic in various cultural practices through which people do not just reproduce existing cultures but also modify, develop, and innovate. This approach helps us see American gun culture in all its complexity today, as well as the major ways in which it has evolved over time.

Emphasizing the material aspect of culture reminds us that culture is not only grounded in interaction between people, but it also is formally produced

---

[16] Battani et al., *Sociology on Culture*, 7; Clifford Geertz, *The Interpretation of Cultures* (New York: Basic Books, 1973), 92–93.

and disseminated. Understanding the production and distribution of culture requires examining the "complex apparatus which is interposed between cultural creators and consumers." According to sociologist Wendy Griswold, "This apparatus includes facilities for production and distribution; marketing techniques such as advertising, co-opting mass media, or targeting; and the creation of situations that bring potential cultural consumers in contact with cultural objects."[17] This is to say that some cultural products circulate as commodities in the consumer marketplace, and the Concealed Carry Expo can be understood as a key situation in which cultural producers make their products available to cultural consumers.

In the end, a real strength of this working definition is that it recalls the origins of the term culture, from the Medieval Latin *cultivare*—to tend or to cultivate. Put briefly, "Culture, in this sense, amounts to ways of taking care of things."[18] This understanding of culture gives us analytical leverage in explaining the movement of armed citizenship to the center of American gun culture as a whole, a movement which has facilitated the practice of concealed carry by an increasing number of ordinary Americans, but which also creates certain challenges for those who wish to "take care of things" with guns.

The balance of this chapter complements Harel Shapira's contribution to this volume. Where Shapira focuses on the individual and embodied aspects of gun carrying, this work highlights the business end of guns and gun-related accessories as objects of material culture. It focuses on technologies that are designed to solve the kinds of practical problems Shapira highlights, which are faced by those who would carry concealed firearms in public. These technologies are developed by "the gun industry"—companies small and large—into products like guns, holsters, clothing, and bags which are sold to the public as commodities in venues like the Concealed Carry Expo.

Guns

A unique aspect of the CCX is the opportunity to live-fire handguns on site, inside the exhibition hall. This is made possible by the Mobile Tactics semi-trailer, an armor plated, sound insulated three lane gun range on wheels. Seven of the nine exhibiting firearms manufacturers have made their guns available to be shot. Surveying the row of tables displaying the options, the guns appear to be

---

[17] Richard A. Peterson, "The Production of Cultural Change: The Case of Contemporary Country Music," *Social Forces* 45 (1978), 295; Griswold, *Cultures and Societies in a Changing World*, 73.

[18] Battani et al., *Sociology on Culture*, 7.

revolutionary. And in certain ways they are, especially in the lightweight alloys and polymers now routinely used in the manufacturing process.

But the use of handheld weapons for personal defense was not invented by Gun Culture 2.0. The handguns on display at the CCX are part of an unbroken thread of personal weaponry stretching back to rocks in the hands of Paleolithic humans.[19] As objects of material culture, personal weapons are tools created to address problems. In this case the main problem addressed is the need for a tool for fighting—animals or other human beings—that is sufficiently lethal yet allows the user to maintain distance from the intended target. At each stage of development, humans have sought to craft weapons that are more effective at accomplishing this end: larger and lighter axes, sharper knives, more aerodynamic spear points.

The ability to deliver a lethal blow from a distance was greatly advanced by the discovery and harnessing of the power of gunpowder, and its eventual application to handheld firearms. In his 1917 *Book of the Pistol & Revolver,* Hugh B. C. Pollard observes as follows:

> From the earliest period of the invention of firearms, mankind has desired a short, easily portable, and easily concealed means of defence, and to this common desire we owe the pistol, the revolver, the "automatic," and all their kindred. The pistol—by which term I include all pistols, revolvers, automatics, and repeating or single-shot weapons meant for use in one hand—was essentially designed as a weapon for quick use at close quarters.

Put more abstractly, as philosophers David DeGrazia and Lester Hunt do, "A gun is a tool, a product of human technology; and like any technological device, it exists to solve problems."[20]

Although the desire for effective fighting tools has remained constant, the technologies developed by gun manufacturers for realizing this desire have evolved over time. This is driven not only by technological advances, but also the specific cultural conditions under which the guns will be used. As CCW is a dominant trend in Gun Culture 2.0, gun manufacturers are motivated to develop technologies into products that will help gun carriers solve the problem of armed self-defense in public. Here, however, the demands of concealed carry

---

[19] In her contribution to this volume, Joanna Bourke makes a similar observation about the parallels between dum-dum bullets and "stone throwing" as "innovations" in their own times.

[20] Hugh B. C. Pollard, *The Book of the Pistol and Revolver,* reprint (Pittsburgh, PA: Sportsman's Vintage Press, 2014 [1917]); David DeGrazia and Lester H. Hunt, *Debating Gun Control: How Much Regulation Do We Need?* (New York: Oxford University Press, 2016), 8.

are at odds with the ideals of the gun as a weapon. From the perspective of the weapon itself, lethality is key. A more lethal weapon is one that holds more rounds of ammunition in a larger caliber, and is more accurate due to a longer barrel and sight radius (for aiming) and heavier weight to absorb recoil (to get back on target more quickly). This sounds very much like a description of a rifle rather than a handgun, hence the common refrain in gun culture: "The only purpose of a pistol is to fight your way back to your rifle." But of course you cannot conceal and carry a rifle, practically (for most) or legally (for all). Not only that, but in order to carry a handgun in public on a regular basis, portability, comfort, and concealability are essential attributes in a weapon. This is achieved primarily by reducing the gun's size and weight by chambering it for a smaller caliber, having fewer rounds in the magazine, reducing the length of the barrel and grip, and constructing the frame out of lighter materials. In a word, making the weapon less lethal.

Perhaps no gun manufacturer exhibiting at the CCX exemplifies these developments in gun technologies for concealed carry better than the Austrian firm Glock GmbH. On its black cloth covered table, in front of a large banner showing a picture of a woman receiving shooting instruction on a gun range, are five of its best-selling pistols. This includes the iconic Glock 17, the semi-automatic pistol which revolutionized the gun industry in the 1980s. Created in 1982 by Gaston Glock, a curtain-rod manufacturer in Austria with no background in firearms design or manufacturing, the Glock 17 is known for its polymer frame, absence of an external safety lever, and 17-round standard capacity magazines. A full-size duty weapon, it was first adopted by the Austrian army, and subsequently became the handgun of choice for many American police departments. Compared to the steel frame revolvers and semi-autos commonly issued at the time, the Glock was both lighter and had carried more rounds of ammunition.[21] It was so successful that for many today, "Glock" is to high-capacity, polymer frame semi-automatic handguns as "Kleenex" is to facial tissues.

The success of the Glock 17 notwithstanding, it was designed for military use, not concealed carry. This is obvious when compared to the other four, smaller pistols on the Glock table. One of these smaller pistols is the Glock 19. Released in 1988, it is a more compact version of the Glock 17, though not much more so. It was not until 1995 that Glock got into the concealed-carry market in earnest with the subcompact Glock 26, known as the "Baby Glock." Just looking at the full size Glock 17 next to the compact Glock 19 and subcompact Glock 26 highlights the trade-offs necessary in designing firearms for concealed carry. To aid concealability, the Glock 26 is more than an inch shorter than the Glock 17

---

[21] Paul M. Barrett, *Glock: The Rise of America's Gun* (New York: Random House, 2012).

in both length and height. The Glock 26's weight also makes it easier to carry; it is 10% lighter unloaded and 20% lighter loaded than the Glock 17. But this concealability and carry-ability is achieved in large part by sacrificing magazine capacity and hence lethality or "stopping power." Although both guns are chambered in 9mm, the Glock 26 has a 10-round standard magazine capacity in comparison to the larger gun's 17 rounds—fully 40% fewer.

The two other guns on the table, the Glock 42 and 43, are visibly smaller than even the Baby Glock. Despite being very popular with the public and critics alike, Glock went into a sort of twenty-year hibernation relative to the civilian concealed-carry market after the introduction of the Glock 26. Its deep sleep was broken in 2014 by its introduction of the Glock 42. A baby "Baby Glock," the Model 42 is smaller than the Model 26 in every way. It is less than 6 inches long, barely 4 inches tall, only 0.94 inches wide, and weighs just over a pound (17.29 ounces) fully loaded. Its lightweight, "slimline" design makes it extremely convenient to carry, but at a cost. The Glock 42 is made slimmer and lighter by reducing magazine capacity another 40%, from 10 to just 6 rounds in a "single stack" magazine, and it is chambered for the lower-power .380 ACP (Automatic Colt Pistol or AUTO) cartridge.[22]

Although James Bond's legendary Walther PPK was chambered in .380 ACP, many in the self-defense firearms community historically looked down on .380 caliber guns, seeing them as "sub-caliber" (i.e., ineffective) for personal defense and disparaging them as mere "mouse guns."[23] Not surprisingly, the year after the Model 42 was introduced, Glock unveiled what it has called the "most highly desired and anticipated release" in the company's history: the Glock 43. Fractionally larger than the Glock 42, the Model 43 is also a single-stack micro-compact but is chambered for the more powerful 9mm cartridge. At just 1.02 inches wide, the Glock 43 weighs less than 23 ounces fully loaded, with 6 rounds in the magazine and one in the chamber. According to the Glock representative at the Concealed Carry Expo, the most popular choices among those shooting in the Mobile Tactics trailer are the Glock 42 and 43, reflecting the caption on the Glock banner: "Confidence. It's what you carry."

Although Glock has certainly not been on the cutting edge of concealed-carry weapon technologies—following the lead of more innovative manufacturers like Kahr Arms, Kel-Tec, and Sturm Ruger—the development of the Glock line

---

[22] In the slimmer "single stack" magazine, the cartridges sit on top of each other in a single row as opposed to being staggered in the wider "double stack" magazine. Another technological development that facilitated smaller pistol designs was the locked-breech system, which was used in place of a straight-blowback design that required larger pistols.

[23] Although many still favor the more powerful ballistics of the 9mm cartridge, technological improvements in bullet design have reduced the bias against the supposedly underpowered .380 ACP.

is still a microcosm of the rise of Gun Culture 2.0. As reported by *The Trace*, production of .380 ACP caliber pistols like the Glock 42 has increased in tandem with the increasing percentage of the American population with concealed-carry permits.[24] Microcompact guns the size of the Glock 42 and 43 are commonly called "pocket pistols" because they are small enough to be carried in most pants or jacket pockets. As such, they maximize the concealability and carry-ability components of the CCW equation. These benefits, however, come at the cost of the weapon part of the equation: 6 to 10 rounds of either 9mm or .380 ACP in a pocket pistol's magazine is less lethal than more rounds in the same caliber or the same number of rounds in a larger caliber, *ceteris paribus*. Even this trade-off, however, has been addressed by one gun manufacturer at the Concealed Carry Expo: Heizer Defense.

Heizer Defense, LLC, was founded in 2011 as an offshoot of Heizer Aerospace, a fifty-plus year old company founded by Charles K. Heizer and headquartered in Pevely, Missouri. The company is introducing its new PKO-45 to the public at the Concealed Carry Expo and allowing it to be test-fired in the Mobile Tactics trailer. Like other concealed-carry pistols on display, the PKO-45 is a subcompact, magazine-fed semi-automatic. But it is unique in being made not from the ubiquitous polymers but from airplane grade stainless steel. This results in a handgun that is comparatively heavy at twenty-eight ounces. But Heizer Defense also uses its parent company's expertise in machining components for the aerospace industry to make the PKO-45 just 0.8 inches wide—slimmer than even the Glock 42. This is particularly impressive considering, as the gun's name suggests, that the PKO-45 shoots the .45 ACP cartridge. Although the weight makes this gun slightly less carry-able, its slim design makes it quite concealable, and the .45 caliber amps up the potential stopping power of the gun.

Indeed, the .45 ACP is a venerable old cartridge invented by legendary gun designer John Moses Browning early in the twentieth century. Legend has it that during the Philippine-American War (1899–1902), and the Moro Rebellion which succeeded it (to 1913), US Army troops found their .38 Long Colt handguns and .30-40 Krag rifle cartridges inadequate to stop the Filipino and Moro warriors; only the .45 Colt cartridge was effective. This experience was reinforced by ammunition tests run by Colonel John T. Thompson and Major Louis Anatole LaGarde using live cattle and human cadavers. Thompson and LaGarde concluded that "a bullet, which will have the shock effect and stopping effect at short ranges necessary for a military pistol or revolver, should have a

---

[24] Alex Yablon, "Concealed Carriers Have Made a Tiny Pistol with a Sketchy Past a Big Seller for Gun Makers," *The Trace*, March 13, 2016, https://www.thetrace.org/2016/03/380-pistol-big-seller-for-gun-manufacturers/.

caliber not less than .45."[25] In response, Browning discontinued his work on a .41 caliber cartridge and developed the .45 Automatic Colt Pistol (ACP) cartridge instead in 1904. The .45 ACP was subsequently paired with the Colt M1911 pistol, which was adopted by the US Army in 1911 and remained the standard US service pistol until the late 1980s.

A government model 1911 pistol weighs in at three pounds loaded, is over eight inches long and five inches tall. Such a gun is easily worn in plain view but is extremely difficult to conceal. Thus, the remarkable potential of the PKO-45 is that it puts the power of the .45 caliber cartridge into the frame of a pocket pistol. Like other pocket pistols, the PKO-45's shorter height is achieved primarily by making the grip shorter, such that the pinky finger of the firing hand does not fit on the grip. This represents yet another trade-off in gun design as it compromises the accuracy (or "shootability") of the weapon, including the ability to aim, manage recoil, and put additional rounds on target quickly.

As Shapira also observes in his chapter in this volume, the inability to grip a semi-automatic pistol tightly enough can also lead to malfunctions if the gun does not "cycle" properly. In a magazine-fed pistol, the explosion which propels the bullet through the barrel also drives the slide of the gun backward, helping to eject the empty cartridge case. A recoil spring then brings the slide back forward and as it does it pulls an unspent cartridge from the magazine into the empty chamber. Now back "in battery," the gun can be fired again (and again, until the magazine is empty). This process, however, requires that the shooter provide enough resistance that the recoil spring takes up the energy from the explosion. If the shooter's body—hands, wrists, arms—absorb too much of the recoil energy, the slide will not cycle properly causing a malfunction known as a "failure to eject" (FTE). One such FTE is colloquially called a "stovepipe" because the spent case gets trapped in the ejection port by the slide and protrudes like a stovepipe from the gun. If the grip on the PKO-45 is so thin and short that a shooter cannot get an adequate handle on the gun, malfunctions are likely. In a self-defense situation, such a malfunction could be fatal.

These developments in handgun technology highlight the balancing act performed by manufacturers designing guns for the concealed-carry market as they attempt to meet the competing demands of concealability/carry-ability and lethality. But changing the technical attributes of guns themselves is just one way the gun industry attempts to strike a balance between these competing demands. As is abundantly clear to Concealed Carry Expo attendees, many other

---

[25] Louis Anatole LaGarde, *Gunshot Injuries: How They Are Inflicted, Their Complications and Treatment* (New York: William Wood, 1914), 72.

technologies are being developed by the gun industry to address the challenge of living the concealed-carry lifestyle.

Holsters

Alongside the gun manufacturers, the Georgia International Convention Center exhibition hall is filled with booth after booth for companies like Fast Holsters, PDA Holsters, HolsterSmith.com, Sticky Holsters, Andre's Holsters, Clip Draw, Kinetic Concealment, Versa Carry, Smart Carry, Holster Partners, and Clinger Holsters. Because it is easier to get into the gun industry as an accessory maker than a gun manufacturer, these smaller companies have proliferated as people try to tap into the growing concealed-carry market. As important as the gun is in the CCW equation, no hardware is more important than the holster to being able to "carry your damn gun" every day as part of the concealed-carry lifestyle promoted by the USCCA. At some point every person who wants to carry a concealed weapon in public needs to figure out *how* to carry it. In the words of Oklahoma-based holster-maker Spencer Keepers, "If you're going to conceal [a gun] and carry it safely, then the holster is the thing you need to research most."[26]

In contrast to Hollywood depictions, carrying a gun every day is far from cool or sexy. The hand-tooled leather belt holster carrying a foot-long Colt "Peacemaker" revolver worn by Gary Cooper in *High Noon* is as impractical for the civilian concealed carrier of Gun Culture 2.0 today as it is iconic of the old Gun Culture 1.0. Equally impractical for most are the shoulder holsters worn by "Dirty Harry" Callahan for his Smith & Wesson Model 29 .44 Magnum revolver and Miami Vice's Sonny Crockett for his Bren Ten (10mm) semi-auto. The technology of a holster for armed citizens is very different than for law enforcement officers, who can carry guns openly in holsters on their sides or shoulders. The concealed-carry holster has to emphasize concealment. Even though accidentally displaying an inadequately concealed firearm is not a crime in most places, it can cause concern among other members of the public with potentially devastating consequences.

In 2010, Erik Scott was shopping at a Las Vegas area Costco when he inadvertently exposed the handgun he was carrying in a holster inside the waistband of his jeans. Scott identified himself as a Nevada concealed-weapons permit holder, and the store manager informed him of Costco's "no guns" policy. The manager allowed Scott to finish his shopping, but at the same time another

---

[26] Spencer Keepers, "The In's and Out's of Concealed Carry," The Polite Society Tactical Conference, Memphis, Tennessee, February 21, 2014.

store employee had called the police to report an armed individual acting erratically. The Las Vegas Metro Police Department reacted swiftly and in great strength. When the store was evacuated, Scott and his girlfriend exited with other shoppers, only to be pointed out and confronted by police officers who shot and killed him.

Consequently, many holster makers put a premium on technologies to keep the weapon being carried completely concealed. This includes avoiding "printing"—a situation in which the outline of the concealed gun shows ("prints") through the gun carrier's clothing. At the same time, a holster that conceals a gun completely but is uncomfortable to wear is an impediment to everyday gun carrying. Moreover, a gun that is so deeply concealed that it cannot be drawn quickly negates the main defensive purpose of carrying a gun. In response to these competing demands, a number of holster technologies have been developed specifically for concealed carry. Among the companies at the Concealed Carry Expo figuring out a way to "build a better mousetrap" and sell it to the concealed-carry consumer are N8^2 Tactical, Crossbreed Holsters, and Urban Carry. All three companies sell variants of the "inside-the-waistband" (IWB) holster. Rather than being secured on a belt "outside-the-waistband" (OWB), as military and police typically wear their holstered handguns, IWB holsters are made to conceal the majority of a firearm inside a person's pants or shorts, with only enough of the grip exposed above the belt to allow the gun to be drawn.

Pronounced "Nate Squared," N8^2 Tactical is named after the two Nates that founded the company back in 2009. Nate Beard and Nate Johnson were friends who shared, among other things, an interest in concealed carry. They also shared a frustration with finding a holster that was comfortable enough "to be worn all day, every day," as their advertising puts it. A holster that would do the job would need to be worn inside-the-waistband but also shield the entire gun from contact with the body. At the same time, that shield could not be so stiff or rough that it could not come in direct contact with the wearer's bare skin. Because it could be in direct contact with skin, the holster would also need to create a moisture barrier to protect the gun. A phone conversation between the two Nates led to a joking suggestion that they just make the holster they were looking for. The joke became a serious endeavor after they bought a sewing machine, took sewing lessons, and cobbled together some initial prototypes. The prototypes met their needs in testing and they brought their product to market. From the original design, N8^2 now sells six different versions of its IWB holster, which accommodate hundreds of guns from twenty-three different manufacturers.

Although the original N8^2 Tactical IWB holster is designed to be "comfortable enough to wear all day, every day," the gun must still be concealed by some "cover garment" (in CCW parlance). That is, an untucked shirt or vest/jacket must be worn to cover the grip of the gun which needs to protrude above the belt line in order for it to be accessible. For anyone who needs to keep their shirt tucked in or cannot wear a jacket all the time, this is an inadequate solution to the CCW puzzle. Enter CrossBreed Holsters.

While most exhibitors have just one or two people working at a time, CrossBreed has half-a-dozen reps on hand to help sell the dozens of products the company is displaying. This large presence suggests tremendous growth in the decade since its founding in the garage of Mark Craighead's home near Springfield, Missouri. Craighead's goal was to produce a holster for concealed carry that would maximize the benefits of existing designs and minimize the liabilities. The "cross" in the company name is a clear allusion to the cross of Christianity, as evidenced by the modified Celtic cross which is a central symbol in their company logo. But it also refers to the hybrid materials used in their flagship IWB holsters. While many holsters are made entirely of leather or plastic, the CrossBreed holster is a combination of a leather backing onto which is riveted a pocket for the gun itself made from a moldable plastic called kydex. The large piece of leather provides comfort for the wearer, and the kydex pocket is molded to fit the exact gun being carried for safety and security. But the major innovation that got my attention is captured in the name of its first and best known holster: the SuperTuck. The tucking here refers not only to "tucking" the holster into one's pants, but also to the design of the belt clips. There is a space between the clips and the leather backing of the holster that allows the wearer to tuck in her or (more likely) his shirt over the gun so it is entirely covered.

An upstart challenger to now established companies like N8[2] Tactical and CrossBreed Holsters is Urban Carry. Although the bare wooden board displays seem at odds with the "urban" in the company name, its promise of "total concealment" fits seamlessly with the concealed-carry lifestyle. The concept of concealability through tuck-ability seen in the CrossBreed SuperTuck is central to the innovative design of the Urban Carry holster, and taken one step further. The Urban Carry is essentially a belt-mounted leather pouch that holds the firearm inside the gun carrier's pants, behind the front pocket. A belt is looped through the top of the holster and a flap connected to the back of the pouch folds over the belt and secures to the loop with a magnet. To draw the gun, the carrier grabs the flap and pulls upward, which draws the entire pouch up out of the pants and reveals the gun.

Beyond just an inside-the-waistband holster, this is a "below-the-waistband" holster. The handle of the gun does not protrude above the beltline, as it does with the N8[2] or CrossBreed IWB holsters. Consequently, a shirt can be tucked completely in the pants without any need to fit the ends of the shirt behind the clips and blouse it around the handle for fear of the gun printing. David Foster, the holster's designer and a self-described "serial inventor," says, "I got sick of my gun digging into my waist when I was sitting at my desk." He figured that others probably did not carry their guns for this same reason. So, he spent about a year developing the product, going through 114 prototypes. When he finally settled on the Urban Carry design, Foster posted a video on YouTube in July 2015 demonstrating its use. The video went viral, and when he demonstrates the procedure at the CCX, it is easy to see why. Wearing a T-shirt tucked into tight-fitting jeans, in one swift movement he draws a very large gun—a full-size 1911, in fact—from his Urban Carry holster. Just as quickly he re-holsters and the gun disappears back into his pants, and then it is back out again. Like a street magician pulling a rabbit out of a hat, Foster repeats the action over and over to a growing and amazed audience.

Whether the Urban Carry holster in practice lives up to its motto, "SAFE • HIDDEN • READY," who knows? But like the N8² Tactical, CrossBreed, and other holsters being exhibited at the Concealed Carry Expo, it represents a technology developed to solve part of the challenge of concealed carry. Each of these holster designs attempts to incorporate technological innovations that strike a better balance between the need for safe accessibility, concealability, and comfort in a concealed-carry holster. This is especially true for those in Gun Culture 2.0 who want to carry something larger than a pocket pistol. Those who solve the riddle of concealed carry with more emphasis on the lethality found in larger guns like the Springfield Armory EMP4 or FN FNS-9 Compact, or even a full-size duty weapon like the Glock 17. For those who emphasize lethality, Stephen Sharp provides a cautionary tale. Attempting to stop a co-worker's rampage at a St. Louis power plant in 2010, Sharp fired all seven rounds from his .380 caliber Walther PPK/S and missed seven times, only to be fatally injured by return fire from the homicidal maniac's AK-47 rifle. Even though the first rule of gunfighting is have a gun, the ability to put rounds on target matters too. Sharp might have been better served by a larger, more shootable handgun than by his compact Walther.

David Foster's performance highlights the fact that the Urban Carry holster, like the N8² Tactical and CrossBreed holsters, are designed by men, for men. They work well with a man's typical body type and attire. This, of course, makes sense at one level. American gun culture, old and new, has been heavily identified with men and masculinity.[27] Still, it is impossible not to notice the large number of vendors at the Concealed Carry Expo selling products specifically designed by women for women. Although the problems to be addressed by those who

<hr>

[27] Carlson, *Citizen-Protectors*; Stroud, *Good Guys with Guns*; and Melzer, *Gun Crusaders*; but see Laura Browder, *Her Best Shot: Women and Guns in America* (Chapel Hill: University of North Carolina Press, 2008); and Martha McCaughey, *Real Knockouts: The Physical Feminism of Self-Defense* (New York: New York University Press, 1997).

want to live the CCW lifestyle are gender-neutral, the specific technologies for addressing those problems often differ between men and women.

Women's Specific Carry Needs

Sociologist Jennifer Carlson begins a very interesting essay on the complexity of women's involvement in gun culture recounting her first day carrying a concealed handgun in public:

> I remember looking at myself in the mirror that first morning, the familiar feminine ritual of checking my looks before heading out for the day disrupted by a new concern. I examined my hip for an unsightly bulge, hoping I had adequately concealed the handgun holstered on my right side.[28]

This scene highlights two significant realities of Gun Culture 2.0: the growing number of women who are arming themselves for self-defense and the special challenges women face when they decide to carry concealed firearms.

Although data on who has concealed-carry permits are scarce, Carlson notes that 20% of the 400,000+ Michigan Concealed Pistol License holders are women. In Florida, as the number of concealed weapon licenses has grown, so too has the percentage of women with them. In February 2014, women held 23% of the 1.237 million valid state concealed weapon licenses, according to the Florida Department of Agriculture and Consumer Services. This is up from 15% in 2004. In Texas, for calendar year 2014, 27% of the 246,000 concealed handgun licenses issued by the Department of Public Safety were to women. Ten years earlier, just 17% of the licenses issued went to women. The place of women in the gun culture is actively promoted by organizations like the National Rifle Association, from their 1990s "Refuse to be a Victim" seminars to today's online NRA Women's Channel. The Concealed Carry Expo also has two seminars on women in the gun culture, including "Why Women Hate Guns: Encouraging Women to Accept, Own, Use & Carry Firearms." Of the seventy-five attendees at this seminar, about 40% are women.

As women become a larger part of the concealed-carry story, the practical challenges they face are increasingly noticeable. The leading female gun trainer today, Kathy Jackson (aka, "The Cornered Cat") observes, "As many women have discovered, the curvier you are, the more painful it can be to hold an

---

[28] Jennifer Dawn Carlson, "Carrying Guns, Contesting Gender," *Contexts* 14:1 (2015): 21.

unyielding chunk of metal firmly against your waistline. Faced with this simple biological fact, a lot of women simply give up on the idea of carrying a concealed handgun on the belt."[29] The common practice of "pocket carry" facilitated by the miniaturizing of handguns discussed earlier is also not an ideal option for many women. Take Kristen Zeh-Franke, for example. After having her Florida concealed-carry permit for two months, her husband asked her why she was not carrying her gun. Zeh-Franke replied with a question of her own for her husband: How do *you* carry? Which she answered for herself. "In your pocket! Look at my pocket—I can't even get a credit card in there!" So Zeh-Franke looked at the various purses available for women who want to carry guns. Concealed-carry purses typically look like any other purse but have a special compartment built in designed to hold a gun.

A purse aficionado herself, Zeh-Franke was not satisfied with any of the existing options. "Give me a little time and I can fix this. It will only take a long weekend," she told herself. "Well, it went from a long weekend to 18 months developing it." Zeh-Franke did not like that the existing concealed-carry purses require you to abandon your existing purses and that the typical horizontal placement of the gun in one of the purse's pockets forces you to "muzzle" people (i.e., point the muzzle end of the gun at people). She solved her own carry problem and created a product to sell to others by inventing a purse insert that gives the owner flexibility to use as many of their current purses as they want. At the Concealed Carry Expo, Zeh-Franke demonstrates her invention in one of her own Coach purses, but she also has one of her Louis Vuitton and two Michael Kors handbags on display for those interested. The insert also keeps the gun pointing down to prevent the owner from inadvertently muzzling people as they walk around, and the gun pocket sits above the side of the insert so the gun is always the highest thing in the purse for easy access. The "Packin' Neat" purse holster system was developed in late 2012 and Zeh-Franke's company, Packin' Neat by Kristen, was online by the fourth quarter of 2013. To protect her invention, Zeh-Franke has a utility patent pending on any bag inserts with pockets and a holster.

Packin' Neat by Kristen is just one of four exhibitors in Atlanta selling purse-carry options for women. Although purse carry maximizes comfort and concealability, these benefits can come at the cost of safety and security due to too much accessibility. It is easier to lose control of one's firearms when it is carried "off body" as opposed to "on body." Someone who has their purse stolen or simply loses track of it also loses their firearm. In the worst case scenario, that

[29] Kathy Jackson, "Straight Talk about Curves," n.d., http://www.corneredcat.com/article/practical-issues/straight-talk-about-curves/.

firearm can then be used against the person who was carrying it for personal protection in the first place. Although not a common scenario, the case of Veronica Rutledge serves as a cautionary tale for women considering this option.[30] A twenty-nine-year-old research chemist and concealed-carry permit holder, Rutledge received a concealed-carry handbag from her husband as a Christmas gift in December 2014. Like the typical concealed-carry purse, it had a separate, dedicated pocket for a gun with a zippered closure. A few days after Christmas, Rutledge took four children with her to a Walmart in Hayden, Idaho. One of the children was her two-year-old son, who was sitting in the shopping cart with her handbag, an unremarkable sight in grocery stores all over the world. But in this case, the two-year-old somehow managed not only to retrieve Rutledge's Smith & Wesson M&P Shield 9mm handgun from the purse, but he also was able to fire a round that struck Rutledge in the head, killing her.

Janet Sheriff was living in Coeur d'Alene, Idaho, a mile from the Hayden Walmart when Veronica Rutledge was killed. In that moment, Sheriff got the idea for a concealed-carry purse with some locking mechanism. A Canadian by birth, Sheriff's professional background is in government relations and private business in the mining industry. She had no real experience with firearms until she "married a guy with lots of guns." Even then, it took her three years to pick up a gun, and once she obtained her concealed-carry permit she took another year trying various carry options. Here Sheriff's story dovetails with Kristen Zeh-Franke's. A slight woman, on-body carry did not work for Sheriff. She needed to find a way to carry off body—safely. Like Zeh-Franke, she wanted a concealed-carry purse that was both fashionable and functional and was unable to find one that she was willing to carry publicly. As Sheriff puts it, "Like so many products in our lives, necessity is the mother of invention." So, she spent a year developing the ShePax organizer insert, and had been in business just a month when she debuted the product at the Concealed Carry Expo. The ShePax functions exactly like the Packin' Neat insert, with one small but significant difference: the pocket designed to hold the gun is zippered and lockable. Here, the peace of mind that comes from having a gun quickly accessible in a moment of need is traded off against the peace of mind that comes from knowing the gun is safe and secure, particularly from children.

Janet Sheriff's innovation notwithstanding, a woman carrying off body in a purse or purse insert still runs the risk of losing control of her firearm. Consequently, there are several exhibitors at the Concealed Carry Expo who address the challenge of concealed carry for women with various technologies for on-body carry. But rather than simply modifying traditional holster designs,

---

[30] And men, too, though "off body" carry is not as common for men as women.

which are separate from and attach to the body—as we have seen, typically to a belt worn on the waist—these female-centric products modify the types of clothing typically worn by women to integrate gun carry. Like Kristen Zeh-Franke and Janet Sheriff, the women who developed these technologies typically got their impetus from their own struggles to address the challenge of concealed carry in their own lives.

A fashionably dressed woman with short, styled blonde hair and a statement necklace energetically greets visitors to the Dene Adams booth. She is not Dene Adams. She is Anna Taylor, the founder and CEO of Dene Adams LLC, which is named after Taylor's grandfather who was her role model especially when it came to guns. In the fall of 2012, Taylor received her Missouri concealed-carry permit and was immediately confronted with the challenge of integrating gun carrying into her everyday life. She says it only took one trip to Walmart with her four young children to decide that one common option, a concealed-carry purse, was too heavy and impractical to use. So, Taylor says, "I ended up not carrying." She tried six or seven other carry options and none worked. "It pissed me off that I couldn't carry my gun and I wanted to solve the problem." Like many women, especially after she had given birth several times, Taylor appreciated products designed with compression, like Spanx undergarments. Some thought and time at her sewing machine led to the creation of a concealed-carry corset. It is specifically designed to allow women like her to carry a gun safely, comfortably, and accessibly—without having the change her wardrobe. Like David Foster's YouTube video for his Urban Carry holster for men, a twelve-second video of Taylor demonstrating her design went viral and her concealed-carry corset business was off and running.

Although their solution differs from Taylor's, Julene Franklin and Patty McConnell's story of founding Silver State Apparel does not. As Franklin says a bit sheepishly when asked how they got started in the concealed-carry clothing business, "It's cliché, but necessity is the mother of invention." When McConnell received her Nevada concealed-carry permit in 2009, the only clothing she could find for concealed carry were tactical pants. The kind of concealed-carry clothing she envisioned, by contrast, would be "stylish," she says. "Boutique, not Cabela's"—referring to the big box outdoor recreation store. The clothes she would produce with her business partner would be tactical in the sense of allowing the wearer to carry a firearm covertly, but at the same time would embody "three Fs: feminine, fashionable, and functional." While McConnell is a shooter, her friend Franklin has a background in clothing design, not guns. Her unfamiliarity with guns became an advantage of sorts, she claims, because she had no preconceptions about what concealed-carry clothing for women should look like. McConnell just advised her that the garment needed to be able to fit a compact gun and that the gun needed to be readily accessible. Luckily, the fit model that Franklin used while testing various designs happened to be a concealed-carry permit holder, so the model was able to give practical input as they went along. In the end, McConnell and Franklin brought to market a concealed-carry shirt for women that allows for on-body carry of a pocket size pistol with no holster.

Silver State Apparel was founded in 2012, but McConnell observes that since then she has seen the rise of more companies started by women designing concealed-carry clothing for women. One such company made its debut at the Concealed Carry Expo: Incognito Wear IX. The company's founder, Jan Wolbrecht, describes its origin on the company's website:

> It was around 2013 when my husband bought me my first pistol. I began training and learning about gun safety and concealed carry. As I learned, I became very conscious of how to dress. I felt as if my firearm plainly showed through whatever I was wearing. It seemed to me that "concealed" carry wasn't an effective form of protection when it was so obvious that I was carrying. My mind began to seek a solution—a discreet way to carry protection with clothing that was functional, fashionable, and would camouflage a weapon.[31]

Using language identical to McConnell, Wolbrecht explains to me that she "didn't want to be tactical," telling herself, "There has to be a way to make a dress that is professional and allows me to carry." She "spent a lot of time thinking about the problem and how to solve it" and came up with her line of dress casual wear for women. At the CCX, Wolbrecht is wearing one of her designs, "The Boardwalk." As befits the company's Georgia roots, the full-length dress is available in khaki or grey seersucker, and ties at the waist to gather the fabric at the midsection. The gathering is a key functional element as it allows the wearer to conceal a firearm in the ambidextrous pockets just above the waist.

Without downplaying the importance of large, multinational corporations in today's global gun industry, the smaller scale of the Concealed Carry Expo allows upstart companies like Packin' Neat by Kristen, ShePax, Dene Adams, Silver State Apparel, and Incognito Wear IX a more prominent place. Here, the "who" of the gun industry really stands out, as do the particular technologies they have developed for other women who face the same challenge of living the concealed-carry lifestyle they did.

---

[31] Incognito Wear IX, http://incognitowearix.com/my-story/.

Conclusion

Although it runs through Sunday, the Concealed Carry Expo actually culminates on Saturday night with a "Concealed Carry Fashion Show." It is the brain child of Marilyn Smolenski, founder of Chicago-based concealed-carry clothier Nickel & Lace. Smolenski and Karen Bartuch, a former police officer and founder of Alpha Girls LLC, teamed up to host the first annual Firearms and Fashion show in Chicago in 2013. After two years in Chicago, they joined forces with the USCCA at the first Concealed Carry Expo in 2015, and that partnership was reprised in 2016 in Atlanta. The spectacle is emceed by Mark Walters, the host of the USCCA's weekly radio program "Armed American Radio." The runway itself, lighting, two large projection screens, and loud but clear music all give the show a very professional feel.

The runway models are both male and female, professional and amateur. Among the female models are Beth Alcazar, the USCCA staff writer who earlier in the day led the aforementioned seminar on "Why Women Hate Guns," and the wife of one of the holster makers whose products are featured in the show. Seven companies in all participate: three clothing companies (Nickel and Lace, Silver State Apparel, and UnderTech UnderCover), two holster makers (CrossBreed and MTR Custom Leather), and two bag companies (ShePax and Man-PACK). Suggestive of the mainstreaming of concealed carry, the fashion show is co-sponsored by the publicly-traded retail men's apparel giant Men's Warehouse (founded by George "You're gonna like the way you look, I guarantee it" Zimmer), which supplied the male models' attire.

The Concealed Carry Fashion Show emphasizes the *lifestyle* element of concealed carry, to be sure. But what is enacted on the runway is anything but frivolous. It is a glamorized presentation of addressing a practical challenge: How to make carrying a concealed firearm part of one's *everyday life*—while wearing a suit or a skirt, carrying a purse or a murse, going to the office or grocery store. To hybridize the words of Mark Moritz and Tom Givens, the fashion show, like the Concealed Carry Expo in general, show potential gun carriers in attendance how to ensure they obey the first rule of gunfighting by having their damn guns on them when they need it.

The very existence of the United States Concealed Carry Association and its Concealed Carry Expo reflects a profound change that has taken place in American gun culture over the past half century, from Gun Culture 1.0 to Gun Culture 2.0. Led by scholars such as Jennifer Carlson and Angela Stroud, and continued by Elisabeth Anker and Harel Shapira (in this volume), social scientists have begun to explain this emerging culture of armed citizenship, facilitated by a dramatic liberalization of concealed-carry laws and embodied in the growing number of Americans with concealed-carry permits. By focusing not on the problems that gun carry solves for those Anker calls "mobile sovereigns," but on the technologies that seek to address the problems that carrying a concealed weapon creates, this chapter builds on their work. In focusing on "the gun industry"—companies large and small that seek to develop products to meet the competing demands of carrying a lethal weapon in public safely, accessibly, comfortably, and concealed—it highlights the dynamic, creative, problem-solving nature of culture itself, including Gun Culture 2.0.

8

How to Use the Bathroom with a Gun and Other Techniques of the Armed Body

HAREL SHAPIRA

In his canonical essay "Techniques of the Body,"[1] Marcel Mauss urges us to consider the significant role that the body plays in human behavior. Whether eating, driving, or dancing with someone, a key part of what makes our activities and interactions possible are the movements of our arms and legs, as well as the gestures of our hands and the expressions on our faces. In addition to calling attention to the fact that bodies are a key part of human behavior, Mauss shows that the movements and dispositions of the body are not a natural occurrence, born of internal drives and instincts, but rather learned through a process of socialization. As Mauss puts it, after describing a mother berating her young daughter for not walking with the proper gait, "there is perhaps no natural way for an adult [to walk]."[2] In such a manner it is not only minds that are socialized but also bodies, and just as we learn to think in particular ways we learn how to use our bodies in particular ways.

Like minds, bodies are socialized in historically and culturally specific ways. Consequentially, the movements of bodies as they carry out behaviors show variance across time and social groups: women walk differently from men; the French military marches one way, while the British another. This variance emerges not simply because of differing ideas of how to accomplish a behavior in the most efficient and effective way, but also because of different cultural ideas and values which become inscribed onto the body; in learning how to walk we are learning to embody gender, race, nationality, and so forth. Indeed, Mauss's

---

[1] Marcel Mauss, "Techniques of the Body," *Economy and Society* 2, no. 1 (1973): 70–88.
[2] Ibid., 74.

claim is that cultural categories intervene not simply at the level of discourses about bodies, but rather at the level of practice, in terms of how a body practically and physically moves and functions. Consequentially, by calling attention to the variability in the way people use their bodies, Mauss calls attention to the possibilities of being able to read the social off of the body. That is, Mauss establishes the important analytic point that by analyzing the different ways that people use their bodies to undertake various social practices—what Mauss calls "techniques of the body"—we can understand society itself.

In this chapter, I employ Mauss' framework in order to analyze the techniques of the armed body. That is, to examine how people use their bodies when they hold, shoot, and carry guns. In the pages that follow, I show that a particular kind of society is inscribed onto the armed body, one that is gendered, racialized, and fearful.

Data and Methods

This chapter draws on thirty months of fieldwork carried out at gun schools, places where people train their minds and bodies to use guns. Many people come to gun schools to take the mandatory class to get their license to carry (LTC)[3], but these schools offer a range of classes. Some are meant for beginners in which students learn the basics of how to hold a gun, while some are more advanced, in which instructors teach how to shoot on the move or while holding a flashlight.

Although the data presented here are principally focused on central Texas, some of the fieldwork was conducted in different locations across the United States. I spent a total of 104 hours in firearms training classes as a participant observer, taking a range of classes, in both a group setting as well as private one-on-one instruction. I participated in beginner's classes, concealed-carry licensing classes, and advanced tactical classes. I also conducted participant observation at shooting ranges (where you also often see training taking place informally), shooting competitions, gun shows, and organizational meetings. Within these other settings I have spent just under 250 hours.

The students and instructors at these schools are part of a relatively new and growing population: people who have obtained a license to carry and who carry their guns with them on a regular basis for the purpose of self-defense. The

---

[3] While states use different terms for licenses or permits to carry a concealed firearm, such as a Concealed Handgun Permit (CHP), Concealed Carry Permit/License (CCP/CCL), Concealed Handgun License (CHL), Carry of Concealed Deadly Weapon license (CCDW), or Concealed Pistol License (CPL), we use License to Carry (LTC) to refer to all such policies which allow gun owners to carry their handguns in public in a concealed manner.

rise of LTC represents a change in what gun ownership is—both at the level of attitudes connected to gun ownership as well as the sets of practices in which gun owners engage.[4] By enlarging the scope of where people can carry guns, and creating a large civilian population that carries their guns every day, the rise of LTC requires that we consider the processes by which individuals are socialized into gun ownership as an embodied everyday activity.

While the existing body of research on gun ownership has documented the sets of attitudes that are connected to gun ownership and gun carry, the meanings that people attach to guns, as well as the structural conditions that may foster those attitudes and meanings, these accounts provide a limited understanding of contemporary gun ownership because they do not examine the embodied dimensions of gun carrying as an everyday practice.[5] While holding a set of attitudes about guns is a key part of gun ownership, we need a greater understanding of the actual practice of owning and carrying a gun as an embodied everyday activity in which having a gun on your body becomes a key aspect of one's identity.

By analyzing the physical techniques learned at gun schools, I reveal not only how gun ownership and gun carry is accomplished as a practical matter, but the sets of cultural ideas that become inscribed onto the gun owner's body. In what follows, I present three ethnographic vignettes, each one focusing on one bodily technique that gun owners learn: the first focuses on a technique for loading

[4] In terms of attitudes, there has been a dramatic shift away from hunting to self-defense as the primary motivation for gun ownership. A recent study conducted by the Pew Research Center documents the enormity of this transformation: whereas in 1999, the primary reason gun owners gave for owning a gun was hunting (49%) with only a minority (26%) claiming "protection" as their motivation, by 2013 these figures were reversed, with protection becoming the number one reason (48%), and hunting dropping down to a secondary motivation (32%). Pew Research Center, "Why Own a Gun? Protection Is Now Top Reason," March 12, 2013, http://www.people-press.org/2013/03/12/why-own-a-gun-protection-is-now-top-reason/.

[5] On the attitudes of gun owners, see, for example, Katarzyna Celinka, "Individualism and Collectivism in America: The Case of Gun Ownership and Attitudes Toward Gun Control," *Sociological Perspectives* 50, no. 2 (2007): 229–247; David Hemenway et al., "Firearms and Community Feelings of Safety," *The Journal of Criminal Law & Criminology* 86 (1995): 121–132; Kerry O'Brien et al., "Racism, Gun Ownership, and Gun Control: Biased Attitudes in US Whites May Influence Policy Decisions," *PLoS ONE* 8, no. 10 (October 31, 2013); Jo Dixon and Alan J. Lizotte, "Gun Ownership and the 'Southern Subculture of Violence,'" *American Journal of Sociology* 93, no. 2 (1987): 383–405. On the meanings that gun owners attach to guns, see for example, Bernard Harcourt, *Language of the Gun: Youth, Crime, and Public Policy* (Chicago: University of Chicago Press, 2006); Jennifer Carlson, *Citizen Protectors: The Everyday Politics of Guns in an Age of Decline* (New York: Oxford University Press, 2015); Angela Stroud, *Good Guys with Guns: The Appeal and Consequences of Concealed Carry* (Chapel Hill: University of North Carolina Press, 2016). Lastly, on how structural conditions influence people's attitudes about guns, see Carlson, *Citizen Protectors*; Nicholas Johnson, *Negroes and the Gun: The Black Tradition of Arms* (New York: Prometheus Books, 2014).

ammunition; the second, on a technique for holding a gun; and the third on a technique for carrying a gun. From each one of these techniques I pull out a different characteristic of gun culture: through the technique for loading ammunition I reveal how the gendered dimensions of gun culture are inscribed on the armed body; through the technique for holding a gun I reveal how the racist dimensions of gun culture are inscribed on the armed body; and through the technique for carrying a gun I reveal how a culture of fear is inscribed on the gun owners body. I begin where many novice gun owners begin, which is with learning how to load a gun.

Loading a Gun

Recent graduates of Kansas State University, Katie and her boyfriend Chris moved to Austin a little over year ago when Chris got a job at a tech firm. Having spent most of their lives living in small towns in Kansas, they find Austin to be at once exciting and frightening. "When we moved down here," Chris tells me, "we decided to go all in and get a place downtown."

Sometimes Chris works late nights, leaving Katie all alone. "There are a bunch of bars on our street," Chris tells me, "and guys are always drunk, urinating in public, and constantly harassing her."

A few months ago, while Chris was working late on a Friday night, Katie decided to go out on her own for dinner. A group of men started shouting profanities at her. Feeling unsafe, Katie went back inside the house.

A week later Chris and Katie purchased a Beretta .45 ACP handgun. Chris had done some research and the Beretta seemed like a very good option. "It's what the military uses," he tells me.

I met Chris and Katie at a beginner's firearms class. When the indoor lecture portion of the class ended and it came to go to the firing range, the instructor asked us to load our guns with ammo.

For those without much experience, loading ammo is not an easy task. First, it is not entirely obvious which direction of the magazine is the front and which is the back. While the experienced shooters, those who have loaded thousands of rounds of ammo don't even need to think about it, for the beginner it's unclear which direction the bullets go in. Second, loading ammo into the magazine requires holding the individual bullets between your thumb and index finger, and pushing them down with a rarely used set of finger muscles. While it does not require that much force, it's a force that is hard to generate. This is particularly the case once there are already a couple of rounds of ammo in the magazine, and the spring at the bottom builds up resistance to the addition of new ones. While the experienced shooters have developed callouses on their thumbs and forefingers, and can load ammo quickly and without much strain, for novices like Chris and Katie, it is a stressful and time-consuming task.

Chris and Katie have two magazines. They each take responsibility for loading one of them. Both are having issues. Exasperated, Katie says she can't do it. Another female student who is standing nearby tells Katie that she too used to have trouble loading ammo. She tells her that there is a great little contraption you can buy that helps you do it.

The contraption she is referring to, known as a speed loader, is a square piece of plastic that fits on top of the magazine. A bullet is inserted into an opening on top, and an easy downward tug loads the bullet into the magazine. Having purchased one of these myself, I can attest that they make loading ammo quite easy.

The student asks Katie if she wants to try it out.

She shows Katie how it works. "See that," she says, "it just pushes the ammo down into the magazine for you."

Katie takes hold of the speed loader. She begins loading her magazine with ease. She asks Chris if he wants to try it out, "it makes it so much easier" she tells him. Chris says that he doesn't need it. And as he does so, I notice that while a couple of other women are using speed loaders, I am in fact the only man to be using one.

My experiences with Chris and Katie began to raise my awareness of the varied ways that men and women go about loading ammo, and as I became attuned to them, I noted examples everywhere I looked.

A few months after meeting Chris and Katie I was at a shooting range with two very experienced and avid male gun owners, Adam Gonzalez and Hank Crawford. Adam and Hank are close friends with their friendship mostly revolving around a mutual love for guns. Every Saturday morning, they wake up early, meet at an outdoor firing range located about forty-five minutes from each of their houses, shoot guns for a couple of hours, and then have lunch together. They both say Saturday is the highlight of their week.

One Friday, Adam contacted Hank and I very early in the morning. He had recently purchased a brand new, very expensive, and highly sought-after handgun. Adam was going to bring it with him to the range on Saturday. He told us he wanted us to help him "break it in."

Adam says that you need to fire about 350–500 rounds in a gun in order for it to be "broken in." When I ask Adam what he means by "breaking in" a gun, he tells me that it has to do with firing enough rounds to test the gun out and make sure the ammunition is feeding and ejecting properly, and that the tension on the trigger of the gun is the same after the last shot as it is on the first shot.

Texas winter mornings can get cold. And that Saturday was a particularly cold one, with record setting temperatures hovering below freezing. The cold was a recurring topic of conversation among the three of us, and within thirty minutes of firing guns in the outdoors, each of us began commenting on how cold our hands were and how difficult it was to load ammunition. But Adam badly wanted to break in his gun, and encouraged us to help him keep loading ammo and firing his new gun. We proceeded to help Adam for the next thirty minutes, but with our fingers slowly numbing, our enthusiasm was waning. But Adam was undeterred; loading round after round of ammo into his gun, and firing shot after shot.

Adam's hands began to bleed. The space between his thumb and index finger was cut up from the incessant recoil of the gun, while the thumbs themselves were badly bruised and swollen, trembling, and disfigured from all the ammo he had loaded over the past hour. Adam showed us his hands, clasping them, and noting the blood that was trickling down one of his knuckles in a performance of masculinity. And then, after showing us his bleeding hands, and after nearly an hour manually loading roughly 300 rounds of ammunition, Adam went to his car, and brought a speedloader. He began to load his gun with the help of the speedloader. "Ah, much better," he told us.

Why didn't Adam just use the speedloader from the beginning? Clearly the gendered nature of gun culture, permeated with notions of hegemonic masculinity, prevented him from doing so. According to the gendered script, Adam is "allowed" to use the speedloader only after his hands, openly displayed to myself and Hank, were bruised and bleeding. Adam ends up using the speedloader, but in so doing, he only re-affirms the gendered dimensions of its use.

It has been well-documented that cultural norms about gender inform people's decisions to carry guns. For example, as Angela Stroud shows in *Good Guys with Guns*, carrying a gun is a way for men to achieve idealized notions of masculinity in which manhood is attached to protecting women and children.[6] The previous vignettes illustrate that such gender norms inform not only the decision to acquire or carry a gun, but the very way that one goes about doing so. Furthermore, beyond merely showing that gender norms are expressed in how men and women load guns, by analyzing the techniques of the armed body we can see how men and women experience and relate to guns in ways that articulate radically different forms of embodiment. Specifically, what we see is that gun culture promotes men to have a much more physically embodied relationship to guns, and that the techniques they learn are organized around developing that sense of embodiment.

---

[6] Stroud, *Good Guys with Guns*.

The speed loader can be conceptualized as an intermediary object, inserting itself between the gun owner and the gun. And, as I have found, men seek out a relationship to guns that tries to deny all kinds of mediating agents. Indeed, men embrace an experience of guns in which the gun is an extension of the body, and the men I have talked to over the past thirty months are much more likely than women to talk about "feeling naked" when they are not carrying their guns. Indeed, even the women I have met who carry guns with them nearly every-where they go rarely articulate the same sense of embodiment of the gun as men. Furthermore, if we consider *how* men and women carry guns, we find that like the speed loader, a kind of intermediary object, in this case the purse, mediates between women's bodies and guns. While some women will carry guns on their hips, they very rarely do so, whereas for men, carrying a gun literally on the body is the primary technique.

In such ways, gender norms find expression in the differing ways in which male and female bodies operate and carry guns. It is not simply the felt need, desire, or meaning of gun ownership that is stratified along gender lines, but the very way that the body carries out and experiences the behavior.

While gender norms of hegemonic masculinity can be read off the way that people learn to load a gun, when it comes to learning how to hold a gun, we can see how racism can sometimes inform the techniques of the armed body.

Holding a Gun

Like many gun instructors, Steve Babic likes to point out that the movies don't accurately portray how guns work. He often talks about scenes from movies where the gun will fire off a shot when it's dropped—something he says will almost never happen in reality—or scenes where people are able to take cover behind objects that, in realty, would be easily penetrated by a bullet. But more than anything, Steve likes to point out the poor gun-holding techniques of actors on TV: "You always see them holding it with one hand, you just don't do that." In fact, Steve says that you can tell which TV shows actually have their actors go through proper training by the way in which they hold their guns. "When you see them with the right grip, two handed, high on the frame, you can tell they actually got their actors to take some real instruction."

What does it mean to hold a gun the right way? The idea of there being a proper way to hold a gun can be interpreted simply as a matter of practical knowl-edge and proper use. Holding a gun one way as opposed to another can lead to better accuracy, control, and safety. But the discourse of proper gun hand-ling functions as part of a much broader dynamic within gun culture, which establishes a boundary between those who should and those who should not have guns. It is a boundary whose contours are often marked by race.

"Don't hold your gun like the gang bangers," Steve tells a student when they grip their gun with only one hand. The image of the uncouth "gang banger"— who keeps his gun inside his waistband and holds it with one hand, tilted to the side—is a common trope among gun instructors. "They do it because they think it looks cool," he announces in one of his classes, "but you don't own guns because they are cool. You own them because they will save your life. . . . Owning a gun comes with responsibility and part of that [responsibility] means getting proper training." For people like Steve, the "gang-banger," uneducated in the proper techniques of gun ownership, stands as the epitome of the "bad" gun owner, the one who should not have a gun, the one who gives people like him a "bad name."

But for people like Steve, there are still instances in which learning how to shoot with one hand is important. They are instances in which training to do so is not a mark of misconduct, but precisely the mark of a properly trained gun owner. And those are moments in which you need to hold your gun with one hand because your other hand has been injured during a "gunfight."

Steve says that when you are in a gunfight, the hand that is most likely to be injured is your "dominant" hand. That is, the hand that you normally shoot with. The reason for this, he says, is that the dominant hand is fully extended and exposed, providing a target for the "bad guy" to hit. For this reason, Steve says, it is important to learn to shoot with both hands.

The most challenging aspect of shooting with one hand is the fact that you don't have the support of your second hand to hold your gun in place. The key to learning how to shoot with one hand is to overcome this lack of support by "using skeletal support, instead of muscle support." The technique used to address this involves holding the gun at a sideways angle—that is, tilting or canting the gun. You extend your arm as you normally would, but instead of having the gun perpendicular to the target, you turn it sideways, at about a 45 degree angle. This helps steady the gun and provide greater balance.

Steve says you don't want to tilt the gun sideways too much. Critiquing a student in the class who practiced the motion of firing with one hand, Steve says the student had his hand angled far too much. Except, Steve doesn't use the words "tilt" or "angle." Instead he says "homey." "That was too much homey," he laughs; "straighten it a bit—you want *some* homey, but not *that much* homey."

Part of what the training for shooting with one hand shows us is that guns are used by gun owners to tell stories. Stories about themselves as well as about others. In Norbert Elias's account of the civilizing process, before even considering the content of a behavior as a determining factor in whether or not it is deemed "civilized," he points out that the very dichotomy of civilized and un-civilized, that is the very establishment of these categories, is part of the mark of the civilizing process.

And we begin to see the marks of this process in the distinction that gun instructors make between the "thuggish" way to carry a gun and the way "good guys" carry a gun. That is, that there are different *kinds* of gun owners (the responsible one: usually coded as white) and the irresponsible one (usually coded as black). And in this way we see how race overlaps with notions of there being civilized and uncivilized gun owners. But the discourse of civilization that gets articulated at gun schools, a discourse about the proper ways to embody gun ownership, is not simply reducible to racism. While the figure of the "homey" or "gang banger" is the ultimate expression of the improper ways of holding guns, instructors like Steve and Hank also criticize other white gun owners for not having proper "technique."

Beyond the articulation of racism, then, the important point that we can learn when looking at the techniques of the armed body, particularly connected to the discourse surrounding how to hold one's gun, is that gun ownership becomes entwined in a discourse of professionalism and etiquette, in which there becomes legitimate and illegitimate ways of owning a gun and embodying its violent capabilities. And at the heart of this idea of proper and improper ways of carrying guns, is the idea of professionalism, of the fact that these different ways are rooted in teaching, in training, in technique. That is, the very articulation of a "technique" for the armed body does important work of redefining the activity, shifting it from a purely brutal behavior, in which violence is very present, to one in which that brutality and violence is recast as a civilized behavior. Indeed, when it comes to gun ownership, and violence more broadly, the discourse of technique helps integrate the brutality of the behavior in society by recasting it as a civilized one.

Carrying a Gun

Adam Gonzalez says that for the first two months he carried a gun, he was very uncomfortable. "It was so uncomfortable . . . I was so self-conscious," Adam explains. "I kept feeling this thing on my hip. I kept thinking that people could see that I was carrying a gun." Although uncomfortable, Adam forced himself to keep carrying his gun. "I just forced myself to carry," Adam explains. "Everyone told me that I needed to just push through and eventually it would become a habit." These days, nearly two years after he first obtained his concealed handgun license, Adam says that he feels uncomfortable when he is *not* carrying his gun, "I just feel totally naked."

The truth is, these days, Adam rarely doesn't have his gun with him, carrying it everywhere he goes, and avoiding those places where he is not allowed to carry his gun. For Adam, becoming comfortable carrying a gun involved a cognitive process in which he came to think of guns as inanimate "tools," with life-saving capabilities, that are no more violent or dangerous than other objects in the world. It had to with a process of learning to think of the potential threat—the "bad guy"—as so utterly dangerous and immoral, that killing him is a virtuous action. But beyond all these cognitive framings which helped make Adam feel comfortable with his gun, Adam also learned techniques for how to physically comport his body in such a way that he could continue to engage in day-to-day interactions.[7]

These day-to-day interactions are varied, as are the specific techniques and tools they call upon. Consider the basic need of concealing a gun. Beyond simply a matter of following the law, gun owners talk about the importance of concealment in terms of tactics—specifically, the importance of the "bad guys" not knowing that you have a firearm because (1) you want to have the element of surprise; (2) the first person who will be attacked by a "bad guy" in a shooting will be the person with the gun; (3) you want to prevent someone from coming up to you and taking your gun from you. In these ways, a combination of fears and tactical beliefs motivate the techniques of concealment.

Adam has nearly twenty handguns. And as a sales manager for a tech company located in central Texas who frequently travels, every morning Adam wakes up, thinks about where he needs to be that day for work, the kinds of clothing he needs to wear—whether formal business suit or casual attire—and picks a gun based on that. Smaller guns for a business suit. But when he is casual he can wear cargo pants and choose among a larger array of guns. But beyond this, the very selection of clothing that Adam chooses when he wakes up in the morning is different than used to be. Over the past two years, Adam has acquired completely new clothing, clothing that, as he says, "makes carrying a gun easier." Furthermore, beyond buying different kinds of clothes—for example Adam now owns multiple pairs of cargo pants and other pants with multiple pockets— Adam now buys all his shirts in larger sizes; that way, the shirt can hang down lower and cover the gun on his hip. Relatedly, unless he needs to go to a business meeting and tuck in his shirt, these days Adam always lets his shirt hang out over his pants.

Beyond changing his clothing, Adam has also changed how he sits. The changes in how he sits have to do with the development of "situational

---

[7] The relationship between the cognitive and physical training a person undergoes in the process of becoming a gun owner is examined in more detail in a forthcoming essay: Harel Shapira and Samantha Simon, "Becoming a Gun Owner" (forthcoming).

awareness"—that is, seeking to have knowledge about one's surroundings so as to be able to notice potential threats. Adam says that situational awareness requires one always having an unobstructed view of his surroundings. This is why when he sits at a restaurant or coffee shop, he always does so facing the entrance. "You never want to have your back turned to the door," Adam explains, "You always want to be able to see people coming in." Furthermore, if a restaurant or coffee shop has multiple floors, he will always request to sit at the top floor. "If a shooter comes in, you have time to prepare and use your position for tactical advantage." But it is not only "situational awareness" and the desire for tactical advantage that has lead Adam to sit differently. It is also the very weight and size of the gun that he carries on his hip. These days, Adam says he sits high up on chairs, with his weight shifted slightly to his left side, and leaning forward. That way the gun does not does not touch the bottom of the chair and dig into his hip.

Adam had to learn how to sit with a gun by himself. He says that while the classes he has taken, around forty by his count, have been very good in terms of teaching him about how to use his gun and prepare for dangerous scenarios, none of the classes went through the basics of day-to-day life with a gun on your hip. "It was mostly by trial and error," Adam says, in regards to how he learned to sit. "I sort of did it one way and it didn't work, then tried something else out, kept positioning my body in different ways until I found something that worked."

While sitting in a chair at a restaurant is challenging in itself, Adam says it doesn't compare to the challenge of sitting on a toilet seat. Something else he mostly had to learn on his own.

Adam says that the first time he had to use the bathroom while carrying a gun, he stopped himself on the way to bathroom and thought about what he was going to do. "I'm like half way to the bathroom at this restaurant," Adam recalls, "and suddenly I realized I wasn't sure what I was going to do with my gun." Adam decided that first time to unholster his gun and place it on top of the toilet paper dispenser. In retrospect, Adam says that it was mistake, "You always want to be able to be in control of the gun, and I was putting it somewhere where it could have fallen very easily." The next time Adam used the bathroom, he developed a technique which involves unholstering the gun, pulling down your pants, and then placing the gun in the space between your legs. Adam used this technique for nearly a year, until he read on an online gun forum that this was a dangerous thing to do for two reasons: first, you always want to keep your gun in the holster so that it cannot move around; and, second you don't want the person in the bathroom stall next to you to be able to see the gun. Adam says that the reason for not wanting the person in the stall next to you to see your gun is two-fold: first, the person may "freak-out" and call the police; and second, and Adam says, "more importantly," you never want another person to be able to access your gun and take it away from you. The website suggested the following technique: first, to keep your gun holstered, then to pull down your pants—but only down to knees. Adam adds that its "very important to do this slowly, and to keep your hands on your gun while you pull down your pants. . . when you unbuckle your pants the weight of that gun will make them drop down fast." In this scenario then, gravity was not on the gun owner's side, and Adam explains that after slowly pulling down your pants, you want to push your knees out, extending them so to make a V-shape, so that your pants are tightened. This way, the gun will remain in place. And moreover, this way, the gun will remain above the line of sight of the person in the stall next to you.

Adam used this technique for a few months until a friend of his who is a gun instructor suggested he add another element: rebuckling his belt once his pants are pulled down to his knees. This way, Adam says, the pants are tightened, completely held in place, and the gun is steadied in its holster.

Adam says that one of the challenges of using the bathroom is being able to keep the gun concealed from the person in the stall next to you, while simultaneously also being able to access it should you need it. He says that the technique of keeping the pants at the knees with the belt buckled, addresses both these challenges. And when he is at home, he says he often unloads his gun when he goes to the bathroom and practices drawing his gun with his pants down at his knees. He says he has gotten to the point where he feels comfortable, that, in the event that something should happen, he would be able to quickly draw his gun while seated on the toilet.

Furthermore, Adam says that just as there are better, safer, more tactically strategic places to sit at a restaurant, there are better, safer, more tactically strategic places to sit in a bathroom. "You want to go to the stall furthest away from the door," Adam tells me; "that way if a shooter barges in, you have that extra time to prepare. It's just a few seconds, but every second counts." There is a second reason for choosing the stall furthest away: "If you are in the middle stall," Adam explains, "you have to worry about the person to your left and the person to your right. Either one could see your gun or reach for it if it falls, but if you're in that furthest stall, you've only got to worry about one person."

In *The Culture of Fear*, Barry Glassner examines the ways in which life in America is permeated by an overwhelming sense of fear—a fear that is connected not to actual increases in danger or risk, but rather an increase in people's perceptions of risk and danger.[8] What we see in the various techniques that gun owners like Adam employ to undertake the banal activities of their everyday

---

[8] Barry Glassner, *The Culture of Fear: Why Americans Are Afraid of the Wrong Things: Crime, Drugs, Minorities, Teen Moms, Killer Kids, Mutant Microbes, Plane Crashes, Road Rage, & So Much More* (New York: Basic Books, 2010).

lives is how perceptions of risk and danger radically transform those banal activities. Indeed, we see how a culture of fear not only permeates gun culture, but also the very bodies of gun owners. That is, we see how a sense of danger materializes, very physically, and in a remarkable, everyday way, in the manner in which gun owners must relearn such basic activities as using the bathroom.

Conclusion

In "Techniques of the Body," Marcel Mauss provides an important avenue for understanding society: by looking at how people use their bodies. In examining the ways in which people use their bodies, Mauss undertakes an analysis of embodiment that is truly corporal in its focus—that is, his focus is not on how bodies are understood or represented, but on how the bodies are used to carry out a behavior—indeed, on the physical dimensions of various social behaviors.

But the body must be trained to undertake its motions and maneuverings. What appears often as merely somatic and instinctual—the movement of an arm or flexing of a muscle—is in fact the product of socialization. And in the process of being socialized to use our bodies, we are socialized into using our bodies *in particular ways*, ways that reflect cultural ideas about race, class, gender, and so on. Indeed, as Mauss points out, the body is never used simply in a practical matter, but in a social one.

In this chapter, I have explored the ways in which people learn to use their bodies in the process of learning to become gun owners. Each of the techniques of the armed body articulates an important aspect of gun culture. In the process of looking at the technique for loading a gun, we see how gun culture is invested with hegemonic masculinity and how those ideas become inscribed in the way men and women use their bodies when they load ammunition and carry guns on their bodies. In the process of looking at the technique for holding a gun, we see the ways in which racial tropes inform boundaries within gun culture around proper and improper ways of embodying guns. Furthermore, when it comes to the embodiment of gun ownership, we see how ideas about "proper" technique help promote certain forms of violence as mannered or civilized, and others, as unmannered and brutal. Finally, in looking at the techniques for carrying a gun as an everyday behavior, and specifically by examining how a person uses the bathroom with a gun, we see how the culture of fear that permeates gun culture manifests itself in the very way that a person sits on a toilet.

Index

Tables and figures are indicated by an italic *t* and *f* following the page number.